Practice*Planners*®

Arthur E. Jongsma, Jr., Series Editor

Helping therapists help their clients . . .

Treatment Planners cover all the necessary elements for developing formal treatment plans, including detailed problem definitions, long-term goals, short-term objectives, therapeutic interventions, and DSM-IV™ diagnoses.

- ❑ **The Complete Adult Psychotherapy Treatment Planner,** Fourth Edition..........0-471-76346-2 / $49.95
- ❑ **The Child Psychotherapy Treatment Planner,** Fourth Edition..........0-471-78535-0 / $49.95
- ❑ **The Adolescent Psychotherapy Treatment Planner,** Fourth Edition..........0-471-78539-3 / $49.95
- ❑ **The Addiction Treatment Planner,** Third Edition..........0-471-72544-7 / $49.95
- ❑ **The Couples Psychotherapy Treatment Planner**..........0-471-24711-1 / $49.95
- ❑ **The Group Therapy Treatment Planner,** Second Edition..........0-471-66791-9 / $49.95
- ❑ **The Family Therapy Treatment Planner**..........0-471-34768-X / $49.95
- ❑ **The Older Adult Psychotherapy Treatment Planner**..........0-471-29574-4 / $49.95
- ❑ **The Employee Assistance (EAP) Treatment Planner**..........0-471-24709-X / $49.95
- ❑ **The Gay and Lesbian Psychotherapy Treatment Planner**..........0-471-35080-X / $49.95
- ❑ **The Crisis Counseling and Traumatic Events Treatment Planner**..........0-471-39587-0 / $49.95
- ❑ **The Social Work and Human Services Treatment Planner**..........0-471-37741-4 / $49.95
- ❑ **The Continuum of Care Treatment Planner**..........0-471-19568-5 / $49.95
- ❑ **The Behavioral Medicine Treatment Planner**..........0-471-31923-6 / $49.95
- ❑ **The Mental Retardation and Developmental Disability Treatment Planner**..........0-471-38253-1 / $49.95
- ❑ **The Special Education Treatment Planner**..........0-471-38872-6 / $49.95
- ❑ **The Severe and Persistent Mental Illness Treatment Planner**..........0-471-35945-9 / $49.95
- ❑ **The Personality Disorders Treatment Planner**..........0-471-39403-3 / $49.95
- ❑ **The Rehabilitation Psychology Treatment Planner**..........0-471-35178-4 / $49.95
- ❑ **The Pastoral Counseling Treatment Planner**..........0-471-25416-9 / $49.95
- ❑ **The Juvenile Justice and Residential Care Treatment Planner**..........0-471-43320-9 / $49.95
- ❑ **The School Counseling and School Social Work Treatment Planner**..........0-471-08496-4 / $49.95
- ❑ **The Psychopharmacology Treatment Planner**..........0-471-43322-5 / $49.95
- ❑ **The Probation and Parole Treatment Planner**..........0-471-20244-4 / $49.95
- ❑ **The Suicide and Homicide Risk Assessment and Prevention Treatment Planner**..........0-471-46631-X / $49.95
- ❑ **The Speech-Language Pathology Treatment Planner**..........0-471-27504-2 / $49.95
- ❑ **The College Student Counseling Treatment Planner**..........0-471-46708-1 / $49.95
- ❑ **The Parenting Skills Treatment Planner**..........0-471-48183-1 / $49.95
- ❑ **The Early Childhood Education Intervention Treatment Planner**..........0-471-65962-2 / $49.95
- ❑ **The Co-Occurring Disorders Treatment Planner**..........0-471-73081-5 / $49.95
- ❑ **The Sexual Abuse Victim and Sexual Offender Treatment Planner**..........0-471-21979-7 / $49.95

The **Complete Treatment and Homework Planners** series of books combines our bestselling *Treatment Planners* and *Homework Planners* into one easy-to-use, all-in-one resource for mental health professionals treating clients suffering from the most commonly diagnosed disorders.

- ❑ **The Complete Depression Treatment and Homework Planner**..........0-471-64515-X / $39.95
- ❑ **The Complete Anxiety Treatment and Homework Planner**..........0-471-64548-6 / $39.95

Over 500,000 Practice*Planners*® sold . . .

WILEY

Practice*Planners*®

Homework Planners feature dozens of behaviorally based, ready-to-use assignments that are designed for use between sessions, as well as a disk or CD-ROM (Microsoft Word) containing all of the assignments—allowing you to customize them to suit your unique client needs.

- ❑ **Brief Couples Therapy Homework Planner** .... 0-471-29511-6 / $49.95
- ❑ **Child Psychotherapy Homework Planner,** Second Edition .... 0-471-78534-2 / $49.95
- ❑ **Child Therapy Activity and Homework Planner** .... 0-471-25684-6 / $49.95
- ❑ **Adolescent Psychotherapy Homework Planner,** Second Edition .... 0-471-78537-7 / $49.95
- ❑ **Addiction Treatment Homework Planner,** Third Edition .... 0-471-77461-8 / $49.95
- ❑ **Brief Employee Assistance Homework Planner** .... 0-471-38088-1 / $49.95
- ❑ **Brief Family Therapy Homework Planner** .... 0-471-38512-3 / $49.95
- ❑ **Grief Counseling Homework Planner** .... 0-471-43318-7 / $49.95
- ❑ **Divorce Counseling Homework Planner** .... 0-471-43319-5 / $49.95
- ❑ **Group Therapy Homework Planner** .... 0-471-41822-6 / $49.95
- ❑ **School Counseling and School Social Work Homework Planner** .... 0-471-09114-6 / $49.95
- ❑ **Adolescent Psychotherapy Homework Planner II** .... 0-471-27493-3 / $49.95
- ❑ **Adult Psychotherapy Homework Planner,** Second Edition .... 0-471-76343-8 / $49.95
- ❑ **Parenting Skills Homework Planner** .... 0-471-48182-3 / $49.95

Practice Planners
Arthur E. Jongsma, Jr., Series Editor
SECOND EDITION
Companion to The Addiction Treatment Planner, 3e
The Addiction
PROGRESS NOTES PLANNER
DAVID J. BERGHUIS AND ARTHUR E. JONGSMA, JR.

Progress Notes Planners contain complete prewritten progress notes for each presenting problem in the companion Treatment Planners.

- ❑ **The Adult Psychotherapy Progress Notes Planner** .... 0-471-76344-6 / $49.95
- ❑ **The Adolescent Psychotherapy Progress Notes Planner** .... 0-471-78538-5 / $49.95
- ❑ **The Severe and Persistent Mental Illness Progress Notes Planner** .... 0-471-21986-X / $49.95
- ❑ **The Child Psychotherapy Progress Notes Planner** .... 0-471-78536-9 / $49.95
- ❑ **The Addiction Progress Notes Planner** .... 0-471-73253-2 / $49.95
- ❑ **The Couples Psychotherapy Progress Notes Planner** .... 0-471-27460-7 / $49.95
- ❑ **The Family Therapy Progress Notes Planner** .... 0-471-48443-1 / $49.95

Client Education Handout Planners contain elegantly designed handouts that can be printed out from the enclosed CD-ROM and provide information on a wide range of psychological and emotional disorders and life skills issues. Use as patient literature, handouts at presentations, and aids for promoting your mental health practice.

- ❑ **Adult Client Education Handout Planner** .... 0-471-20232-0 / $49.95
- ❑ **Child and Adolescent Client Education Handout Planner** .... 0-471-20233-9 / $49.95
- ❑ **Couples and Family Client Education Handout Planner** .... 0-471-20234-7 / $49.95

Name ______________________
Affiliation ______________________
Address ______________________
City/State/Zip ______________________
Phone/Fax ______________________
E-mail ______________________
❑ Check enclosed ❑ Visa ❑ MasterCard ❑ American Express
Card # ______________________
Expiration Date ______________________
Signature ______________________

**Add $5 shipping for first book, $3 for each additional book. Please add your local sales tax to all orders. Prices subject to change without notice.*

- **To order by phone in the US: Call toll free 1-877-762-2974**
- **Online: www.practiceplanners.wiley.com**
- **Mail this order form to: John Wiley & Sons, Attn: J. Knott, 111 River Street, Hoboken, NJ 07030**

The Complete Adult Psychotherapy Treatment Planner

Practice*Planners*® Series

Treatment Planners

The Complete Adult Psychotherapy Treatment Planner, Fourth Edition
The Child Psychotherapy Treatment Planner, Fourth Edition
The Adolescent Psychotherapy Treatment Planner, Fourth Edition
The Addiction Treatment Planner, Third Edition
The Continuum of Care Treatment Planner
The Couples Psychotherapy Treatment Planner
The Employee Assistance Treatment Planner
The Pastoral Counseling Treatment Planner
The Older Adult Psychotherapy Treatment Planner
The Behavioral Medicine Treatment Planner
The Group Therapy Treatment Planner, Second Edition
The Gay and Lesbian Psychotherapy Treatment Planner
The Family Therapy Treatment Planner
The Severe and Persistent Mental Illness Treatment Planner
The Mental Retardation and Developmental Disability Treatment Planner
The Social Work and Human Services Treatment Planner
The Crisis Counseling and Traumatic Events Treatment Planner
The Personality Disorders Treatment Planner
The Rehabilitation Psychology Treatment Planner
The Special Education Treatment Planner
The Juvenile Justice and Residential Care Treatment Planner
The School Counseling and School Social Work Treatment Planner
The Sexual Abuse Victim and Sexual Offender Treatment Planner
The Probation and Parole Treatment Planner
The Psychopharmacology Treatment Planner
The Speech-Language Pathology Treatment Planner
The Suicide and Homicide Risk Assessment & Prevention Treatment Planner
The College Student Counseling Treatment Planner
The Parenting Skills Treatment Planner
The Early Childhood Education Intervention Treatment Planner
The Co-Occurring Disorders Treatment Planner

Progress Notes Planners

The Child Psychotherapy Progress Notes Planner, Third Edition
The Adolescent Psychotherapy Progress Notes Planner, Third Edition
The Adult Psychotherapy Progress Notes Planner, Third Edition
The Addiction Progress Notes Planner, Second Edition
The Severe and Persistent Mental Illness Progress Notes Planner
The Couples Psychotherapy Progress Notes Planner
The Family Therapy Progress Notes Planner

Homework Planners

Brief Therapy Homework Planner
Brief Couples Therapy Homework Planner
Brief Employee Assistance Homework Planner
Brief Family Therapy Homework Planner
Grief Counseling Homework Planner
Group Therapy Homework Planner
Divorce Counseling Homework Planner
School Counseling and School Social Work Homework Planner
Child Therapy Activity and Homework Planner
Addiction Treatment Homework Planner, Third Edition
Adolescent Psychotherapy Homework Planner, Second Edition
Adult Psychotherapy Homework Planner, Second Edition
Child Psychotherapy Homework Planner, Second Edition
Parenting Skills Homework Planner

Client Education Handout Planners

Adult Client Education Handout Planner
Child and Adolescent Client Education Handout Planner
Couples and Family Client Education Handout Planner

Complete Planners

The Complete Depression Treatment and Homework Planner
The Complete Anxiety Treatment and Homework Planner

Arthur E. Jongsma, Jr., Series Editor

The Complete Adult Psychotherapy Treatment Planner, Fourth Edition

Arthur E. Jongsma, Jr.

L. Mark Peterson

Timothy J. Bruce, Contributing Editor

JOHN WILEY & SONS, INC.

This book is printed on acid-free paper. ♾

Published by John Wiley & Sons, Inc., Hoboken, New Jersey.
Published simultaneously in Canada.

For general information on our other products and services please contact our Customer Care Department within the United States at (800) 762-2974, outside the United States at (317) 572-3993 or fax (317) 572-4002.

Wiley also publishes its books in a variety of electronic formats. Some content that appears in print may not be available in electronic books. For more information about Wiley products, visit our web site at www.wiley.com.

ISBN-13: 978-0-471-76346-8 (pbk.)
ISBN-10: 0-471-76346-2 (pbk.)

Printed in the United States of America.

10 9 8 7 6 5 4 3 2 1

We dedicate this book to our most influential teachers
and mentors early in our professional journey:

Dr. Solomon E. Feldman
Dr. Richard A. Westmaas
Dr. Richard Brown
Dr. Jack Carr
Dr. David H. Barlow
Dr. Jerome A. Cerny

CONTENTS

ℰℬ indicates that selected Objective/Interventions are consistent with those found in evidence-based treatments.

PRACTICE*PLANNERS*® SERIES PREFACE

Accountability is an important dimension of the practice of psychotherapy. Treatment programs, public agencies, clinics, and practitioners must justify and document their treatment plans to outside review entities in order to be reimbursed for services. The books and software in the Practice*Planners*® series are designed to help practitioners fulfill these documentation requirements efficiently and professionally.

The Practice*Planners*® series includes a wide array of treatment planning books including not only the original *Complete Adult Psychotherapy Treatment Planner, Child Psychotherapy Treatment Planner,* and *Adolescent Psychotherapy Treatment Planner,* all now in their fourth editions, but also *Treatment Planners* targeted to a wide range of specialty areas of practice, including:

- Addictions
- Co-occurring disorders
- Behavioral medicine
- College students
- Couples therapy
- Crisis counseling
- Early childhood education
- Employee assistance
- Family therapy
- Gays and lesbians
- Group therapy
- Juvenile justice and residential care
- Mental retardation and developmental disability
- Neuropsychology
- Older adults
- Parenting skills
- Pastoral counseling
- Personality disorders
- Probation and parole
- Psychopharmacology

- School counseling
- Severe and persistent mental illness
- Sexual abuse victims and offenders
- Special education
- Suicide and homicide risk assessment

In addition, there are three branches of companion books which can be used in conjunction with the *Treatment Planners,* or on their own:

- ***Progress Notes Planners*** provide a menu of progress statements that elaborate on the client's symptom presentation and the provider's therapeutic intervention. Each *Progress Notes Planner* statement is directly integrated with the behavioral definitions and therapeutic interventions from its companion *Treatment Planner.*
- ***Homework Planners*** include homework assignments designed around each presenting problem (such as anxiety, depression, chemical dependence, anger management, eating disorders, or panic disorder) that is the focus of a chapter in its corresponding *Treatment Planner.*
- ***Client Education Handout Planners*** provide brochures and handouts to help educate and inform clients on presenting problems and mental health issues, as well as life skills techniques. The handouts are included on CD-ROMs for easy printing from your computer and are ideal for use in waiting rooms, at presentations, as newsletters, or as information for clients struggling with mental illness issues. The topics covered by these handouts correspond to the presenting problems in the *Treatment Planners.*

The series also includes:

- **Thera*Scribe*®**, the #1 selling treatment planning and clinical record-keeping software system for mental health professionals. Thera*Scribe*® allows the user to import the data from any of the *Treatment Planner, Progress Notes Planner,* or *Homework Planner* books into the software's expandable database to simply point and click to create a detailed, organized, individualized, and customized treatment plan along with optional integrated progress notes and homework assignments.

Adjunctive books, such as *The Psychotherapy Documentation Primer* and *The Clinical Documentation Sourcebook* contain forms and resources to aid the clinician in mental health practice management.

The goal of our series is to provide practitioners with the resources they need in order to provide high quality care in the era of accountability. To put it simply: we seek to help you spend more time on patients, and less time on paperwork.

Arthur E. Jongsma, Jr.
Grand Rapids, Michigan

ACKNOWLEDGMENTS

I have learned that it is better to acknowledge your weaknesses and to seek out those who complement you with their strengths. I was fortunate enough to have found the right person who brings his expertise in Evidence-Based Treatment to this project. He has contributed wisely and thoughtfully to greatly improve our *Complete Adult Psychotherapy Treatment Planner* through his well-informed edits and additions to our content, to bring it in line with the latest psychotherapy research. He has been thoroughly professional in his approach while being a joy to work with, due to his wonderful sense of humor. I have said to many people since beginning this revision, "This guy really knows the literature!" For a person like me, who has spent his career in the psychotherapy trenches, it is a pleasure to get back in touch with my science-based roots by working with a Boulder Model clinician-scientist. I take my hat off to you, Dr. Tim Bruce. You have taken our product to a new level of contribution to the clinicians who are looking for Evidence-Based Treatment guidance. Your students are fortunate to have you for a mentor and we are fortunate to have you for a Contributing Editor. Thank you!

AEJ

I want to acknowledge how honored I am to have had this chance to work with Art Jongsma, his colleague Sue Rhoda, and the staff at John Wiley and Sons on these, their well-known and highly regarded, treatment planners. These planners are widely recognized as works of enormous value to practicing clinicians as well as great educational tools for students of our profession. I didn't know Art when he asked me if I would join him on these editions, and the task he had in mind, to help empirically inform objectives and interventions, was daunting. I knew it would be a challenge to retain the rich breadth of options that Art has offered in past editions while simultaneously trying to identify and describe the fundamental features of identified empirically supported treatments. Although I have trained in empirically supported treatment approaches, contributed to this literature, and used them throughout my professional career, I recognize that our product will be open to criticism. I can say that we have done our best to offer a resource to our colleagues and their clients that is practical, flexible, and appreciates the complexities of any of the treatment approaches it conveys. And in the process of working with Art and Sue toward these goals, I have found them not only to be consummate professionals, but also thoughtful, conscientious, and kind persons. It has been a great pleasure working with you, Art and Sue, and a privilege to call you my friends.

TJB

The Complete Adult Psychotherapy Treatment Planner

INTRODUCTION

ABOUT PRACTICE*PLANNERS*® TREATMENT PLANNERS

Pressure from third-party payors, accrediting agencies, and other outside parties has increased the need for clinicians to quickly produce effective, high-quality treatment plans. *Treatment Planners* provide all the elements necessary to quickly and easily develop formal treatments plans that satisfy the needs of most third-party payors and state and federal review agencies.

Each *Treatment Planner:*

- Saves you hours of time-consuming paperwork.
- Offers the freedom to develop customized treatment plans.
- Includes over 1,000 clear statements describing the behavioral manifestations of each relational problem, and includes long-term goals, short-term objectives, and clinically tested treatment options.
- Has an easy-to-use reference format that helps locate treatment plan components by behavioral problem or DSM-IV™ diagnosis.

As with the rest of the books in the Practice*Planners*® series, our aim is to clarify, simplify, and accelerate the treatment planning process, so you spend less time on paperwork, and more time with your clients.

HOW TO USE THIS TREATMENT PLANNER

Use this *Treatment Planner* to write treatment plans according to the following progression of six steps:

1. **Problem Selection.** Although the client may discuss a variety of issues during the assessment, the clinician must determine the most significant problems on which to focus thc treatment process. Usually a primary problem will surface, and secondary problems may also be evident. Some other problems may have to be set aside as not urgent enough to require treat-

ment at this time. An effective treatment plan can only deal with a few selected problems or treatment will lose its direction. Choose the problem within this *Planner* which most accurately represents your client's presenting issues.

2. **Problem Definition.** Each client presents with unique nuances as to how a problem behaviorally reveals itself in his or her life. Therefore, each problem that is selected for treatment focus requires a specific definition about how it is evidenced in the particular client. The symptom pattern should be associated with diagnostic criteria and codes such as those found in the *DSM-IV* or the International Classification of Diseases. This *Planner* offers such behaviorally specific definition statements to choose from or to serve as a model for your own personally crafted statements.
3. **Goal Development.** The next step in developing your treatment plan is to set broad goals for the resolution of the target problem. These statements need not be crafted in measurable terms but can be global, long-term goals that indicate a desired positive outcome to the treatment procedures. This *Planner* provides several possible goal statements for each problem, but one statement is all that is required in a treatment plan.
4. **Objective Construction.** In contrast to long-term goals, objectives must be stated in behaviorally measurable language so that it is clear to review agencies, health maintenance organizations, and managed care organizations when the client has achieved the established objectives. The objectives presented in this *Planner* are designed to meet this demand for accountability. Numerous alternatives are presented to allow construction of a variety of treatment plan possibilities for the same presenting problem.
5. **Intervention Creation.** Interventions are the actions of the clinician designed to help the client complete the objectives. There should be at least one intervention for every objective. If the client does not accomplish the objective after the initial intervention, new interventions should be added to the plan. Interventions should be selected on the basis of the client's needs and the treatment provider's full therapeutic repertoire. This *Planner* contains interventions from a broad range of therapeutic approaches, and we encourage the provider to write other interventions reflecting his or her own training and experience.

   Some suggested interventions listed in the *Planner* refer to specific books that can be assigned to the client for adjunctive bibliotherapy. Appendix A contains a full bibliographic reference list of these materials, including these two popular choices: *Read Two Books and Let's Talk Next Week: Using Bibliotherapy in Clinical Practice* (2000) by Maidman and DiMenna and *Rent Two Films and Let's Talk in the Morning: Using Popular Movies in Psychotherapy, Second Edition* (2001) by Hesley and Hesley (both books are published by Wiley). For further information about self-help books, mental health professionals may wish to consult *The Au-*

thoritative Guide to Self-Help Resources in Mental Health, Revised Edition (2003) by Norcross et al (available from The Guilford Press, New York).

6. **Diagnosis Determination.** The determination of an appropriate diagnosis is based on an evaluation of the client's complete clinical presentation. The clinician must compare the behavioral, cognitive, emotional, and interpersonal symptoms that the client presents with the criteria for diagnosis of a mental illness condition as described in *DSM-IV*. Despite arguments made against diagnosing clients in this manner, diagnosis is a reality that exists in the world of mental health care, and it is a necessity for third-party reimbursement. It is the clinician's thorough knowledge of *DSM-IV* criteria and a complete understanding of the client assessment data that contribute to the most reliable, valid diagnosis.

Congratulations! After completing these six steps, you should have a comprehensive and individualized treatment plan ready for immediate implementation and presentation to the client. A sample treatment plan for borderline personality is provided at the end of this introduction.

INCORPORATING EVIDENCE-BASED TREATMENT INTO THE *TREATMENT* PLANNER

Evidence-based treatment (that is, treatment which is scientifically shown in research trials to be efficacious) is rapidly becoming of critical importance to the mental health community as insurance companies are beginning to offer preferential pay to organizations using it. In fact, the APA Division 12 (Society of Clinical Psychology) lists of empirically supported treatments have been referenced by a number of local, state and federal funding agencies, which are beginning to restrict reimbursement to these treatments, as are some managed-care and insurance companies.

In this fourth edition of *The Complete Adult Psychotherapy Treatment Planner* we have made an effort to empirically inform some chapters by highlighting Short-term Objectives (STOs) and Therapeutic Interventions (TIs) that are consistent with therapies that have demonstrated efficacy through empirical study. Watch for this icon as an indication that an Objective/Intervention is consistent with those found in evidence-based treatments.

EB

References to their empirical support have been included in the reference section as Appendix B. Reviews of efforts to identify evidence-based therapies (EBT), including the effort's benefits and limitations can be found in Bruce and Sanderson (2005), Chambless and colleagues (1996, 1998), and Chambless and Ollendick (2001). References have also been included to therapist- and client-oriented treatment manuals and books that describe the step-by-step use of noted EBTs or treatments consistent with their objectives and interventions. Of course, recognizing that there are STOs and TIs that practicing clinicians have found useful but that have not yet received empirical scrutiny, we have included those that reflect common practice among experienced clinicians. The goal is to provide a range of treatment plan options, some studied empirically, others reflecting common clinical practice, so the user can construct what they believe to be the best plan for their particular client.

In many instances, EBTs are short-term, problem-oriented treatments that focus on improving current problems/symptoms related to a client's current distress and disability. Accordingly, STOs and TIs of that type have been placed earlier in the sequence of STO and TI options. In addition, some STOs and TIs reflect core components of the EBT approach that are always delivered (e.g., exposure to feared objects and situations for a phobic disorder; behavioral activation for depression). Others reflect adjuncts to treatment that are commonly used to address problems that may not always be a feature of the clinical picture (e.g., assertive communication skills training for the social anxious or depressed client whose difficulty with assertion appears contributory to the primary anxiety or depressive disorder). Most of the STOs and TIs associated with the EBTs are described at a level of detail that permits flexibility and adaptability in their specific application. As with previous editions of this *Treatment Planner,* each chapter also includes the option to add STOs and TIs that are not listed.

Criteria for Inclusion of Evidence-Based Therapies

Not every treatment that has undergone empirical study for a mental health problem is included in this edition. In general, we have included EBTs the empirical support for which has either been well established or demonstrated at more than a preliminary level as defined by those authors who have undertaken the task of identifying EBTs, such as Chambless and colleagues (1996, 1998) and Nathan and Gorman (1998, 2002). At minimum, this requires demonstration of efficacy through a clinical trial or large clinical replication series that have features reflective of good experimental design (e.g., random assignment, blind assignments, reliable and valid measurement, clear inclusion and exclusion criteria, state-of-the-art diagnostic methods, and adequate sample size). Well established EBTs typically have more than one of these types of studies demonstrating their efficacy as well as other desirable features, such as demonstration of efficacy by independent research groups and specification of client characteristics for which the treatment was effective. Because treatment literatures for various problems develop at different paces, treatment STOs and TIs that have been included may have the most empirical support for their problem area, but less than that found in more heavily studied areas. For example, Dialectical Behavior Therapy (DBT) has the highest level of empirical support of tested psychotherapies for Borderline Personality Disorder (BPD), but that level of evidence is lower than that supporting, for example, exposure-based therapy for phobic fear and avoidance. The latter has simply been studied more extensively, so there are more controlled trials, independent replications, and the like. Nonetheless, within the psychotherapy outcome literature for BPD, DBT clearly has the highest level of evidence supporting its efficacy and usefulness. Accordingly, STOs and TIs consistent with DBT have been included in this edition. Lastly, just as some of the STOs and TIs included in this edition reflect common clinical practices of experienced clinicians, those associated with EBTs reflect what is commonly practiced by clinicians that use EBTs.

Summary of Required and Preferred EBT Inclusion Criteria

Required

- Demonstration of efficacy through at least one randomized controlled trial with good experimental design, or
- Demonstration of efficacy through a large, well-designed clinical replication series.

Preferred

- Efficacy has been shown by more than one study.
- Efficacy has been demonstrated by independent research groups.
- Client characteristics for which the treatment was effective were specified.
- A clear description of the treatment was available.

There does remain considerable debate regarding evidence-based treatment amongst mental health professionals who are not always in agreement regarding the best treatments or how to weigh the factors that contribute to good outcomes. Some practitioners are skeptical about the wisdom of changing their practice on the basis of research evidence, and their reluctance is fuelled by the methodological problems of psychotherapy research. Our goal in this book is to provide a range of treatment plan options, some studied empirically, others reflecting common clinical practice, so the user can construct what they believe to be the best plan for their particular client. As indicated earlier, recognizing that there are interventions which practicing clinicians have found useful but that have not yet received empirical scrutiny, we have included those that reflect common practice among experienced clinicians.

A FINAL NOTE ON TAILORING THE TREATMENT PLAN TO THE CLIENT

One important aspect of effective treatment planning is that each plan should be tailored to the individual client's problems and needs. Treatment plans should not be mass-produced, even if clients have similar problems. The individual's strengths and weaknesses, unique stressors, social network, family circumstances, and symptom patterns must be considered in developing a treatment strategy. Drawing upon our own years of clinical experience, we have put together a variety of treatment choices. These statements can be combined in thousands of permutations to develop detailed treatment plans. Relying on their own good judgment, clinicians can easily select the statements that are appropriate for the individuals whom they are treating. In addition, we encourage readers to add their own definitions, goals, objectives, and interventions to the existing samples. As with all of the books in the *Treatment Planners* series, it is our hope that this book will help promote effective, creative treatment planning—a process that will ultimately benefit the client, clinician, and mental health community.

SAMPLE TREATMENT PLAN

BORDERLINE PERSONALITY

Definitions: A minor stress leads to extreme emotional reactivity (anger, anxiety, or depression) that usually lasts from a few hours to a few days.

Exhibits a pattern of intense, chaotic interpersonal relationships.

Engages in recurrent suicidal gestures, threats, or self-mutilating behavior.

Reports chronic feelings of emptiness and boredom.

Exhibits frequent eruptions of intense, inappropriate anger.

Easily feels unfairly treated and believes that others can't be trusted.

Analyzes most issues in simple terms (e.g., right/wrong, black/white, trustworthy/deceitful) without regard for extenuating circumstances or complex situations.

Goals: Develop and demonstrate coping skills to deal with mood swings.

Replace dichotomous thinking with the ability to tolerate ambiguity and complexity in people and issues.

Learn and practice interpersonal relationship skills.

Terminate self-damaging behaviors (such as substance abuse, reckless driving, sexual acting out, binge eating, or suicidal behaviors).

OBJECTIVES

1. Discuss openly the history of difficulties that have led to seeking treatment.

INTERVENTIONS

1. Assess the client's experiences of distress and disability, identifying behaviors (e.g., parasuicidal acts, angry outbursts, overattachment), affect (e.g., mood swings, emotional overreactions, painful emptiness), and cognitions (e.g., biases such as dichotomous thinking, overgeneralization, catastrophizing) that will become the targets of therapy.

2. Explore the client's history of abuse and/or abandonment, particularly in childhood years.

2. Verbalize an accurate and reasonable understanding of the process of therapy and what the therapeutic goals are.

1. Orient the client to dialectical behavior therapy (DBT), highlighting its multiple facets (e.g., support, collaboration, challenge, problem-solving, skill-building) and discuss dialectical/biosocial view of borderline personality, emphasizing constitutional and social influences on its features (see *Cognitive-Behavioral Treatment of Borderline Personality* by Linehan).

3. Verbalize any history of self-mutilative and suicidal urges and behavior.

1. Probe the nature and history of the client's self-mutilating behavior.
2. Assess the client's suicidal gestures as to triggers, frequency, seriousness, secondary gain, and onset.
3. Arrange for hospitalization, as necessary, when the client is judged to be harmful to self.

4. Reduce actions that interfere with participating in therapy.

1. Continuously monitor, confront, and problem-solve client actions that threaten to interfere with the continuation of therapy, such as missing appointments, noncompliance, and/or abruptly leaving therapy.

5. Reduce the frequency of maladaptive behaviors, thoughts, and feelings that interfere with attaining a reasonable quality of life.

1. Use validation, dialectical strategies (e.g., metaphor, devil's advocate), and problem-solving strategies (e.g., behavioral and solution analysis, cognitive restructuring, skills training, exposure) to help the client manage, reduce, or stabilize maladaptive behaviors (e.g., angry outbursts, binge drinking, abusive relationships, high-risk sex, uncontrolled

spending), thoughts (e.g., all-or-nothing thinking, catastrophizing, personalizing), and feelings (e.g., rage, hopelessness, abandonment; see *Cognitive-Behavioral Treatment of Borderline Personality* by Linehan).

6. Participate in a group (preferably) or individual personal skills development course.

1. Conduct group or individual skills training tailored to the client's identified problem behavioral patterns (e.g., assertiveness for abusive relationships, cognitive strategies for identifying and controlling financial, sexual, and other impulsivity).

7. Identify, challenge, and replace biased, fearful self-talk with reality-based, positive self-talk.

1. Explore the client's schema and self-talk that mediate their trauma-related and other fears; identify and challenge biases; assist him/her in generating thoughts that correct for negative biases and build confidence.
2. Assign the client a homework exercise in which he/she identifies fearful self-talk and creates reality-based alternatives; review and reinforce success, providing corrective feedback for failure (see "Journal and Replace Self-Defeating Thoughts" in *Adult Psychotherapy Homework Planner,* 2nd ed. by Jongsma, or "Daily Record of Dysfunctional Thoughts" in *Cognitive Therapy of Depression* by Beck, Rush, Shaw, and Emery).
3. Reinforce the client's positive, reality-based cognitive messages, which enhance self-confidence and increase adaptive action.

Diagnosis: 301.83 Borderline Personality Disorder

ANGER MANAGEMENT

BEHAVIORAL DEFINITIONS

1. History of explosive, aggressive outbursts out of proportion with any precipitating stressors, leading to assaultive acts or destruction of property.
2. Overreactive hostility to insignificant irritants.
3. Swift and harsh judgmental statements made to or about others.
4. Body language suggesting anger, including tense muscles (e.g., clenched fist or jaw), glaring looks, or refusal to make eye contact.
5. Use of passive-aggressive patterns (e.g., social withdrawal, lack of complete or timely compliance in following directions or rules, complaining about authority figures behind their backs, uncooperative in meeting expected behavioral norms) due to anger.
6. Consistent pattern of challenging or disrespectful attitudes toward authority figures.
7. Use of abusive language meant to intimidate others.

__. ____

____

__. ____

____

__. ____

____

LONG-TERM GOALS

1. Decrease overall intensity and frequency of angry feelings, and increase ability to recognize and appropriately express angry feelings as they occur.
2. Develop an awareness of current angry behaviors, clarifying origins of and alternatives to aggressive anger.

3. Come to an awareness and acceptance of angry feelings while developing better control and more serenity.
4. Become capable of handling angry feelings in constructive ways that enhance daily functioning.
5. Demonstrate respect for others and their feelings.

__. ____

____

__. ____

____

__. ____

____

SHORT-TERM OBJECTIVES

1. Identify situations, thoughts, feelings that trigger anger, angry verbal and/or behavioral actions and the targets of those actions. (1)

2. (EB) Cooperate with a medical evaluation to assess possible organic contributors to poor anger control. (2)

3. (EB) Cooperate with a physician evaluation for possible treatment with psychotropic medications to assist in anger control and take medications consistently, if prescribed. (3, 4)

THERAPEUTIC INTERVENTIONS

1. Thoroughly assess the various stimuli (e.g., situations, people, thoughts) that have triggered the client's anger and the thoughts, feelings, and actions that have characterized his/her anger responses.

2. Refer the client to a physician for a complete physical exam to rule out organic contributors (e.g., brain damage, tumor, elevated testosterone levels) to poor anger control. (EB)

3. Assess the client for the need for psychotropic medication to assist in control of anger; refer him/her to a physician for an evaluation and prescription of medication, if needed. (EB)

(EB) indicates that the Objective/Intervention is consistent with those found in evidence-based treatments.

4. Monitor the client for prescription compliance, effectiveness, and side effects; provide feedback to the prescribing physician. ♥

♥ 4. Keep a daily journal of persons, situations, and other triggers of anger; record thoughts, feelings, and actions taken. (5, 6)

5. Ask the client to keep a daily journal in which he/she documents persons, situations, and other triggers of anger, irritation, or disappointment (or assign "Anger Journal" in *Adult Psychotherapy Homework Planner,* 2nd ed. by Jongsma); routinely process the journal toward helping the client understand his/her contributions to generating his/her anger. ♥

6. Assist the client in generating a list of anger triggers; process the list toward helping the client understand the causes and extent of his/her anger. ♥

♥ 5. Verbalize increased awareness of anger expression patterns, their possible origins, and their consequences. (7, 8, 9, 10)

7. Assist the client in coming to the realization that he/she is angry by reviewing triggers and frequency of angry outbursts. ♥

8. Assist the client in identifying ways that key life figures (e.g., father, mother, teachers) have expressed angry feelings and how these experiences have positively or negatively influenced the way he/she handles anger. ♥

9. Ask the client to list ways anger has negatively impacted his/her daily life (e.g., injuring others or self, legal conflicts, loss of respect from self and others, destruction of property); process this list. ♥

10. Expand the client's awareness of the negative effects that anger has on his/her psychical health (e.g., increased susceptibilty to disease, injuries, headaches).

6. Agree to learn alternative ways to think about and manage anger. (11, 12)

11. Assist the client in reconceptualizing anger as involving different components (cognitive, physiological, affective, and behavioral) that go through predictable phases (e.g., demanding expectations not being met leading to increased arousal and anger leading to acting out) that can be managed.

12. Assist the client in identifying the positive consequences of managing anger (e.g., respect from others and self, cooperation from others, improved physical health); ask the client to agree to learning new ways to conceptualize and manage anger.

7. Learn and implement calming strategies as part of managing reactions to frustration. (13, 14)

13. Teach the client calming techniques (e.g., muscle relaxation, paced breathing, calming imagery) as part of a tailored strategy for responding appropriately to angry feelings when they occur.

14. Assign the client to implement calming techniques in his/her daily life when facing anger trigger situations; process the results, reinforcing success and redirecting for failure.

8. Identify, challenge, and replace anger-inducing self-talk with self-talk that facilitates a less angry reaction. (15, 16)

15. Explore the client's self-talk that mediates his/her angry feelings and actions (e.g., demanding expectations reflected in should, must, or have to statements); identify and challenge biases, assisting

him/her in generating appraisals and self-talk that corrects for the biases and facilitates a more flexible and temperate response to frustration. ▼

16. Assign the client a homework exercise in which he/she identifies angry self-talk and generates alternatives that help moderate angry reactions; review; reinforce success, providing corrective feedback toward improvement. ▼

▼ 9. Learn and implement thought-stopping to manage intrusive unwanted thoughts that trigger anger. (17)

17. Assign the client to implement a "thought-stopping" technique on a daily basis between sessions (or assign "Making Use of the Thought-Stopping Technique" in *Adult Psychotherapy Homework Planner,* 2nd ed. by Jongsma); review implementation; reinforce success, providing corrective feedback toward improvement. ▼

▼ 10. Verbalize feelings of anger in a controlled, assertive way. (18, 19)

18. Use instruction, modeling, and/or role-playing to teach the client assertive communication; if indicated, refer him/her to an assertiveness training class/group for further instruction. ▼

19. Conduct conjoint sessions to help the client implement assertion, problem-solving, and/or conflict resolution skills in the presence of his/her significant others. ▼

▼ 11. Learn and implement problem-solving and/or conflict resolution skills to manage interpersonal problems. (19, 20)

19. Conduct conjoint sessions to help the client implement assertion, problem-solving, and/or conflict resolution skills in the presence of his/her significant others. ▼

20. Teach the client conflict resolution skills (e.g., empathy, active listening, "I messages," respectful communication, assertiveness

without aggression, compromise); use modeling, role-playing, and behavior rehearsal to work through several current conflicts. ▽

▽12. Practice using new anger management skills in session with the therapist and during homework exercises. (21, 22, 23)

21. Assist the client in constructing a client-tailored strategy for managing anger that combines any of the somatic, cognitive, communication, problem-solving, and/or conflict resolution skills relevant to his/her needs. ▽

22. Select situations in which the client will be increasingly challenged to apply his/her new strategies for managing anger. ▽

23. Use any of several techniques, including relaxation, imagery, behavioral rehearsal, modeling, role-playing, or in vivo exposure/behavioral experiments to help the client consolidate the use of his/her new anger management skills. ▽

▽13. Decrease the number, intensity, and duration of angry outbursts, while increasing the use of new skills for managing anger. (24)

24. Monitor the client's reports of angry outbursts toward the goal of decreasing their frequency, intensity, and duration through the client's use of new anger management skills (or assign "Alternatives to Destructive Anger" in *Adult Psychotherapy Homework Planner,* 2nd ed. by Jongsma); review progress, reinforcing success and providing corrective feedback toward improvement. ▽

▽14. Identify social supports that will help facilitate the implementation of anger management skills. (25)

25. Encourage the client to discuss his/her anger management goals with trusted persons who are likely to support his/her change. ▽

15. Implement relapse prevention strategies for managing possible future trauma-related symptoms. (26, 27, 28, 29, 30)

26. Discuss with the client the distinction between a lapse and relapse, associating a lapse with an initial and reversible angry outburst and relapse with the choice to return routinely to the old pattern of anger.

27. Identify and rehearse with the client the management of future situations or circumstances in which lapses back to anger could occur.

28. Instruct the client to routinely use the new anger management strategies learned in therapy (e.g., calming, adaptive self-talk, assertion, and/or conflict resolution) to respond to frustrations.

29. Develop a "coping card" or other reminder on which new anger management skills and other important information (e.g., calm yourself, be flexible in your expectations of others, voice your opinion calmly, respect others' point of view) are recorded for the client's later use.

30. Schedule periodic "maintenance" sessions to help the client maintain therapeutic gains.

16. Read a book or treatment manual that supplements the therapy by improving understanding of anger and anger management. (31)

31. Assign the client to read material that educates him/her about anger and its management (e.g., *Overcoming Situational and General Anger: Client Manual* by Deffenbacher and McKay, *Of Course You're Angry* by Rosselini and Worden, or *The Anger Control Workbook* by McKay).

17. Identify the advantages and disadvantages of holding on to anger and of forgiveness; discuss with therapist. (32, 33)

32. Discuss with the client forgiveness of the perpetrators of pain as a process of letting go of his/her anger.

33. Assign the client to read *Forgive and Forget* (Smedes).

18. Write a letter of forgiveness to the perpetrator of past or present pain and process this letter with the therapist. (34)

34. Ask the client to write a forgiving letter to the target of anger as a step toward letting go of anger; process this letter in session.

___. ______________________________

___. ______________________________

___. ______________________________

___. ______________________________

___. ______________________________

___. ______________________________

DIAGNOSTIC SUGGESTIONS

Axis I:	312.34	Intermittent Explosive Disorder
	296.xx	Bipolar I Disorder
	296.89	Bipolar II Disorder
	312.8	Conduct Disorder
	310.1	Personality Change Due to Axis III Disorder
	309.81	Posttraumatic Stress Disorder
	V61.12	Physical Abuse of Adult (by Partner)
	V61.83	Physical Abuse of Adult (by non-Partner)
	______	______________________
	______	______________________
Axis II:	301.83	Borderline Personality Disorder
	301.7	Antisocial Personality Disorder
	301.0	Paranoid Personality Disorder
	301.81	Narcissistic Personality Disorder
	301.9	Personality Disorder NOS
	______	______________________
	______	______________________

ANTISOCIAL BEHAVIOR

BEHAVIORAL DEFINITIONS

1. An adolescent history of consistent rule-breaking, lying, stealing, physical aggression, disrespect for others and their property, and/or substance abuse resulting in frequent confrontation with authority.
2. Failure to conform with social norms with respect to the law, as shown by repeatedly performed antisocial acts (e.g., destroying property, stealing, pursuing an illegal job) for which he/she may or may not have been arrested.
3. Pattern of interacting in a confrontive, aggressive, and/or argumentative way with authority figures.
4. Little or no remorse for causing pain to others.
5. Consistent pattern of blaming others for what happens to him/her.
6. Little regard for truth, as reflected in a pattern of consistently lying to and/or conning others.
7. Frequent initiation of verbal or physical fighting.
8. History of reckless behaviors that reflect a lack of regard for self or others and show a high need for excitement, fun, and living on the edge.
9. Pattern of sexual promiscuity; has never been totally monogamous in any relationship for a year and does not take responsibility for children resulting from relationships.
10. Pattern of impulsive behaviors, such as moving often, traveling with no goal, or quitting a job without having secured another one.
11. Inability to sustain behavior that would maintain consistent employment.
12. Failure to function as a consistently concerned and responsible parent.

__. ____

____

__. ____

____

—. ____

____

LONG-TERM GOALS

1. Accept responsibility for own behavior and keep behavior within the acceptable limits of the rules of society.
2. Develop and demonstrate a healthy sense of respect for social norms, the rights of others, and the need for honesty.
3. Improve method of relating to the world, especially authority figures; be more realistic, less defiant, and more socially sensitive.
4. Come to an understanding and acceptance of the need for conforming to prevailing social limits and boundaries on behavior.
5. Maintain consistent employment and demonstrate financial and emotional responsibility for children.

—. ____

____

—. ____

____

—. ____

____

SHORT-TERM OBJECTIVES

1. Admit to illegal and/or unethical behavior that has trampled on the law and/or the rights and feelings of others. (1, 2)
2. Verbalize an understanding of the benefits for self and others of living within the laws and rules of society. (3, 4)

THERAPEUTIC INTERVENTIONS

1. Explore the history of the client's pattern of illegal and/or unethical behavior and confront his/her attempts at minimization, denial, or projection of blame.
2. Review the consequences for the client and others of his/her antisocial behavior.
3. Teach the client that the basis for all relationships is trust that the other person will treat one with respect and kindness.

4. Teach the client the need for lawfulness as the basis for trust that forestalls anarchy in society as a whole.

3. Make a commitment to live within the rules and laws of society. (5, 6)

5. Solicit a commitment from the client to conform to a prosocial, law-abiding lifestyle.
6. Emphasize the reality of negative consequences for the client if he/she continues to practice lawlessness.

4. List relationships that have been broken because of disrespect, disloyalty, aggression, or dishonesty. (7, 8)

7. Review relationships that have been lost due to the client's antisocial attitudes and practices (e.g., disloyalty, dishonesty, aggression).
8. Confront the client's lack of sensitivity to the needs and feelings of others.

5. Acknowledge a pattern of self-centeredness in virtually all relationships. (8, 9)

8. Confront the client's lack of sensitivity to the needs and feelings of others.
9. Point out the self-focused, me-first, look-out-for-number-one attitude that is reflected in the client's antisocial behavior.

6. Make a commitment to be honest and reliable. (10, 11, 12)

10. Teach the client the value for self of honesty and reliability in all relationships, since he/she benefits from social approval as well as increased trust and respect.
11. Teach the client the positive effect that honesty and reliability have for others, since they are not disappointed or hurt by lies and broken promises.
12. Ask the client to make a commitment to be honest and reliable.

7. Verbalize an understanding of the benefits to self and others of being empathetic and sensitive to the needs of others. (3, 13, 14)

3. Teach the client that the basis for all relationships is trust that the other person will treat one with respect and kindness.

13. Attempt to sensitize the client to his/her lack of empathy for others by revisiting the consequences of his/her behavior on others. Use role reversal techniques.

14. Confront the client when he/she is rude or not being respectful of others and their boundaries.

8. List three actions that will be performed that will be acts of kindness and thoughtfulness toward others. (15)

15. Assist the client in listing three actions that he/she will perform as acts of service or kindness for others.

9. Indicate the steps that will be taken to make amends or restitution for hurt caused to others. (16, 17, 18)

16. Assist the client in identifying those who have been hurt by his/her antisocial behavior.

17. Teach the client the value of apologizing for hurt caused as a means of accepting responsibility for behavior and of developing sensitivity to the feelings of others.

18. Encourage the client's commitment to specific steps that will be taken to apologize and make restitution to those who have suffered from his/her hurtful behaviors.

10. Verbally demonstrate an understanding of the rules and duties related to employment. (19)

19. Review the rules and expectations that must govern the client's behavior in the work environment.

11. Attend work reliably and treat supervisors and coworkers with respect. (20, 21)

20. Monitor the client's attendance at work and reinforce reliability as well as respect for authority.

21. Ask the client to make a list of behaviors and attitudes that must be modified in order to decrease his/her conflict with authorities; process the list.

12. Verbalize the obligations of parenthood that have been ignored. (22, 23)

22. Confront the client's avoidance of responsibilities toward his/her children.

23. Assist the client in listing the behaviors that are required to be a responsible, nurturing, consistently reliable parent.

13. State a plan to meet responsibilities of parenthood. (24)

24. Develop a plan with the client that will begin to implement the behaviors of a responsible parent.

14. Increase statements of accepting responsibility for own behavior. (25, 26, 27)

25. Confront the client when he/she makes blaming statements or fails to take responsibility for own actions, thoughts, or feelings.

26. Explore the client's reasons for blaming others for his/her own actions (e.g., history of physically abusive punishment, parental modeling, fear of rejection, shame, low self-esteem, avoidance of facing consequences).

27. Give verbal positive feedback to the client when he/she takes responsibility for his/her own behavior.

15. Verbalize an understanding of how childhood experiences of pain have led to an imitative pattern of self-focused protection and aggression toward others. (28, 29)

28. Explore the client's history of abuse, neglect, or abandonment in childhood; explain how the cycle of abuse or neglect is repeating itself in the client's behavior.

29. Point out that the client's pattern of emotional detachment in relationships and self-focused behavior is related to a dysfunctional attempt to protect self from pain.

16. Verbalize a desire to forgive perpetrators of childhood abuse. (30)

30. Teach the client the value of forgiving the perpetrators of hurt versus holding on to hurt and rage and using the hurt as an excuse to continue antisocial practices.

17. Practice trusting a significant other with disclosure of personal feelings. (31, 32, 33)

31. Explore the client's fears associated with placing trust in others.

32. Identify some personal thoughts and feelings that the client could share with a significant other as a means of beginning to demonstrate trust in someone.

33. Process the experience of the client making self vulnerable by self-disclosing to someone.

__. ____________________

__. ____________________

__. ____________________

__. ____________________

__. ____________________

__. ____________________

DIAGNOSTIC SUGGESTIONS

Axis I:	303.90	Alcohol Dependence
	304.20	Cocaine Dependence
	304.80	Polysubstance Dependence
	309.3	Adjustment Disorder With Disturbance of Conduct
	312.8	Conduct Disorder
	312.34	Intermittent Explosive Disorder
	_______	____________________
	_______	____________________
Axis II:	301.7	Antisocial Personality Disorder
	301.81	Narcissistic Personality Disorder
	799.9	Diagnosis Deferred
	V71.09	No Diagnosis
	_______	____________________
	_______	____________________

ANXIETY

BEHAVIORAL DEFINITIONS

SYMPTOMS

1. Excessive and/or unrealistic worry that is difficult to control occurring more days than not for at least 6 months about a number of events or activities.
2. Motor tension (e.g., restlessness, tiredness, shakiness, muscle tension).
3. Autonomic hyperactivity (e.g., palpitations, shortness of breath, dry mouth, trouble swallowing, nausea, diarrhea).
4. Hypervigilance (e.g., feeling constantly on edge, experiencing concentration difficulties, having trouble falling or staying asleep, exhibiting a general state of irritability).

—. ____

—. ____

—. ____

LONG-TERM GOALS

1. Reduce overall frequency, intensity, and duration of the anxiety so that daily functioning is not impaired.
2. Stabilize anxiety level while increasing ability to function on a daily basis.
3. Resolve the core conflict that is the source of anxiety.
4. Enhance ability to effectively cope with the full variety of life's anxieties.

—. ____

__. ______________________________

____

__. ______________________________

____

SHORT-TERM OBJECTIVES

Patient will

1. Describe current and past experiences with the worry and anxiety symptoms, complete with their impact on functioning and attempts to resolve it. (1)

2. Complete psychological tests designed to assess worry and anxiety symptoms. (2)

3. Cooperate with an evaluation by a physician for psychotropic medication. (3, 4)

4. Verbalize an understanding of the cognitive, physiological, and behavioral components of anxiety and its treatment. (5, 6, 7)

THERAPEUTIC INTERVENTIONS

1. Assess the focus, excessiveness, and uncontrollability of the client's worry and anxiety the type, frequency, intensity, and duration of his/her anxiety symptoms (e.g., *The Anxiety Disorders Interview Schedule for the DSM-IV* by DiNardo, Brown, and Barlow).

2. Administer a client-report measure to help assess the nature and degree of the client's worry and anxiety symptoms (e.g., *The Penn State Worry Questionnaire* by Meyer, Miller, Metzger, and Borkovec).

3. Refer the client to a physician for a psychotropic medication consultation.

4. Monitor the client's psychotropic medication compliance, side effects, and effectiveness; confer regularly with the physician.

5. Discuss how generalized anxiety typically involves excessive worry about unrealistic threats, various bodily expressions of tension, overarousal, and hypervigilance, and avoidance of what is threatening that interact to maintain

---

indicates that the Objective/Intervention is consistent with those found in evidence-based treatments.

the problem (see *Mastery of Your Anxiety and Worry—Therapist Guide* by Craske, Barlow, and O'Leary). ▽

6. Discuss how treatment targets worry, anxiety symptoms, and avoidance to help the client manage worry effectively and reduce overarousal and unnecessary avoidance. ▽

7. Assign the client to read psychoeducational sections of books or treatment manuals on worry and generalized anxiety (e.g., *Mastery of Your Anxiety and Worry—Client Guide* by Zinbarg, Craske, Barlow, and O'Leary). ▽

▽ 5. Pt. will Learn and implement calming skills to reduce overall anxiety and manage anxiety symptoms. (8, 9, 10, 11)

8. Teach the client relaxation skills (e.g., progressive muscle relaxation, guided imagery, slow diaphragmatic breathing) and how to discriminate better between relaxation and tension; teach the client how to apply these skills to his/her daily life (e.g., *Progressive Relaxation Training* by Bernstein and Borkovec; *Treating GAD* by Rygh and Sanderson). ▽

9. Assign the client homework each session in which he/she practices relaxation exercises daily; review and reinforce success while providing corrective feedback toward improvement. ▽

10. Assign the client to read about progressive muscle relaxation and other calming strategies in relevant books or treatment manuals (e.g., *Progressive Relaxation Training* by Bernstein

and Borkovec; *Mastery of Your Anxiety and Worry—Client Guide* by Zinbarg, Craske, Barlow, and O'Leary). EB

11. Use biofeedback techniques to facilitate the client's success at learning relaxation skills. EB

6. Verbalize an understanding of the role that cognitive biases play in excessive irrational worry and persistent anxiety symptoms. (12, 13, 14) EB

12. Discuss examples demonstrating that unrealistic worry typically overestimates the probability of threats and underestimates or overlooks the client's ability to manage realistic demands (or assign "Past Successful Anxiety Coping" in *Adult Psychotherapy Homework Planner,* 2nd ed. by Jongsma). EB

13. Assist the client in analyzing his/her fear by examining the probability of the negative expectation occurring, the real consequences of it occurring, his/her ability to control the outcome, the worst possible outcome, and his/her ability to accept it (see "Analyze the Probability of a Feared Event" in *Adult Psychotherapy Homework Planner,* 2nd ed. by Jongsma, and *Anxiety Disorders and Phobias* by Beck and Emery). EB

14. Help the client gain insight into the notion that worry is a form of avoidance of a feared problem and that it creates chronic tension. EB

7. Identify, challenge, and replace biased, fearful self-talk with positive, realistic, and empowering self-talk. (15, 16, 17) EB

15. Explore the client's schema and self-talk that mediate his/her fear response; challenge the biases; assist him/her in replacing the distorted messages with reality-based alternatives and positive

self-talk that will increase his/her self-confidence in coping with irrational fears. ▼

16. Assign the client a homework exercise in which he/she identifies fearful self-talk and creates reality-based alternatives; review and reinforce success, providing corrective feedback toward improvement. ▼

17. Teach the client to implement a thought-stopping technique (thinking of a stop sign and then a pleasant scene) for worries that have been addressed but persist (or assign "Making Use of the Thought-Stopping Technique" in *Adult Psychotherapy Homework Planner,* 2nd ed. by Jongsma); monitor and encourage the client's use of the technique in daily life between sessions. ▼

▼ 8. Undergo gradual repeated imaginal exposure to the feared negative consequences predicted by worries and develop alternative reality-based predictions. (18, 19, 20, 21)

18. Direct and assist the client in constructing a hierarchy of two to three spheres of worry for use in exposure (e.g., worry about harm to others, financial difficulties, relationship problems). ▼

19. Select initial exposures that have a high likelihood of being a success experience for the client; develop a plan for managing the negative affect engendered by exposure; mentally rehearse the procedure. ▼

20. Ask the client to vividly imagine worst-case consequences of worries, holding them in mind until anxiety associated with them weakens (up to 30 minutes); generate reality-based alternatives to

that worst case and process them (see *Mastery of Your Anxiety and Worry—Therapist Guide* by Craske, Barlow, and O'Leary).

21. Assign the client a homework exercise in which he/she does worry exposures and records responses (see *Mastery of Your Anxiety and Worry—Client Guide* by Zinbarg, Craske, Barlow, and O'Leary or *Generalized Anxiety Disorder* by Brown, O'Leary, and Barlow); review, reinforce success, and provide corrective feedback toward improvement.

9. Learn and implement problem-solving strategies for realistically addressing worries. (22, 23)

22. Teach problem-solving strategies involving specifically defining a problem, generating options for addressing it, evaluating options, implementing a plan, and reevaluating and refining the plan.

23. Assign the client a homework exercise in which he/she problem-solves a current problem (see *Mastery of Your Anxiety and Worry—Client Guide* by Zinbarg, Craske, Barlow, and O'Leary or *Generalized Anxiety Disorder* by Brown, O'Leary, and Barlow); review, reinforce success, and provide corrective feedback toward improvement.

10. Learn and implement relapse prevention strategies for managing possible future anxiety symptoms. (24, 25, 26, 27)

24. Discuss with the client the distinction between a lapse and relapse, associating a lapse with an initial and reversible return of worry, anxiety symptoms, or urges to avoid, and relapse with the decision to continue the fearful and avoidant patterns.

25. Identify and rehearse with the client the management of future situations or circumstances in which lapses could occur.

26. Instruct the client to routinely use relaxation, cognitive restructuring, exposure, and problem-solving exposures as needed to address emergent worries, building them into his/her life as much as possible.

27. Develop a "coping card" on which coping strategies and other important information (e.g., "Breathe deeply and relax," "Challenge unrealistic worries," "Use problem-solving") are written for the client's later use.

11. Utilize a paradoxical intervention technique to reduce the anxiety response. (28)

28. Develop a paradoxical intervention (see *Ordeal Therapy* by Haley) in which the client is encouraged to have the problem (e.g., anxiety) and then schedule that anxiety to occur at specific intervals each day (at a time of day/night when the client would be clearly wanting to do something else) in a specific way and for a defined length of time.

12. Complete a Cost Benefit Analysis of maintaining the anxiety. (29)

29. Ask the client to evaluate the costs and benefits of worries (e.g., complete the Cost Benefit Analysis exercise in *Ten Days to Self-Esteem!* by Burns) in which he/she lists the advantages and disadvantages of the negative thought, fear, or anxiety; process the completed assignment.

13. Identify the major life conflicts from the past and present that form the basis for present anxiety. (30, 31, 32)

30. Assist the client in becoming aware of key unresolved life conflicts and in starting to work toward their resolution.

31. Reinforce the client's insights into the role of his/her past emotional pain and present anxiety.

32. Ask the client to develop and process a list of key past and present life conflicts that continue to cause worry.

14. Maintain involvement in work, family, and social activities. (33)

33. Support the client in following-through with work, family, and social activities rather than escaping or avoiding them to focus on panic.

15. Return for a follow-up session to track progress, reinforce gains, and problem-solve barriers. (34)

34. Schedule a "booster session" for the client for 1 to 3 months after therapy ends.

___. ____________________

___. ____________________

___. ____________________

___. ____________________

___. ____________________

___. ____________________

DIAGNOSTIC SUGGESTIONS

Axis I:	300.02	Generalized Anxiety Disorder
	300.00	Anxiety Disorder NOS
	309.24	Adjustment Disorder With Anxiety
	______	____________________
	______	____________________

ATTENTION DEFICIT DISORDER (ADD)—ADULT

BEHAVIORAL DEFINITIONS

1. Childhood history of Attention Deficit Disorder (ADD) that was either diagnosed or later concluded due to the symptoms of behavioral problems at school, impulsivity, temper outbursts, and lack of concentration.
2. Unable to concentrate or pay attention to things of low interest, even when those things are important to his/her life.
3. Easily distracted and drawn from task at hand.
4. Restless and fidgety; unable to be sedentary for more than a short time.
5. Impulsive; has an easily observable pattern of acting first and thinking later.
6. Rapid mood swings and mood lability within short spans of time.
7. Disorganized in most areas of his/her life.
8. Starts many projects but rarely finishes any.
9. Has a "low boiling point and a short fuse."
10. Exhibits low stress tolerance; is easily frustrated, hassled, or upset.
11. Chronic low self-esteem.
12. Tendency toward addictive behaviors.

__. ______________________________

____

__. ______________________________

____

__. ______________________________

____

LONG-TERM GOALS

1. Reduce impulsive actions while increasing concentration and focus on low-interest activities.

2. Minimize ADD behavioral interference in daily life.
3. Accept ADD as a chronic issue and need for continuing medication treatment.
4. Sustain attention and concentration for consistently longer periods of time.
5. Achieve a satisfactory level of balance, structure, and intimacy in personal life.

__. ____

____

__. ____

____

__. ____

____

SHORT-TERM OBJECTIVES

1. Cooperate with and complete psychological testing. (1)
2. Cooperate with and complete a psychiatric evaluation. (2)
3. Comply with all recommendations based on the psychiatric and/or psychological evaluations. (3, 4)
4. Take medication as prescribed, on a regular, consistent basis. (5, 6)

THERAPEUTIC INTERVENTIONS

1. Arrange for the administration of psychological testing to the client to establish or rule out Attention-Deficit Disorder (ADD); provide feedback as to testing results.
2. Arrange for a psychiatric evaluation of the client to assess his/her need for psychotropic medication.
3. Process the results of the psychiatric evaluation and/or psychological testing with the client and answer any questions that may arise.
4. Conduct a conjoint session with significant others and the client to present the results of the psychological and psychiatric evaluations. Answer any questions they may have and solicit their support in dealing with the client's condition.
5. Monitor and evaluate the client's psychotropic medication prescription compliance and the

effectiveness of the medications on his/her level of functioning.

6. Confer with the client's psychiatrist on a regular basis regarding the effectiveness of the medication regime.

5. Identify specific benefits of taking prescribed medications on a long-term basis. (7, 8, 9)

7. Ask the client to make a "pros and cons" spreadsheet regarding staying on medications after doing well; process the results.

8. Encourage and support the client in remaining on medications and warmly but firmly confront thoughts of discontinuing when they surface.

9. Assign the client to list the positive effects that have occurred for him/her since starting on medication.

6. Read material that is informative regarding ADD to gain knowledge about the condition. (10)

10. Ask the client to read material on ADD (e.g., *Driven to Distraction* by Hallowell and Ratey; *The Hyperactive Child, Adolescent and Adult* by Wender; *Putting on the Brakes* by Quinn and Stern; *You Mean I'm Not Lazy, Stupid or Crazy* by Kelly and Ramundo); process the material read.

7. Identify the specific ADD behaviors that cause the most difficulty. (11, 12, 13)

11. Assist the client in identifying the specific behaviors that cause him/her the most difficulty.

12. Review the results of psychological testing and/or psychiatric evaluation again with the client assisting in identifying or in affirming his/her choice of the most problematic behavior(s) to address.

13. Ask the client to have extended family members and close collaterals complete a ranking of the

three behaviors they see as interfering the most with his/her daily functioning (e.g., mood swings, temper outbursts, easily stressed, short attention span, never completes projects).

8. List the negative consequences of the ADD problematic behavior. (14)

14. Assign the client to make a list of negative consequences that he/she has experienced or that could result from a continuation of the problematic behavior; process the list.

9. Apply problem-solving skills to specific ADD behaviors that are interfering with daily functioning. (15, 16)

15. Teach the client problem-solving skills (i.e., identify problem, brainstorm all possible options, evaluate each option, select best option, implement course of action, and evaluate results) that can be applied to his/her ADD behaviors.

16. Assign problem-solving homework to the client specific to the identified behavior (i.e., impulse control, anger outbursts, mood swings, staying on task, attentiveness); process the completed assignment and give appropriate feedback to the client.

10. Utilize cognitive strategies to curb impulsive behavior. (17)

17. Teach the client the self-control strategies of "stop, listen, think, and act" and "problem-solving self-talk." Role-play these techniques to improve his/her skill level.

11. Implement a specific, time-limited period if indulging impulses that are not self-destructive. (18)

18. Structure a "blowout" time each week when the client can do whatever he/she likes to do that is not self-destructive (e.g., blast themselves with music, gorge on ice cream).

12. Use "time out" to remove self from situations and think about behavioral reaction alternatives and their consequences. (19)

19. Train the client to use a "time out" intervention in which he/she settles down by going away from the situation and calming down

to think about behavioral alternatives and their consequences.

13. Implement relaxation procedures to reduce tension and physical restlessness. (20)

20. Instruct the client in various relaxation techniques (e.g., deep breathing, meditation, guided imagery) and encourage him/her to use them daily or when stress increases.

14. Reward self when impulsivity, inattention, or forgetfulness are replaced by positive alternatives. (21, 22)

21. Design and implement a self-administered reward system to reinforce and encourage the client's decreased impulsiveness, loss of temper, inattentiveness, and so on.

22. Teach the client to utilize external structure (e.g., lists, reminders, files, daily rituals) to reduce the effects of his/her inattention and forgetfulness; encourage the client to reward himself/herself for successful recall and follow-through.

15. Cooperate with brainwave biofeedback to improve impulse control and reduce distractibility. (23, 24)

23. Refer for or administer brainwave biofeedback to improve attention span, impulse control, and mood regulation.

24. Encourage the client to transfer the biofeedback training skills of relaxation and cognitive focusing to everyday situations (e.g., home, work, social).

16. Report a decrease in statements and feelings of negativity regarding self and life. (25)

25. Conduct conjoint sessions in which positive aspects of the relationship, the client, and significant other are identified and affirmed.

17. Introduce behaviors into life that improve health and/or serve others. (26, 27)

26. Direct the client toward healthy addictions (e.g., exercise, volunteer work, community service).

27. After clearance from the client's personal physician, refer client to a physician fitness trainer who can design an aerobic exercise routine for him/her.

18. Attend an ADD support group. (28)

28. Refer the client to a specific group therapy for adults with ADD to increase the client's understanding of ADD, to boost his/her self-esteem, and to obtain feedback from others.

19. Use a "coach" who has been trained by therapist to increase organization and task focus. (29, 30)

29. Direct the client to pick a "coach" who is a friend or colleague to assist him/her in getting organized and staying on task and to provide encouragement and support (see *Driven to Distraction* by Hallowell and Ratey).

30. Instruct the coach in HOPE technique (i.e., Help, Obligations, Plans, and Encouragement) as described in *Driven to Distraction* by Hallowell and Ratey.

20. Report improved listening skills without defensiveness. (31)

31. Use role-playing and modeling to teach the client how to listen and accept feedback from others regarding his/her behavior.

21. Have significant other attend an ADD support group to increase his/her understanding of the condition. (32)

32. Educate the client's significant other on ADD and encourage him/her to attend a support group.

22. Report improved communication, understanding, and feelings of trust between self and significant other. (33, 34, 35, 36)

33. Ask the client and significant other to list the expectations they have for the relationship and each other. Process the list in a conjoint session with a focus on identifying how the expectations can be met and how realistic they are.

34. Assist the client and his/her significant other in removing blocks in their communication and in developing new communication skills.

35. Refer the client and significant other to a skill-based marriage/relationship seminar (e.g., PREP, Marriage Encounter, Engaged Encounter) to improve communication and conflict resolution skills.

36. Assign the client and significant other to schedule a specific time each day to devote to communicating together, expressing affection, having fun, or talking through problems. Move assignment toward becoming a daily ritual.

23. Develop a signal to act as a warning system to indicate when anger levels are escalating with the partner. (37)

37. Assist the client and significant other in developing a signal system as a means of giving feedback when conflict behaviors and anger begin to escalate.

—. ____________________

—. ____________________

—. ____________________

—. ____________________

—. ____________________

—. ____________________

DIAGNOSTIC SUGGESTIONS

Axis I:	314.00	Attention-Deficit/Hyperactivity Disorder, Predominantly Inattentive Type
	314.01	Attention-Deficit/Hyperactivity Disorder, Predominantly Hyperactive-Impulsive Type
	314.9	Attention-Deficit/Hyperactivity Disorder NOS
	296.xx	Bipolar I Disorder
	301.13	Cyclothymic Disorder
	296.90	Mood Disorder NOS
	312.30	Impulse-Control Disorder NOS
	303.90	Alcohol Dependence
	305.00	Alcohol Abuse
	304.30	Cannabis Dependence
	305.20	Cannabis Abuse
	______	____________________
	______	____________________

BORDERLINE PERSONALITY

SYMPTOMS

BEHAVIORAL DEFINITIONS

1. A minor stress leads to extreme emotional reactivity (anger, anxiety, or depression) that usually lasts from a few hours to a few days.
2. A pattern of intense, chaotic interpersonal relationships.
3. Marked identity disturbance.
4. Impulsive behaviors that are potentially self-damaging.
5. Recurrent suicidal gestures, threats, or self-mutilating behavior.
6. Chronic feelings of emptiness and boredom.
7. Frequent eruptions of intense, inappropriate anger.
8. Easily feels unfairly treated and believes that others can't be trusted.
9. Analyzes most issues in simple terms (e.g., right/wrong, black/white, trustworthy/deceitful) without regard for extenuating circumstances or complex situations.
10. Becomes very anxious with any hint of perceived abandonment in a relationship.

—. ____

____

—. ____

____

—. ____

____

LONG-TERM GOALS

Pt. will

1. Develop and demonstrate coping skills to deal with mood swings.
2. Develop the ability to control impulsive behavior.
3. Replace dichotomous thinking with the ability to tolerate ambiguity and complexity in people and issues.

4. Develop and demonstrate anger management skills.
5. Learn and practice interpersonal relationship skills.
6. Terminate self-damaging behaviors (such as substance abuse, reckless driving, sexual acting out, binge eating, or suicidal behaviors).

—. ______________________________

—. ______________________________

—. ______________________________

SHORT-TERM OBJECTIVES

1. Discuss openly the history of difficulties that have led to seeking treatment. (1, 2, 3)

THERAPEUTIC INTERVENTIONS

1. Assess the client's experiences of distress and disability, identifying behaviors (e.g., parasuicidal acts, angry outbursts, overattachment), affect (e.g., mood swings, emotional overreactions, painful emptiness), and cognitions (e.g., biases such as dichotmous thinking, overgeneralization, catastrophizing) that will become the targets of therapy.
2. Explore the client's history of abuse and/or abandonment particularly in childhood years.
3. Validate the client's distress and difficulties as understandable given his/her particular circumstances, thoughts, and feelings.

EB 2. Verbalize an accurate and reasonable understanding of the process of therapy and what the therapeutic goals are. (4, 5)

4. Orient the client to dialectical behavior therapy (DBT), highlighting its multiple facets (e.g., support, collaboration, challenge,

---

EB indicates that the Objective/Intervention is consistent with those found in evidence-based treatments.

problem-solving, skill-building) and discuss dialectical/biosocial view of borderline personality, emphasizing constitutional and social influences on its features (see *Cognitive-Behavioral Treatment of Borderline Personality* by Linehan).

5. Throughout therapy, ask the client to read selected sections of books or manuals that reinforce therapeutic interventions (e.g., *Skills Training Manual for Treating BPD* by Linehan).

3. Verbalize a decision to work collaboratively with the therapist toward the therapeutic goals. (6)

6. Solicit from the client an agreement to work collaboratively within the parameters of the DBT approach to overcome the behaviors, emotions, and cognitions that have been identified as causing problems in his/her life.

4. Verbalize any history of self-mutilative and suicidal urges and behavior. (7, 8, 9, 10)

7. Probe the nature and history of the client's self-mutilating behavior.

8. Assess the client's suicidal gestures as to triggers, frequency, seriousness, secondary gain, and onset.

9. Arrange for hospitalization, as necessary, when the client is judged to be harmful to self.

10. Provide the client with an emergency helpline telephone number that is available 24 hours a day.

5. Promise to initiate contact with the therapist or helpline if experiencing a strong urge to engage in self-harmful behavior. (11, 12)

11. Interpret the client's self-mutilation as an expression of the rage and helplessness that could not be expressed as a child victim of emotional abandonment or abuse; express the expectation that the client will control the urge for self-mutilation.

12. Elicit a promise (as part of a self-mutilation and suicide prevention contract) from the client that he/she will initiate contact with the therapist or a helpline if a suicidal urge becomes strong and before any self-injurious behavior occurs; throughout the therapy process consistently assess the strength of the client's suicide potential.

6. Reduce actions that interfere with participating in therapy. (13)

13. Continuously monitor, confront, and problem-solve client actions that threaten to interfere with the continuation of therapy such as missing appointments, noncompliance, and/or abruptly leaving therapy.

7. Cooperate with an evaluation by a physician for psychotropic medication and take medication, if prescribed. (14, 15)

14. Assess the client's need for medication (e.g., selective serotonin reuptake inhibitors) and arrange for prescription if appropriate.

15. Monitor and evaluate the client's psychotropic medication prescription compliance and the effectiveness of the medication on his/her level of functioning.

8. Reduce the frequency of maladaptive behaviors, thoughts, and feelings that interfere with attaining a reasonable quality of life. (16)

16. Use validation, dialectical strategies (e.g., metaphor, devil's advocate), and problem-solving strategies (e.g., behavioral and solution analysis, cognitive restructuring, skills training, exposure) to help the client manage, reduce, or stabilize maladaptive behaviors (e.g., angry outbursts, binge drinking, abusive relationships, high-risk sex, uncontrolled spending), thoughts (e.g., all-or-nothing thinking, catastrophizing, personalizing), and feelings (e.g., rage, hopelessness, abandonment; see *Cognitive-Behavioral Treatment of Borderline Personality* by Linehan).

9. Participate in a group (preferably) or individual personal skills development course. (17, 18)

17. Conduct group or individual skills training tailored to the client's identified problem behavioral patterns (e.g., assertiveness for abusive relationships, cognitive strategies for identifying and controlling financial, sexual, and other impulsivity).

18. Use behavioral strategies to teach identified skills (e.g., instruction, modeling, advising), strengthen them (e.g., role-playing, exposure exercises), and facilitate incorporation into the client's everyday life (e.g., homework assignments).

10. Verbalize a decreased emotional response to previous or current posttraumatic stress. (19)

19. After adaptive behavioral patterns and emotional regulation skills are evident, work with the client on remembering and accepting the facts of previous trauma, reducing denial and increasing insight into its effects, reducing maladaptive emotional and/or behavioral responses to trauma-related stimuli, and reducing self-blame.

11. Identify, challenge, and replace biased, fearful self-talk with reality-based, positive self-talk. (20, 21, 22)

20. Explore the client's schema and self-talk that mediate his/her trauma-related and other fears; identify and challenge biases; assist him/her in generating thoughts that correct for the negative biases and build confidence.

21. Assign the client a homework exercise in which he/she identifies fearful self-talk and creates reality-based alternatives; review and reinforce success, providing corrective feedback for failure (see "Journal and Replace Self-Defeating Thoughts" in *Adult Psychotherapy Homework Planner,*

2nd ed. by Jongsma, or "Daily Record of Dysfunctional Thoughts" in *Cognitive Therapy of Depression* by Beck, Rush, Shaw, and Emery).

22. Reinforce the client's positive, reality-based cognitive messages that enhance self-confidence and increase adaptive action.

12. Participate in imaginal and/or in vivo exposure to trauma-related memories until talking or thinking about the trauma does not cause marked distress. (23, 24, 25)

23. Direct and assist the client in constructing a hierarchy of feared and avoided trauma-related stimuli.

24. Direct imaginal exposure to the trauma in session by having the client describe a chosen traumatic experience at an increasing, but client-chosen level of detail; integrate cognitive restructuring and repeat until associated anxiety reduces and stabilizes; record the session and have the client listen to it between sessions (see "Share the Painful Memory" in *Adult Psychotherapy Homework Planner,* 2nd ed. by Jongsma, and *Posttraumatic Stress Disorder* by Resick and Calhoun); review and reinforce progress, problem-solve obstacles.

25. Assign the client a homework exercise in which he/she does an exposure exercise and records responses or listens to a recording of an in-session exposure (see *Posttraumatic Stress Disorder* by Resick and Calhoun); review and reinforce progress, problem-solve obstacles.

13. Verbalize a sense of self-respect that is not dependent on others' opinions. (26)

26. Help the client to value, believe, and trust in his/her evaluations of himself/herself, others, and situations and to examine them nondefensively and independent of others' opinions in a manner that builds self-reliance but does not isolate the client from others.

14. Engage in practices that help enhance a sustained sense of joy. (27)

27. Facilitate the client's personal growth by helping him/her choose experiences that strengthen self-awareness, personal values, and appreciation of life (e.g., insight-oriented therapy, spiritual practices, other relevant life experiences).

__. ______________________________

__. ______________________________

__. ______________________________

__. ______________________________

__. ______________________________

__. ______________________________

DIAGNOSTIC SUGGESTIONS

Axis I:	300.4	Dysthymic Disorder
	296.3x	Major Depressive Disorder, Recurrent
	______	____________________
	______	____________________
Axis II:	301.83	Borderline Personality Disorder
	301.9	Personality Disorder NOS
	799.9	Diagnosis Deferred
	V71.09	No Diagnosis
	______	____________________
	______	____________________

CHEMICAL DEPENDENCE

BEHAVIORAL DEFINITIONS

1. Consistently uses alcohol or other mood-altering drugs until high, intoxicated, or passed out.
2. Unable to stop or cut down use of mood-altering drug once started, despite the verbalized desire to do so and the negative consequences continued use brings.
3. Produces blood study results that reflect a pattern of heavy substance use (e.g., elevated liver enzymes).
4. Denies that chemical dependence is a problem despite direct feedback from spouse, relatives, friends, and employers that the use of the substance is negatively affecting him/her and others.
5. Describes amnestic blackouts that occur when abusing alcohol.
6. Continues drug and/or alcohol use despite experiencing persistent or recurring physical, legal, vocational, social, or relationship problems that are directly caused by the use of the substance.
7. Exhibits increased tolerance for the drug as evidenced by the need to use more to become intoxicated or to attain the desired effect.
8. Exhibits physical symptoms (i.e., shaking, seizures, nausea, headaches, sweating, anxiety, insomnia, depression) when withdrawing from the substance.
9. Suspends important social, recreational, or occupational activities because they interfere with using the mood-altering drug.
10. Makes a large time investment in activities to obtain the substance, to use it, or to recover from its effects.
11. Consumes mood-altering substances in greater amounts and for longer periods than intended.
12. Continues abuse of a mood-altering chemical after being told by a physician that it is causing health problems.

__. ____

____

—. ____

____

—. ____

____

LONG-TERM GOALS

1. Accept the fact of chemical dependence and begin to actively participate in a recovery program.
2. Establish a sustained recovery, free from the use of all mood-altering substances.
3. Establish and maintain total abstinence while increasing knowledge of the disease and the process of recovery.
4. Acquire the necessary skills to maintain long-term sobriety from all mood-altering substances.
5. Improve quality of personal life by maintaining an ongoing abstinence from all mood-altering chemicals.
6. Withdraw from mood-altering substance, stabilize physically and emotionally, and then establish a supportive recovery plan.

—. ____

____

—. ____

____

—. ____

____

SHORT-TERM OBJECTIVES

1. Describe the type, amount, frequency, and history of substance abuse. (1)

THERAPEUTIC INTERVENTIONS

1. Gather a complete drug/alcohol history from the client, including the amount and pattern of his/her use, signs and symptoms of use, and negative life consequences (e.g., social, legal, familial, vocational).

2. Complete psychological tests designed to assess the nature and severity of social anxiety and avoidance. (2)

    2. Administer to the client an objective test of drug and/or alcohol abuse (e.g., the Alcohol Severity Index, the Michigan Alcohol Screening Test [MAST]); process the results with the client.

EB 3. Participate in a medical examination to evaluate the effects of chemical dependence. (3)

    3. Refer the client for a thorough physical examination to determine any physical/medical consequences of chemical dependence. EB

EB 4. Cooperate with an evaluation by a physician for psychotropic medication. (4, 5)

    4. Arrange for an evaluation for a prescription of psychotropic medications (e.g., serotonergic medications). EB

    5. Monitor the client for prescription compliance, side effects, and overall effectiveness of the medication; consult with the prescribing physician at regular intervals. EB

EB 5. Identify the negative consequences of drug and/or alcohol abuse. (3, 6)

    3. Refer the client for a thorough physical examination to determine any physical/medical consequences of chemical dependence. EB

    6. Ask the client to make a list of the ways substance abuse has negatively impacted his/her life; process the medical, relational, legal, vocational, and social consequences (or assign "Substance Abuse Negative Impact versus Sobriety's Positive Impact" in *Adult Psychotherapy Homework Planner,* 2nd ed. by Jongsma). EB

EB 6. Decrease the level of denial around using as evidenced by fewer statements about minimizing amount of use and its negative impact on life. (7, 8)

    7. Assign the client to ask two or three people who are close to him/her to write a letter to the therapist in which they each identify how they saw the client's chemical dependence negatively impacting his/her life. EB

EB indicates that the Objective/Intervention is consistent with those found in evidence-based treatments.

8. Assign the client to complete a First Step paper and then to process it with group, sponsor, or therapist to receive feedback.

7. Verbalize "I statements" that reflect a knowledge and acceptance of chemical dependence. (9)

9. Model and reinforce statements that reflect the client's acceptance of his/her chemical dependence and its destructive consequences for self and others.

8. Verbalize increased knowledge of alcoholism and the process of recovery. (10, 11)

10. Require the client to learn more about chemical dependency and the recovery process (e.g., through assignment of didactic lectures, reading, films); ask the client to identify and process key points.

11. Assign the client to meet with an AA/NA member who has been working the 12-step program for several years and find out specifically how the program has helped him/her to stay sober; afterward, process the meeting.

9. Verbalize a commitment to abstain from the use of mood-altering drugs. (12)

12. Develop an abstinence contract with the client regarding the termination of the use of his/her drug of choice; process client's feelings related to the commitment.

10. Attend Alcoholics Anonymous/Narcotics Anonymous (AA/NA) meetings as frequently as necessary to support sobriety. (13)

13. Recommend that the client attend AA or NA meetings and report on the impact of the meetings; process messages the client is receiving.

11. Verbalize an understanding of factors that can contribute to development of chemical dependence and pose risks for relapse. (14, 15)

14. Assess the client's intellectual, personality, and cognitive vulnerabilities, family history, and life stresses that contribute to his/her chemical dependence.

15. Facilitate the client's understanding of his/her genetic, personality, social, and family factors, including childhood experiences, that led to the development of chemical dependency and serve as risk factors for relapse.

12. Identify the ways being sober could positively impact life. (16)

13. Identify and make changes in social relationships that will support recovery. (17, 18)

14. Identify projects and other social and recreational activities that sobriety will now afford and that will support sobriety. (18, 19)

15. Verbalize how living situation contributes to chemical dependence and acts as a hindrance to recovery. (20)

16. Make arrangements to terminate current living situation and move to a place more conducive to recovery. (21)

16. Ask the client to make a list of how being sober could positively impact his/her life; process the list (or assign "Substance Abuse Negative Impact versus Sobriety's Positive Impact" in *Adult Psychotherapy Homework Planner,* 2nd ed. by Jongsma).

17. Review the negative influence of the client continuing his/her alcohol-related friendships ("drinking buddies") and assist him/her in making a plan to develop new sober relationships including "sobriety buddies"; revisit routinely and facilitate toward development of a new social support system.

18. Assist the client in planning social and recreational activities that are free from association with substance abuse; revisit routinely and facilitate toward development of a new social support system.

18. Assist the client in planning social and recreational activities that are free from association with substance abuse; revisit routinely and facilitate toward development of a new social support system.

19. Plan household, work-related, and/or other free-time projects that can be accomplished to build the client's self-esteem and self-concept as clean and sober.

20. Evaluate the role of the client's living situation in fostering a pattern of chemical dependence; process with the client.

21. Facilitate development of a plan for the client to change his/her living situation to foster recovery; revisit routinely and facilitate toward accomplishing a positive change in living situation.

17. Identify positive impact that sobriety will have on intimate and family relationships. (22)

22. Assist the client in identifying positive changes that will be made in family relationships during recovery.

18. Agree to make amends to significant others who have been hurt by the life dominated by substance abuse. (23, 24)

23. Discuss the negative effects the client's substance abuse has had on family, friends, and work relationships and encourage a plan to make amends for such hurt.

24. Elicit from the client a verbal commitment to make initial amends now to key individuals and further amends when working steps 8 and 9 of the AA program.

19. Participate in Behavioral Marital Therapy to learn and implement ways to resolve conflicts and communicate effectively. (25)

25. Refer the client to or provide Behavioral Marital Therapy (see Intimate Relationship Conflict chapter in this *Planner,* and "Behavioral Marital Therapy" by Holzworth-Munroe and Jacobson in *Handbook of Family Therapy* by Gurman and Knickerson [Eds.]).

20. Learn and implement coping strategies to manage urges to lapse back into chemical use. (26)

26. Teach the client a "coping package" involving calming strategies (e.g., relaxation, breathing), thought stopping, positive self-talk, and attentional focusing skills (e.g., distraction from urges, staying focused on behavioral goals of abstinence) to manage urges to use chemical substances.

21. Identify, challenge, and replace destructive self-talk with positive, strength building self-talk. (27, 28)

27. Explore the client's schema and self-talk that weaken his/her resolve to remain abstinent; challenge the biases; assist him/her in generating realistic self-talk that correct for the biases and build resilience.

28. Rehearse situations in which the client identifies his/her negative self-talk and generates empowering

alternatives (or assign "Negative Thoughts Trigger Negative Feelings" in *Adult Psychotherapy Homework Planner,* 2nd ed. by Jongsma); review and reinforce success.

22. Undergo gradual repeated exposure to triggers of urges to lapse back into chemical substance use. (29, 30)

29. Direct and assist the client in construction of a hierarchy of urge-producing cues to use substances.

30. Select initial in vivo or role-played urge-producing cue exposures that have a high likelihood of being a successful experience for the client, using behavioral (e.g., modeling, rehearsal, social reinforcement) and cognitive restructuring strategies within and after the exposure (or assign "Gradually Reducing Your Phobic Fear" in *Adult Psychotherapy Homework Planner,* 2nd ed. by Jongsma); process the exposure results.

23. Implement personal skills to manage common day-to-day challenges and to build confidence in managing them without the use of substances. (31, 32)

31. Assess the client's current skill in managing common everyday stressors (e.g., work, social, family role demands); use behavioral and cognitive restructuring techniques to build social and/or communication skills to manage these challenges (or assign "Restoring Socialization Comfort" in *Adult Psychotherapy Homework Planner,* 2nd ed. by Jongsma).

32. Assign the client to read about general social and/or communication skills in books or treatment manuals on building social skills (e.g., *Your Perfect Right* by Alberti and Emmons; *Conversationally Speaking* by Garner).

24. Implement relapse prevention strategies for managing possible future situations with high-risk for relapse. (33, 34, 35, 36)

33. Discuss with the client the distinction between a lapse and relapse, associating a lapse with an initial and reversible use of a substance and relapse with the decision to return to a repeated pattern of abuse.

34. Identify and rehearse with the client the management of future situations or circumstances in which lapses could occur.

35. Instruct the client to routinely use strategies learned in therapy (e.g., cognitive restructuring, social skills, exposure) while building social interactions and relationships (or assign "Relapse Triggers" in *Adult Psychotherapy Homework Planner,* 2nd ed. by Jongsma.

36. Recommend that the client read material on how to avoid relapse (e.g., *Staying Sober: A Guide to Relapse Prevention* by Gorski and Miller; *The Staying Sober Workbook* by Gorski).

25. Develop a written aftercare plan that will support the maintenance of long-term sobriety. (37)

37. Assign and review the client's written aftercare plan to ensure it is adequate to maintain sobriety (or assign "Aftercare Plan Components" in *Adult Psychotherapy Homework Planner,* 2nd ed. by Jongsma).

__. ______________________________

__. ______________________________

__. ______________________________

__. ______________________________

__. ______________________________

__. ______________________________

DIAGNOSTIC SUGGESTIONS

Axis I:	303.90	Alcohol Dependence
	305.00	Alcohol Abuse
	304.30	Cannabis Dependence
	304.20	Cocaine Dependence
	305.60	Cocaine Abuse
	304.80	Polysubstance Dependence
	291.2	Alcohol-Induced Persisting Dementia
	291.1	Alcohol-Induced Persisting Amnestic Disorder
	V71.01	Adult Antisocial Behavior
	300.4	Dysthymic Disorder
	312.34	Intermittent Explosive Disorder
	309.81	Posttraumatic Stress Disorder
	304.10	Sedative, Hypnotic, or Anxiolytic Dependence
	________	________________________________
	________	________________________________
Axis II:	301.7	Antisocial Personality Disorder
	________	________________________________
	________	________________________________

CHEMICAL DEPENDENCE—RELAPSE

BEHAVIORAL DEFINITIONS

1. Inability to remain abstinent from mood-altering drugs after receiving treatment for substance abuse.
2. Inability to stay sober even though attending Alcoholics Anonymous (AA) meetings regularly.
3. Relapse into abuse of mood-altering substances after a substantial period of sobriety.
4. Chronic pattern of period of sobriety (six months plus) followed by a relapse, then reestablishing sobriety.

__. ____

____

__. ____

____

__. ____

____

LONG-TERM GOALS

1. Establish a consistently alcohol/drug-free lifestyle.
2. Develop an understanding of personal pattern of relapse in order to help sustain long-term recovery.
3. Develop an increased awareness of relapse triggers and the coping strategies needed to effectively deal with them.
4. Achieve a quality of life that is substance-free on a continuing basis.

__. ____

____

__. ____

____

__. ____

____

SHORT-TERM OBJECTIVES

1. Verbalize a commitment to abstinence/sobriety. (1, 2)
2. Outline and implement a daily routine that is structured and includes AA involvement. (3, 4)
3. Reestablish ongoing relationships with people who are supportive of sobriety. (5, 6)

THERAPEUTIC INTERVENTIONS

1. Discuss with the client the specific behaviors, attitudes, and feelings that led up to the last relapse, focusing on triggers for the relapse. Obtain a clear, firm commitment to renewed sobriety.
2. Assess the client for ability to reestablish total abstinence and refer to more intense level of care if he/she is not able to detox and stay sober.
3. Teach the importance of structure and routine that have either been abandoned or never been present in the client's daily life and then assist the client in developing and implementing a balanced, structured daily routine.
4. Urge the client to attend AA consistently as a part of the routine structure of his/her life.
5. Assist the client in reuniting with his/her AA sponsor.
6. Ask the client to find a second AA/NA sponsor who is an opposite of the primary sponsor (e.g., if the primary is mainly supportive, seek another who is more confrontive) and meet regularly with both sponsors on at least a weekly basis.

4. Verbalize feelings about the loss of sobriety. (7, 8)

7. Assist the client in expanding his/her ability to identify feelings, process them, and then express them in a timely, healthy way.

8. Assign the client to read *The Golden Book of Resentment* (Father John Doe) or readings on resentment from *As Bill Sees It* (Bill Wilson); choose three key concepts that he/she feels relate to him/her and process them together.

5. Identify people and places to be avoided to maintain recovery. (9, 10)

9. Assist the client in identifying the negative influence of people and situations that encourage relapse, and ways to avoid them.

10. Assign the client to read a book or pamphlet on recovery. Select items from it that relate to him/her and process them together.

6. Identify the specific behaviors, attitudes, and feelings that led up to the last relapse, focusing on triggers for the relapse. (11, 12, 13, 14)

11. Assign the client to complete a relapse workbook (e.g., *The Staying Sober Workbook* by Gorski), and process it with him/her.

12. Assign the client to do a focused autobiography dating from his/her first attempt to get sober to the present. Then have him/her read it aloud for feedback as to triggers for relapse.

13. Ask the client to gather from significant others an observation list of the client's behavior or attitudes prior to his/her returning to using; process the feedback in group therapy or in individual session.

14. Develop a symptom line with the client that looks at each relapse in terms of when it happened (i.e., time of year, dates, and their significance) and what was occurring in regard to self, spouse, family, work, and social activities.

7. Identify behavior patterns that will need to be changed to maintain sobriety. (15, 16)

15. Ask the client to develop a list of behaviors, attitudes, and feelings that could have been involved in the relapse, and process it with him/her.

16. Assign the client to read *Many Roads, One Journey: Moving Beyond the 12 Steps* (Kasl-Davis) or *Stage II Recovery* (Larsen), and process the key ideas with him/her.

8. Identify positive rewards associated with abstinence. (17, 18)

17. Assist the client in identifying positive rewards of total abstinence.

18. Assign the client to complete and process with therapist a "Cost-Benefit Analysis" (see *Ten Days to Self-Esteem!* by Burns) on his/her return to substance abuse.

9. Complete medical assessment for Antabuse or antidepressant medications. (19)

19. Refer the client to physician/psychiatrist for an evaluation for Antabuse or antidepressant medication.

10. Cooperate with acupuncturist for treatment to reduce the urge to use mood-altering substances. (20)

20. Refer the client to acupuncturist for treatment on a regular basis and monitor effectiveness.

11. Comply with medication recommendations as prescribed and report any side effects to the therapist and/or physician. (21, 22)

21. Monitor the client for compliance with medication orders or other treatments and possible side effects, and answer any questions he/she may have.

22. Confer with the prescribing physician on a regular basis regarding the effectiveness of the treatment.

12. Verbalize insights learned from talking and listening to successfully recovering chemically dependent people. (23)

23. Ask the client to interview NA/AA members who have been sober for three or more years, focusing on what they have specifically done to accomplish this, and if they have relapsed, what they have done to get back on track to stay. Process the client's findings with him/her.

13. Meet with a spiritual leader to make progress on AA Steps Two, Three, and Five. (24)

24. Refer the client to a pastor, rabbi, priest, or other spiritual leader with knowledge of substance abuse and recovery to work through any blocks regarding Steps Two and Three or to complete Step Five.

14. Report increased tolerance for uncomfortable emotions. (25, 26)

25. Teach the client various methods of stress reduction (e.g., meditation, deep breathing, positive imagery) and assist him/her in implementing them into daily life.

26. Ask the client to develop a list of ways of coping with uncomfortable feelings; process the list with him/her.

15. Implement assertiveness skills to communicate feelings directly. (27)

27. Assist the client in developing assertiveness techniques.

16. Develop in writing two possible coping strategies for each specific relapse trigger. (26, 28)

26. Ask the client to develop a list of ways of coping with uncomfortable feelings; process the list with him/her.

28. Assist the client in developing two coping strategies for each identified trigger to relapse.

17. Verbally describe the family and relationship conflicts that played a role in triggering relapse. (29)

29. Conduct conjoint and/or family sessions that identify and resolve relationship stress that has served as a trigger for relapse.

18. The spouse or significant other verbalize an understanding of constructive actions that can be taken in reaction to the client's relapse and recovery. (30)

30. Conduct sessions with spouse or significant other to educate him/her regarding relapse triggers and instruct them on how to be supportive of sobriety. Encourage him/her to attend Al-Anon on a regular basis.

19. Participate in rituals that support recovery. (31)

31. Assist the client in developing and establishing rituals in life that will enhance sobriety and be a deterrent to relapse (e.g., receiving AA/NA coins, regular membership in a Step Study Group, coffee with sponsor at set date and time).

20. Identify successful sober living strategies of the past. (32)

32. Utilize a brief solution-focused approach with the client to identify specific things he/she did when sobriety was going well and then select and direct the client to increase the use of the identified behaviors. Monitor and adjust direction as needed.

21. Verbalize principles to live by that will support sobriety. (33)

33. Assign the client to read a fable or story such as "The Boy Who Lost His Way," "The Prodigal Son," or "Three Little Pigs" (see *Stories For the 3rd Ear,* by Wallas), and then process it together to identify key concepts connected to staying sober.

22. Develop written continuing aftercare plan with focus on coping with family and other stressors. (34, 35)

34. ~~Ask the client to~~ complete and process a relapse contract with significant other that identifies previous relapse-associated behaviors, attitudes, and emotions, coupling them with agreed-upon warnings from significant other as they are observed.

35. Assign the client to develop and process a written aftercare plan that specifically addresses previously identified relapse triggers.

___. __________________________ ___. __________________________

___. __________________________ ___. __________________________

___. __________________________ ___. __________________________

DIAGNOSTIC SUGGESTIONS

Axis I:	303.90	Alcohol Dependence
	305.00	Alcohol Abuse

	304.30	Cannabis Dependence
	304.20	Cocaine Dependence
	304.80	Polysubstance Dependence
	291.1	Alcohol-Induced Persisting Amnestic Disorder
	300.4	Dysthymic Disorder
	309.81	Posttraumatic Stress Disorder
	______	______________________
	______	______________________
Axis II:	301.7	Antisocial Personality Disorder
	______	______________________
	______	______________________

CHILDHOOD TRAUMAS

BEHAVIORAL DEFINITIONS

1. Reports of childhood physical, sexual, and/or emotional abuse.
2. Description of parents as physically or emotionally neglectful as they were chemically dependent, too busy, absent, etc.
3. Description of childhood as chaotic as parent(s) was substance abuser (or mentally ill, antisocial, etc.), leading to frequent moves, multiple abusive spousal partners, frequent substitute caretakers, financial pressures, and/or many stepsiblings.
4. Reports of emotionally repressive parents who were rigid, perfectionist, threatening, demeaning, hypercritical, and/or overly religious.
5. Irrational fears, suppressed rage, low self-esteem, identity conflicts, depression, or anxious insecurity related to painful early life experiences.
6. Dissociation phenomenon (multiple personality, psychogenic fugue or amnesia, trance state, and/or depersonalization) as a maladaptive coping mechanism resulting from childhood emotional pain.

__. ____

____

__. ____

____

__. ____

____

LONG-TERM GOALS

1. Develop an awareness of how childhood issues have affected and continue to affect one's family life.
2. Resolve past childhood/family issues, leading to less anger and depression, greater self-esteem, security, and confidence.

3. Release the emotions associated with past childhood/family issues, resulting in less resentment and more serenity.
4. Let go of blame and begin to forgive others for pain caused in childhood.

__. ____

____

__. ____

____

__. ____

____

SHORT-TERM OBJECTIVES

1. Describe what it was like to grow up in the home environment. (1, 2)
2. Describe each family member and identify the role each played within the family. (2, 3)
3. Identify patterns of abuse, neglect, or abandonment within the family of origin, both current and historical, nuclear and extended. (4, 5)

THERAPEUTIC INTERVENTIONS

1. Actively build the level of trust with the client in individual sessions through consistent eye contact, active listening, unconditional positive regard, and warm acceptance to help increase his/her ability to identify and express feelings.
2. Develop the client's family genogram and/or symptom line and help identify patterns of dysfunction within the family.
2. Develop the client's family genogram and/or symptom line and help identify patterns of dysfunction within the family.
3. Assist the client in clarifying his/her role within the family and his/her feelings connected to that role.
4. Assign the client to ask parents about their family backgrounds and develop insight regarding patterns of behavior and causes for parents' dysfunction.

5. Explore the client's painful childhood experiences.

4. Identify feelings associated with major traumatic incidents in childhood and with parental child-rearing patterns. (6, 7, 8)

6. Support and encourage the client when he/she begins to express feelings of rage, sadness, fear, and rejection relating to family abuse or neglect.

7. Assign the client to record feelings in a journal that describes memories, behavior, and emotions tied to his/her traumatic childhood experiences.

8. Ask the client to read books on the emotional effects of neglect and abuse in childhood (e.g., *It Will Never Happen To Me* by Black; *Outgrowing the Pain* by Gil; *Healing the Child Within* by Whitfield; *Why I'm Afraid to Tell You Who I Am* by Powell); process insights attained.

5. Identify how own parenting has been influenced by childhood experiences. (9)

9. Ask the client to compare his/her parenting behavior to that of parent figures of his/her childhood; encourage the client to be aware of how easily we repeat patterns that we grew up with.

6. Acknowledge any dissociative phenomena that have resulted from childhood trauma. (10, 11)

10. Assist the client in understanding the role of dissociation in protecting himself/herself from the pain of childhood abusive betrayals (see Dissociation chapter in this *Planner*).

11. Assess the severity of the client's dissociation phenomena and hospitalize as necessary for his/her protection.

7. State the role substance abuse has in dealing with emotional pain of childhood. (12)

12. Assess the client's substance abuse behavior that has developed, in part, as a means of coping with feelings of childhood trauma. If

alcohol or drug abuse is found to be a problem, encourage treatment focused on this issue (see Chemical Dependence chapter of this *Planner*).

8. Decrease feelings of shame by being able to verbally affirm self as not responsible for abuse. (13, 14, 15, 16)

13. Assign writing a letter to mother, father, or other abuser in which the client expresses his/her feelings regarding the abuse.
14. Hold conjoint sessions where the client confronts the perpetrator of the abuse.
15. Guide the client in an empty-chair exercise with a key figure connected to the abuse—that is, perpetrator, sibling, or parent; reinforce the client for placing responsibility for the abuse or neglect on the caretaker.
16. Consistently reiterate that responsibility for the abuse falls on the abusive adults, not the surviving child (for deserving the abuse), and reinforce statements that accurately reflect placing blame on perpetrators and on nonprotective, nonnurturant adults.

9. Identify the positive aspects for self of being able to forgive all those involved with the abuse. (17, 18, 19)

17. Assign the client to write a forgiveness letter to the perpetrator of abuse; process the letter.
18. Teach the client the benefits (i.e., release of hurt and anger, putting issue in the past, opens door for trust of others, etc.) of beginning a process of forgiveness of (not necessarily forgetting or fraternizing with) abusive adults.
19. Recommend the client read books on the topic of forgiveness (e.g., *Forgive and Forget* by Smedes; *When Bad Things Happen to Good People* by Kushner).

10. Decrease statements of being a victim while increasing statements that reflect personal empowerment. (20, 21)

20. Ask the client to complete an exercise that identifies the positives and negatives of being a victim and the positives and negatives of being a survivor; compare and process the lists.

21. Encourage and reinforce the client's statements that reflect movement away from viewing self as a victim and toward personal empowerment as a survivor.

11. Increase level of trust of others as shown by more socialization and greater intimacy tolerance. (22, 23)

22. Teach the client the share-check method of building trust in relationships (sharing a little information and checking as to the recipient's sensitivity in reacting to that information).

23. Teach the client the advantages of treating people as trustworthy given a reasonable amount of time to assess their character.

—. ______________________________

—. ______________________________

—. ______________________________

—. ______________________________

—. ______________________________

—. ______________________________

DIAGNOSTIC SUGGESTIONS

Axis I:	300.4	Dysthymic Disorder
	296.xx	Major Depressive Disorder
	300.3	Obsessive-Compulsive Disorder
	300.02	Generalized Anxiety Disorder
	309.81	Posttraumatic Stress Disorder
	300.14	Dissociative Identity Disorder
	995.53	Sexual Abuse of Child, Victim

	995.54	Physical Abuse of Child, Victim
	995.52	Neglect of Child, Victim
	______	____________________
	______	____________________
Axis II:	301.7	Antisocial Personality Disorder
	301.6	Dependent Personality Disorder
	301.4	Obsessive-Compulsive Personality Disorder
	______	____________________
	______	____________________

CHRONIC PAIN

BEHAVIORAL DEFINITIONS

1. Experiences pain beyond the normal healing process (6 months or more) that significantly limits physical activities.
2. Complains of generalized pain in many joints, muscles, and bones that debilitates normal functioning.
3. Uses increased amounts of medications with little, if any, pain relief.
4. Experiences tension, migraine, cluster, or chronic daily headaches of unknown origin.
5. Experiences back or neck pain, interstitial cystitis, or diabetic neuropathy.
6. Experiences intermittent pain such as that related to rheumatoid arthritis or irritable bowel syndrome.
7. Has decreased or stopped activities such as work, household chores, socializing, exercise, sex, or other pleasurable activities because of pain.
8. Experiences an increase in general physical discomfort (e.g., fatigue, night sweats, insomnia, muscle tension, body aches).
9. Exhibits signs and symptoms of depression.
10. Makes statements like "I can't do what I used to"; "No one understands me"; "Why me?"; "When will this go away?"; "I can't take this pain anymore"; and "I can't go on."

—. ____

____

—. ____

____

—. ____

____

LONG-TERM GOALS

1. Acquire and utilize the necessary pain management skills.
2. Regulate pain in order to maximize daily functioning and return to productive employment.
3. Find relief from pain and build renewed contentment and joy in performing activities of everyday life.
4. Find an escape route from the pain.
5. Accept the chronic pain and move on with life as much as possible.
6. Lessen daily suffering from pain.

—. ____

____

—. ____

____

—. ____

____

SHORT-TERM OBJECTIVES

1. Describe the nature of, history of, impact of, and understood causes of chronic pain. (1, 2)
2. Complete a thorough medical examination to rule out any alternative causes for the pain and reveal any new treatment possibilities. (3)
3. Follow through on a referral to a pain management or rehabilitation program. (4, 5, 6)

THERAPEUTIC INTERVENTIONS

1. Assess the history and current status of the client's chronic pain.
2. Explore the changes in the client's mood, attitude, social, vocational, and familial/marital roles that have occurred as a result of the pain.
3. Refer the client to a physician or clinic to undergo a thorough examination to rule out any undiagnosed condition and to receive recommendations on any further treatment options.
4. Give the client information on the options of pain management specialists or rehabilitation programs that are available and help him/her make a decision on which would be the best for him/her.

5. Make a referral to a pain management specialist or clinic of the client's choice and have him/her sign appropriate releases for the therapist to have updates on progress from the program and to coordinate services.

6. Elicit from the client a verbal commitment to cooperate with pain management specialists, headache clinic, or rehabilitation program.

Ⓔ 4. Complete a thorough medication review by a physician who is a specialist in dealing with chronic pain or headache conditions. (7)

7. Ask the client to complete a medication review with a specialist in chronic pain or headaches; confer with the physician afterward about his/her recommendations and process them with the client. Ⓔ

Ⓔ 5. Participate in a cognitive behavioral group therapy for pain management. (8)

8. Form a small, closed enrollment group (4–8 clients) for pain management (see *Group Therapy for Patients with Chronic Pain* by Keefe, Beaupre, Gil, Rumble, and Aspnes). Ⓔ

Ⓔ 6. Verbalize an understanding of pain. (9)

9. Teach the client key concepts of rehabilitation versus biological healing, conservative versus aggressive medical interventions, acute versus chronic pain, benign versus nonbenign pain, cure versus management, appropriate use of medication, role of selfregulation techniques, and so on. Ⓔ

Ⓔ 7. Verbalize an understanding of the rationale for treatment. (10, 11)

10. Teach the client a rationale for treatment that helps him/her understand that thoughts, feelings, and behavior can affect pain and emphasizes the role that the client can play in managing his/her own pain. Ⓔ

Ⓔ indicates that the Objective/Intervention is consistent with those found in evidence-based treatments.

11. Assign the client to read sections from books or treatment manuals that describe pain conditions and their cognitive behavioral treatment (e.g., *The Chronic Pain Control Workbook* by Catalano and Hardin). ♥

♥ 8. Identify and monitor specific pain triggers. (12)

12. Teach the client self-monitoring of his/her symptoms; ask the client to keep a pain journal that records time of day, where and what he/she was doing, the severity, and what was done to alleviate the pain (or assign "Pain and Stress Journal" in *Adult Psychotherapy Homework Planner,* 2nd ed. by Jongsma); process the journal with the client to increase insight into nature of the pain, cognitive, affective, and behavioral triggers, and the positive or negative effect of the interventions they are currently using. ♥

♥ 9. Learn and implement somatic skills such as relaxation and/or biofeedback to reduce pain level. (13, 14, 15, 16, 17)

13. Teach the client relaxation skills (e.g., progressive muscle, guided imagery, slow diaphragmatic breathing) and how to discriminate better between relaxation and tension; teach the client how to apply these skills to his/her daily life (see *Progressive Relaxation Training* by Bernstein and Borkovec). ♥

14. Refer the client for or conduct biofeedback training (e.g., EMG for muscle tension-related pain, thermal for migraine pain). Assign practice of the skill at home. ♥

15. Identify areas in the client's life that he/she can implement skills learned through relaxation or biofeedback. ♥

16. Assign a homework exercise in which the client implements somatic pain management skills and records the result; review and process during the treatment session. ▼

17. Assign the client to read about progressive muscle relaxation and other calming strategies in relevant books or treatment manuals (e.g., *Progressive Relaxation Training* by Bernstein and Borkovec). ▼

▼10. Incorporate physical therapy into daily routine. (18)

18. Refer the client for physical therapy if pain is heterogeneous. ▼

▼11. Learn mental coping skills and implement with somatic skills for managing acute pain. (19)

19. Teach client distraction techniques (e.g., pleasant imagery, counting techniques, alternative focal point) and how to use them with relaxation skills for the management of acute episodes of pain. ▼

▼12. Increase the level and range of activity by identifying and engaging in pleasurable activities. (20)

20. Ask the client to create a list of activities that are pleasurable to him/her; process the list, developing a plan of increasing the frequency of engaging in the selected pleasurable activities. ▼

▼13. Identify negative pain-related thoughts and replace them with more positive coping-related thoughts. (21, 22, 23)

21. Explore the client's schema and self-talk that mediate his/her pain response, challenging the biases; assist him/her in generating thoughts that correct for the biases, facilitate coping, and build confidence in managing pain. ▼

22. Assign the client a homework exercise in which he/she identifies negative pain-related self-talk and positive alternatives (or assign "Journal and Replace Self-Defeating Thoughts" in *Adult Psychotherapy Homework Planner,* 2nd ed. by Jongsma); review

and reinforce success, providing corrective feedback toward improvement. ▽

23. Assign the client to read about cognitive restructuring in relevant books or treatment manuals (e.g., *The Chronic Pain Control Workbook* by Catalano and Hardin). ▽

▽14. Integrate and implement new mental, somatic, and behavioral ways of managing pain. (24)

24. Assist client in integrating learned pain management skills (e.g., relaxation, distraction, activity scheduling) into a progressively wider range of daily activities; record and review. ▽

▽15. Problem-solve obstacles to implementation of new ways to manage pain. (25)

25. Teach the client problem-solving skills to apply to removal of obstacles to implementing new skills. ▽

▽16. Implement relapse prevention strategies for managing future challenges. (26, 27, 28)

26. Discuss with the client the distinction between a lapse and relapse, associating a lapse with an initial and reversible return of pain or old habits (e.g., a "bad day") and relapse with the persistent return of pain and previous cognitive and behavioral habits that exacerbate pain. ▽

27. Identify and rehearse with the client the management of future situations or circumstances in which lapses could occur, using the strategies learned during therapy. ▽

28. Follow up with the client periodically to problem-solve difficulties and reinforce successes. ▽

17. Incorporate physical exercise into daily routine. (29, 30, 31)

29. Assist the client in recognizing the benefits of regular exercise, encouraging him/her to implement exercise in daily life and monitor results; offer ongoing encouragement to stay with the regimen.

30. Refer the client to an athletic club to develop an individually tailored exercise or physical therapy program that is approved by his/her personal physician.

31. Refer the client to a beginners' yoga class.

18. Make changes in diet that will promote health and fitness. (32)

32. Refer the client to a dietician for consultation around eating and nutritional patterns; process the results of the consultation, identifying changes he/she can make and how he/she might start implementing these changes.

19. Investigate the use of alternative therapies to pain management. (33)

33. Explore the client's openness to alternative therapies for pain management (e.g., acupuncture, hypnosis, therapeutic massage); refer for the services, if indicated.

20. Learn and implement stress management techniques. (34, 35, 36)

34. Teach the client stress management techniques (e.g., deep muscle relaxation, distraction, cognitive restructuring, increased pleasurable activities) to manage stressors that may be exacerbating pain or his/her vulnerability to it.

35. Assist the client in becoming capable of seeing humor in more of his/her daily life; promote this expansion through various means (e.g., increase his/her use of humor, telling jokes), assigning the client to watch one or two comedy movies each week.

36. Assist the client in applying stress management skills to his/her everyday life.

21. Connect with sources in your social network who support your therapeutic changes. (37)

37. Assess the client's social support network and encourage him/her to connect with those who facilitate or support the client's positive change.

__. ______________________________ __. ______________________________

______________________________ ______________________________

__. ______________________________ __. ______________________________

______________________________ ______________________________

__. ______________________________ __. ______________________________

______________________________ ______________________________

DIAGNOSTIC SUGGESTIONS

Axis I:	307.89	Pain Disorder Associated With Both Psychological Factors and a General Medical Condition
	307.80	Pain Disorder Associated With Psychological Factors
	300.81	Somatization Disorder
	300.11	Conversion Disorder
	296.3x	Major Depressive Disorder, Recurrent
	300.3	Obsessive-Compulsive Disorder
	302.70	Sexual Dysfunction NOS
	304.10	Sedative, Hypnotic, or Anxiolytic Dependence
	304.80	Polysubstance Dependence
	________	______________________________
	________	______________________________

COGNITIVE DEFICITS

BEHAVIORAL DEFINITIONS

1. Concrete thinking or impaired abstract thinking.
2. Lack of insight into the consequences of behavior (i.e., impaired judgment).
3. Short-term memory deficits.
4. Long-term memory deficits.
5. Difficulty following complex or sequential directions.
6. Loss of orientation to person, place, or time.
7. Distractibility in attention.
8. Impulsive behavior that violates social mores.
9. Speech and language impairment.

__. ____

____

__. ____

____

__. ____

____

LONG-TERM GOALS

1. Develop an understanding and acceptance of the cognitive impairment.
2. Develop alternative coping strategies to compensate for cognitive limitations.

__. ____

____

__. ____

____

__. ____

____

SHORT-TERM OBJECTIVES

1. Describe all symptoms that may be related to neurological deficit. (1, 2)

2. Cooperate with and complete neuropsychological testing. (3, 4)

3. Obtain a neurological examination. (5)

THERAPEUTIC INTERVENTIONS

1. Explore signs and symptoms of the client's possible neurological impairment (e.g., memory loss, defective coordination, flawed abstract thinking, speech and language deficits, unsound executive functions, disorientation, impaired judgment, inattention, headaches, dizziness, blurry vision).

2. Assess and monitor the client's cognitive behavior in individual sessions.

3. Arrange for the client to have psychological testing administered to determine the nature and degree of cognitive deficits.

4. Administer appropriate psychological tests (e.g., Wechsler Adult Intelligence Scale–III, Booklet Category Test, Trailmaking, Haldstead-Reitan Battery, Michigan Neurological Battery, Luria-Nebraska Battery, Wechsler Memory Scale, Memory Assessment Scales) to determine the nature, extent, and possible origin of the client's cognitive deficits.

5. Refer the client to a neurologist to further assess his/her organic deficits and determine possible causes.

4. Understand and accept cognitive limitations and use alternate coping mechanisms. (6, 7)

6. Inform the client of the results of the cognitive assessment and develop appropriate objectives based on testing.

7. Assist the client in coming to an understanding and acceptance of his/her limitations.

5. Verbalize feelings associated with acceptance of cognitive impairment. (8)

8. Explore the client's feelings of depression and anxiety related to his/her cognitive impairment; provide encouragement and support.

6. Attempt to follow through to completion simple sequential tasks. (9)

9. Assign appropriate sequential tasks for the client to perform and redirect when needed so as to assess his/her cognitive abilities.

7. Implement memory-enhancing mechanisms. (10)

10. Assign and monitor memory-enhancing activities/exercises for the client (e.g., crossword puzzles, card games, TV game shows) and memory-loss coping strategies (e.g., lists, routines, post notes, repeating items aloud to yourself, using mnemonic strategies).

8. Identify when it is appropriate to seek help with a task and when it is not. (7, 11)

7. Assist the client in coming to an understanding and acceptance of his/her limitations.

11. Establish with the client and his/her significant other appropriate points for the client to ask for help.

9. Write a plan identifying who will provide daily supervisory contact and when they will do it. (12, 13)

12. Assist the client in identifying dependable resource people who can provide regular supervision.

13. Develop a written schedule with the client for times of supervisory contact and identify who will provide it.

—. ______________________________
____

—. ______________________________
____

__. ______________________ __. ______________________
______________________ ______________________

__. ______________________ __. ______________________
______________________ ______________________

DIAGNOSTIC SUGGESTIONS

Axis I:	310.1	Personality Change Due to Axis III Disorder
	294.8	Dementia NOS
	294.1	Dementia Due to Axis III Disorder
	291.2	Alcohol-Induced Persisting Dementia
	291.1	Alcohol-Induced Persisting Amnestic Disorder
	294.8	Amnestic Disorder NOS
	303.90	Alcohol Dependence
	304.30	Cannabis Dependence
	294.0	Amnestic Disorder Due to Axis III Disorder
	294.9	Cognitive Disorder NOS
	______	______________________
	______	______________________
Axis II:	799.9	Diagnosis Deferred
	V71.09	No Diagnosis
	______	______________________
	______	______________________

DEPENDENCY

BEHAVIORAL DEFINITIONS

1. Inability to become self-sufficient, consistently relying on parents to provide financial support, housing, or caregiving.
2. A history of many intimate relationships with little, if any, space between the ending of one and the start of the next.
3. Strong feelings of panic, fear, and helplessness when faced with being alone as a close relationship ends.
4. Feelings easily hurt by criticism and preoccupied with pleasing others.
5. Inability to make decisions or initiate actions without excessive reassurance from others.
6. Frequent preoccupation with fears of being abandoned.
7. All feelings of self-worth, happiness, and fulfillment derive from relationships.
8. Involvement in at least two relationships wherein he/she was physically abused but had difficulty leaving.
9. Avoidance of disagreeing with others for fear of being rejected.

—. ____

____

—. ____

____

—. ____

____

LONG-TERM GOALS

1. Develop confidence that he/she is capable of meeting own needs and of tolerating being alone.
2. Achieve a healthy balance between independence and dependence.

3. Decrease dependence on relationships while beginning to meet own needs, build confidence, and practice assertiveness.
4. Establish firm individual self-boundaries and improved self-worth.
5. Break away permanently from any abusive relationships.
6. Emancipate self from emotional and economic dependence on parents.

—. ____

____

—. ____

____

—. ____

____

SHORT-TERM OBJECTIVES

1. Describe the style and pattern of emotional dependence in relationships. (1)
2. Verbalize an increased awareness of own dependency. (2, 3)
3. Verbalize insight into the automatic practice of striving to meet other people's expectations. (4, 5, 6)

THERAPEUTIC INTERVENTIONS

1. Explore the client's history of emotional dependence extending from unmet childhood needs to current relationships.
2. Develop a family genogram to increase the client's awareness of family patterns of dependence in relationships and how he/she is repeating them in the present relationship.
3. Assign the client to read *Codependent No More* (Beattie), *Women Who Love Too Much* (Norwood), or *Getting Them Sober* (Drews). Process key ideas.
4. Explore the client's family of origin for experiences of emotional abandonment.
5. Assist the client in identifying the basis for his/her fear of disappointing others.
6. Read with the client the fable entitled "The Bridge" in *Friedman's Fables* (Friedman). Process the meaning of the fable.

4. List positive things about self. (7, 8)

7. Assist the client in developing a list of his/her positive attributes and accomplishments.
8. Assign the client to institute a ritual of beginning each day with 5 to 10 minutes of solitude where the focus is personal affirmation.

5. Identify and replace distorted automatic thoughts associated with assertiveness, being alone, or keeping personal responsibility boundaries. (5, 9, 10, 11)

5. Assist the client in identifying the basis for his/her fear of disappointing others.
9. Explore and identify the client's distorted, negative automatic thoughts associated with assertiveness, being alone, or not meeting others' needs.
10. Explore and clarify the client's fears or other negative feelings associated with being more independent.
11. Assist the client in developing positive, reality-based messages for self to replace the distorted, negative self-talk.

6. Verbalize a decreased sensitivity to criticism. (12, 13, 14)

12. Explore the client's sensitivity to criticism and help him/her develop new ways of receiving, processing, and responding to it.
13. Assign the client to read books on assertiveness (e.g., *When I Say No I Feel Guilty* by Smith).
14. Verbally reinforce the client for any and all signs of assertiveness and independence.

7. Increase saying no to others' requests. (15, 16)

15. Assign the client to say no without excessive explanation for a period of one week and process this with him/her.
16. Train the client in assertiveness or refer him/her to a group that will facilitate and develop his/her assertiveness skills via lectures and assignments.

8. Report incidents of verbally stating own opinion. (16, 17)

16. Train the client in assertiveness or refer him/her to a group that will facilitate and develop his/her assertiveness skills via lectures and assignments.

17. Assign the client to speak his/her mind for one day, and process the results with him/her.

9. Identify own emotional and social needs and ways to fulfill them. (18, 19)

18. Ask the client to compile a list of his/her emotional and social needs and ways that these could possibly be met; process the list.

19. Ask the client to list ways that he/she could start taking care of himself/herself; then identify two to three that could be started now and elicit the client's agreement to do so. Monitor for follow-through and feelings of change about self.

10. Report examples of receiving favors from others without feeling the necessity of reciprocating. (20)

20. Assign the client to allow others to do favors for him/her and to receive without giving. Process progress and feelings related to this assignment.

11. Verbalize an increased sense of self-responsibility while decreasing sense of responsibility for others. (21, 22, 23)

21. Assist the client in identifying and implementing ways of increasing his/her level of independence in day-to-day life.

22. Assist the client in developing new boundaries for not accepting responsibility for others' actions or feelings.

23. Facilitate conjoint session with the client's significant other with focus on exploring ways to increase independence within the relationship.

12. Verbalize an increased awareness of boundaries and when they are violated. (24, 25, 26)

24. Assign the client to keep a daily journal regarding boundaries for taking responsibility for self and others and when he/she is aware of boundaries being broken by self or others.

25. Assign the client to read the book *Boundaries: Where You End and I Begin* (Katherine) and process key ideas.

26. Ask the client to read the chapter on setting boundaries and limits in the book *A Gift To Myself* (Whitfield) and complete the accompanying survey on personal boundaries. Process the key ideas and results of the survey.

13. Increase the frequency of verbally clarifying boundaries with others. (27)

27. Reinforce the client for implementing boundaries and limits for self.

14. Increase the frequency of making decisions within a reasonable time and with self-assurance. (28, 29)

28. Confront the client's tendency toward decision avoidance and encourage his/her efforts to implement proactive decision making.

29. Give positive verbal reinforcement for each timely thought-out decision that the client makes.

15. Attend an Al-Anon group to reinforce efforts to break dependency cycle with a chemically dependent partner. (30)

30. Refer the client to Al-Anon or another appropriate self-help group.

16. Develop a plan to end the relationship with abusive partner, and implement the plan with therapist's guidance. (31, 32, 33)

31. Assign the client to read *The Verbally Abusive Relationship* (Evans); process key ideas and insights.

32. Refer the client to a safe house.

33. Refer the client to a domestic violence program and monitor and encourage his/her continued involvement in the program.

__. ______________________________

____

__. ______________________________

____

__. ______________________________

____

__. ______________________________

____

__. ______________________________

____

__. ______________________________

____

DIAGNOSTIC SUGGESTIONS

Axis I:	300.4	Dysthymic Disorder
	995.81	Physical Abuse of Adult, Victim
	________	______________________________
	________	______________________________
Axis II:	301.82	Avoidant Personality Disorder
	301.83	Borderline Personality Disorder
	301.6	Dependent Personality Disorder
	________	______________________________
	________	______________________________

DEPRESSION

BEHAVIORAL DEFINITIONS

SYMPTOMS

1. Depressed mood.
2. Loss of appetite.
3. Diminished interest in or enjoyment of activities.
4. Psychomotor agitation or retardation.
5. Sleeplessness or hypersomnia.
6. Lack of energy.
7. Poor concentration and indecisiveness.
8. Social withdrawal.
9. Suicidal thoughts and/or gestures.
10. Feelings of hopelessness, worthlessness, or inappropriate guilt.
11. Low self-esteem.
12. Unresolved grief issues.
13. Mood-related hallucinations or delusions.
14. History of chronic or recurrent depression for which the client has taken antidepressant medication, been hospitalized, or had outpatient treatment, or had a course of electroconvulsive therapy.

__. ____

____

__. ____

____

__. ____

____

LONG-TERM GOALS

1. Alleviate depressed mood and return to previous level of effective functioning.

2. Recognize, accept, and cope with feelings of depression.
3. Develop healthy cognitive patterns and beliefs about self and the world that lead to alleviation and help prevent the relapse of depression symptoms.
4. Develop healthy interpersonal relationships that lead to alleviation and help prevent the relapse of depression symptoms.
5. Appropriately grieve the loss in order to normalize mood and to return to previous adaptive level of functioning.

—. ____

____

—. ____

____

—. ____

____

SHORT-TERM OBJECTIVES

1. Describe current and past experiences with depression complete with its impact on function and attempts to resolve it. (1)
2. Verbally identify, if possible, the source of depressed mood. (2, 3)
3. Complete psychological testing to assess the depth of depression, the need for antidepressant medication, and suicide prevention measures. (4)

THERAPEUTIC INTERVENTIONS

1. Assess current and past mood episodes including their features, frequency, intensity, and duration (e.g., Clinical Interview supplemented by the *Inventory to Diagnose Depression* by Zimmerman, Coryell, Corenthal, and Wilson).
2. Ask the client to make a list of what he/she is depressed about; process the list content.
3. Encourage the client to share his/her feelings of depression in order to clarify them and gain insight as to causes.
4. Arrange for the administration of an objective assessment instrument for evaluating the client's depression and suicide risk (e.g., Beck Depression Inventory–II and/or Beck Hopelessness Scale); evaluate results and give feedback to the client.

4. Verbalize any history of suicide attempts and any current suicidal urges. (5)

5. Explore the client's history and current state of suicidal urges and behavior (see Suicidal Ideation chapter in this *Planner* if suicide risk is present).

5. State no longer having thoughts of self-harm. (6, 7)

6. Assess and monitor the client's suicide potential.

7. Arrange for hospitalization, as necessary, when the client is judged to be harmful to self.

[EB] 6. Take prescribed psychotropic medications responsibly at times ordered by physician. (8, 9)

8. Evaluate the client's possible need for psychotropic medication and arrange for a physician to give him/her a physical examination to rule out organic causes for depression, assess need for antidepressant medication, and order a prescription, if appropriate. [EB]

9. Monitor and evaluate the client's psychotropic medication compliance, effectiveness, and side effects; communicate with prescribing physician. [EB]

[EB] 7. Identify and replace cognitive self-talk that is engaged in to support depression. (10, 11, 12, 13)

10. Assist the client in developing an awareness of his/her automatic thoughts that reflect a depressogenic schemata. [EB]

11. Assign the client to keep a daily journal of automatic thoughts associated with depressive feelings (e.g., "Negative Thoughts Trigger Negative Feelings" in *Adult Psychotherapy Homework Planner,* 2nd ed. by Jongsma, "Daily Record of Dysfunctional Thoughts" in *Cognitive Therapy of Depression* by Beck, Rush, Shaw, and Emery); process the

---

[EB] indicates that the Objective/Intervention is consistent with those found in evidence-based treatments.

journal material to challenge depressive thinking patterns and replace them with reality-based thoughts. ▽

12. Do "behavioral experiments" in which depressive automatic thoughts are treated as hypotheses/predictions, reality-based alternative hypotheses/predictions are generated, and both are tested against the client's past, present, and/or future experiences. ▽

13. Reinforce the client's positive, reality-based cognitive messages that enhance self-confidence and increase adaptive action (see "Positive Self-Talk" in *Adult Psychotherapy Homework Planner,* 2nd ed. by Jongsma). ▽

Pt. will

▽ 8. Utilize behavioral strategies to overcome depression. (14, 15, 16)

14. Assist the client in developing coping strategies (e.g., more physical exercise, less internal focus, increased social involvement, more assertiveness, greater need sharing, more anger expression) for feelings of depression; reinforce success. ▽

15. Engage the client in "behavioral activation" by scheduling activities that have a high likelihood for pleasure and mastery (see "Identify and Schedule Pleasant Activities" in *Adult Psychotherapy Homework Planner,* 2nd ed. by Jongsma); use rehearsal, role-playing, role reversal, as needed, to assist adoption in the client's daily life; reinforce success. ▽

16. Employ self-reliance training in which the client assumes increased responsibility for routine activities (e.g., cleaning, cooking, shopping); reinforce success. ▽

9. Identify important people in your life, past and present, and describe the quality, good and bad, of those relationships. (17)

17. Assess the client's "interpersonal inventory" of important past and present relationships and evidence of potentially depressive themes (e.g., grief, interpersonal disputes, role transitions, interpersonal deficits).

10. Verbalize any unresolved grief issues that may be contributing to depression. (18)

18. Explore the role of unresolved grief issues as they contribute to the client's current depression (see Grief/Loss Unresolved chapter in this *Planner*).

11. Learn and implement problem-solving and/or conflict resolution skills to resolve interpersonal problems. (19, 20, 21)

19. Teach the client conflict resolution skills (e.g., empathy, active listening, "I messages," respectful communication, assertiveness without aggression, compromise) to help alleviate depression; use modeling, role-playing, and behavior rehearsal to work through several current conflicts.

20. Help the client resolve depression related to interpersonal problems through the use of reassurance and support, clarification of cognitive and affective triggers that ignite conflicts, and active problem-solving (or assign "Applying Problem-Solving to Interpersonal Conflict" in *Adult Psychotherapy Homework Planner,* 2nd ed. by Jongsma).

21. In conjoint sessions, help the client resolve interpersonal conflicts.

12. Implement a regular exercise regimen as a depression reduction technique. (22, 23)

22. Develop and reinforce a routine of physical exercise for the client.

23. Recommend that the client read and implement programs from *Exercising Your Way to Better Mental Health* (Leith).

13. Learn and implement relapse prevention skills. (24)

24. Build the client's relapse prevention skills by helping him/her identify early warning signs of relapse, reviewing skills learned during therapy, and developing a plan for managing challenges.

14. Increase assertive communication. (25)

25. Use modeling and/or role-playing to train the client in assertiveness; if indicated, refer him/her to an assertiveness training class/group for further instruction

15. Read books on overcoming depression. (26)

26. Recommend that the client read self-help books on coping with depression (e.g., *Feeling Good* by Burns); process material read.

16. Show evidence of daily care for personal grooming and hygiene with minimal reminders from others. (27)

27. Monitor and redirect the client on daily grooming and hygiene.

17. Increasingly verbalize hopeful and positive statements regarding self, others, and the future (28, 29)

28. Assign the client to write at least one positive affirmation statement daily regarding himself/herself and the future.

29. Teach the client more about depression and to accept some sadness as a normal variation in feeling.

18. Express feelings of hurt, disappointment, shame, and anger that are associated with early life experiences. (30, 31)

30. Explore experiences from the client's childhood that contribute to current depressed state.

31. Encourage the client to share feelings of anger regarding pain inflicted on him/her in childhood that contributed to current depressed state.

19. Verbalize an understanding of the relationship between depressed mood and repression of feelings—that is, anger, hurt, sadness, and so on. (32)

32. Explain a connection between previously unexpressed (repressed) feelings of anger (and helplessness) and current state of depression.

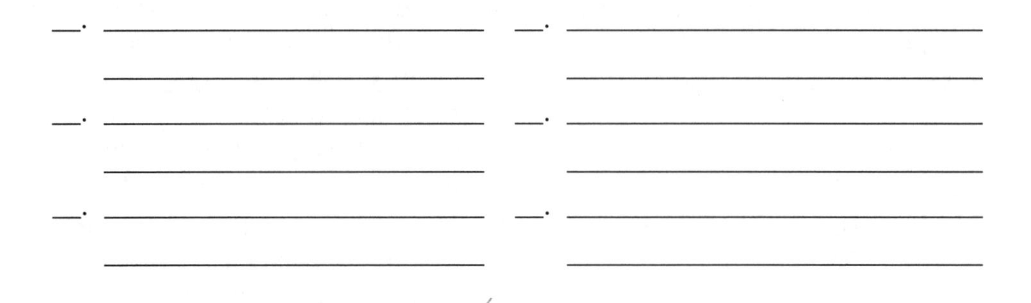

DIAGNOSTIC SUGGESTIONS

Axis I:	309.0	Adjustment Disorder With Depressed Mood
	296.xx	Bipolar I Disorder
	296.89	Bipolar II Disorder
	300.4	Dysthymic Disorder
	301.13	Cyclothymic Disorder
	296.2x	Major Depressive Disorder, Single Episode
	296.3x	Major Depressive Disorder, Recurrent
	295.70	Schizoaffective Disorder
	310.1	Personality Change Due to Axis III Disorder
	V62.82	Bereavement
	_______	_______________________
	_______	_______________________
Axis II:	301.9	Personality Disorder NOS
	799.9	Diagnosis Deferred
	V71.09	No Diagnosis
	_______	_______________________
	_______	_______________________

DISSOCIATION

SYMPTOMS

BEHAVIORAL DEFINITIONS

1. The existence of two or more distinct personality states that recurrently take full control of one's behavior.
2. An episode of the sudden inability to remember important personal identification information that is more than just ordinary forgetfulness.
3. Persistent or recurrent experiences of depersonalization; feeling as if detached from or outside of one's mental processes or body during which reality testing remains intact.
4. Persistent or recurrent experiences of depersonalization; feeling as if one is automated or in a dream.
5. Depersonalization sufficiently severe and persistent as to cause marked distress in daily life.

__. ____

____

__. ____

____

__. ____

____

LONG-TERM GOALS

1. Integrate the various personalities.
2. Reduce the frequency and duration of dissociative episodes.
3. Resolve the emotional trauma that underlies the dissociative disturbance.
4. Reduce the level of daily distress caused by dissociative disturbances.
5. Regain full memory.

adequate

__. ____

____

__. ____

____

__. ____

____

SHORT-TERM OBJECTIVES

1. Identify each personality and have each one tell its story. (1, 2)
2. Complete a psychotropic medication evaluation with a physician. (3)
3. Take prescribed psychotropic medications responsibly at times ordered by the physician. (4)
4. Identify the key issues that trigger a dissociative state. (5, 6, 7)

THERAPEUTIC INTERVENTIONS

1. Actively build the level of trust with the client in individual sessions through consistent eye contact, active listening, unconditional positive regard, and warm acceptance to help increase his/her ability to identify and express feelings.
2. Without undue encouragement or leading, probe and assess the existence of the various personalities that take control of the client.
3. Arrange for an evaluation of the client for a psychotropic medication prescription.
4. Monitor and evaluate the client's psychotropic medication prescription for compliance, effectiveness, and side effects.
5. Explore the feelings and circumstances that trigger the client's dissociative state.
6. Explore the client's sources of emotional pain or trauma, and feelings of fear, inadequacy, rejection, or abuse.
7. Assist the client in accepting a connection between his/her dissociating and avoidance of facing emotional conflicts/issues.

5. Decrease the number and duration of personality changes. (8, 9)

8. Facilitate integration of the client's personality by supporting and encouraging him/her to stay focused on reality rather than escaping through dissociation.

9. Emphasize to the client the importance of a here-and-now focus on reality rather than a preoccupation with the traumas of the past and dissociative phenomena associated with that fixation. Reinforce instances of here-and-now behavior.

6. Practice relaxation and deep breathing as means of reducing anxiety. (10)

10. Train the client in relaxation and deep breathing techniques to be used for anxiety management.

7. Verbalize acceptance of brief episodes of dissociation as not being the basis for panic, but only as passing phenomena. (11)

11. Teach the client to be calm and matter-of-fact in the face of brief dissociative phenomena so as to not accelerate anxiety symptoms, but to stay focused on reality.

8. Discuss the period preceding memory loss and the period after memory returns. (6, 12)

6. Explore the client's sources of emotional pain or trauma, and feelings of fear, inadequacy, rejection, or abuse.

12. Arrange and facilitate a session with the client and significant others to assist him/her in regaining lost personal information.

9. Cooperate with a referral to a neurologist to rule out organic factors in amnestic episodes. (13)

13. Refer the client to a neurologist for evaluation of any organic cause for memory loss experiences.

10. Attend family therapy sessions that focus on the recall of personal history information. (12, 14)

12. Arrange and facilitate a session with the client and significant others to assist him/her in regaining lost personal information.

14. Calmly reassure the client to be patient in seeking to regain lost memories.

11. Utilize photos and other memorabilia to stimulate recall of personal history. (14, 15)

__. ____________________________

__. ____________________________

__. ____________________________

14. Calmly reassure the client to be patient in seeking to regain lost memories.
15. Utilize pictures and other memorabilia to gently trigger the client's memory recall.

__. ____________________________

__. ____________________________

__. ____________________________

DIAGNOSTIC SUGGESTIONS

Axis I:	303.90	Alcohol Dependence
	300.14	Dissociative Identity Disorder
	300.12	Dissociative Amnesia
	300.6	Depersonalization Disorder
	300.15	Dissociative Disorder NOS
	______	____________________
	______	____________________
Axis II:	799.9	Diagnosis Deferred
	V71.09	No Diagnosis
	______	____________________
	______	____________________

EATING DISORDER

BEHAVIORAL DEFINITIONS

1. Refusal to maintain body weight at or above a minimally normal weight for age and height—less than 85% of that expected.
2. Intense fear of gaining weight or becoming fat, even though underweight.
3. Recurrent episodes of binge eating (i.e., rapid consumption of large quantities of high-carbohydrate food).
4. Recurrent inappropriate compensatory behavior to prevent weight gain, such as self-induced vomiting; misuse of laxatives, diuretics, enemas, or other medications; fasting; or excessive exercise.
5. Extreme weight loss (and amenorrhea in females) with refusal to maintain a minimal healthy weight.
6. Undue influence of body weight or shape in self-evaluation.
7. Persistent preoccupation with body image related to grossly inaccurate assessment of self as overweight.
8. Escalating fluid and electrolyte imbalance resulting from eating disorder.
9. Strong denial of seeing self as emaciated even when severely under recommended weight.

__. ______________________________

____

__. ______________________________

____

__. ______________________________

____

LONG-TERM GOALS

1. Restore normal eating patterns, body weight, balanced fluid and electrolytes, and a realistic perception of body size.
2. Terminate the pattern of binge eating and purging behavior with a return to normal eating of enough nutritious foods to maintain a healthy weight.
3. Develop healthy cognitive patterns and beliefs about self that lead to alleviation and help prevent the relapse of the eating disorder.
4. Develop healthy interpersonal relationships that lead to alleviation and help prevent the relapse of the eating disorder.
5. Develop alternate coping strategies (e.g., feeling identification, problem-solving, assertiveness) to address emotional issues that could lead to relapse of the eating disorder.

—. ____

____

—. ____

____

—. ____

____

SHORT-TERM OBJECTIVES

1. Honestly describe the pattern of eating including types, amounts, and frequency of food consumed or hoarded. (1, 2, 3)
2. Describe any regular use of dysfunctional weight control behaviors. (4, 5)

THERAPEUTIC INTERVENTIONS

1. Establish rapport with the client toward building a therapeutic alliance.
2. Assess the amount, type, and pattern of the client's food intake (e.g., too little food, too much food, binge eating, or hoarding food).
3. Compare the client's calorie consumption with an average adult rate of 1,500 calories per day to determine over- or undereating.
4. Assess for the presence of self-induced vomiting behavior by the client to purge himself/herself of calorie intake; monitor on an ongoing basis.

5. Assess for the client's misuse of laxatives, diuretics, enemas, or other medications; fasting; or excessive exercise; monitor on an ongoing basis.

3. Complete psychological tests designed to assess and track eating patterns and unhealthy weight-loss practices. (6)

6. Administer a measure of eating disorders to further assess its depth and breadth (e.g., self-induced vomiting; misuse of laxatives, diuretics, enemas, or other medications; fasting; or excessive exercise) and/or to track treatment progress (e.g., *The Eating Disorders Inventory-2* by Garner, 1991).

EB 4. Cooperate with a complete physical exam. (7)

7. Refer the client to a physician for a physical exam and stay in close consultation with the physician as to the client's medical condition and nutritional habits. EB

EB 5. Cooperate with a dental exam. (8)

8. Refer the client to a dentist for a dental exam. EB

EB 6. Cooperate with an evaluation by a physician for psychotropic medication. (9)

9. ~~Assess the client's need for psychotropic medications (e.g., SSRIs)~~; arrange for a physician to evaluate for and then prescribe psychotropic medications, if indicated. EB

EB 7. Take medications as prescribed and report effectiveness and side effects. (10)

10. Monitor the client's psychotropic medication prescription compliance, effectiveness, and side effects. EB

EB 8. Cooperate with admission to inpatient treatment if indicated. (11)

11. Refer the client for hospitalization, as necessary, if his/her weight loss becomes severe and physical health is jeopardized, if he/she is severely depressed or suicidal. EB

EB indicates that the Objective/Intervention is consistent with those found in evidence-based treatments.

9. Verbalize an accurate understanding of how eating disorders develop. (12)

12. Discuss with the client a model of eating disorders development that includes concepts such as sociocultural pressures to be thin, vulnerability in some individuals to overvalue body shape and size in determining self-image, maladaptive eating habits (e.g., fasting, binging), maladaptive compensatory weight management behaviors (e.g., purging), and resultant feelings of low self-esteem (see *Overcoming Binge Eating* by Fairburn).

10. Verbalize an understanding of the goals of and rationale for treatment. (13, 14)

13. Discuss a rationale for treatment that includes using cognitive and behavioral procedures to break the cycle of thinking and behaving that promotes poor self-image, uncontrolled eating, and unhealthy compensatory actions while building physical and mental health-promoting eating practices.

14. Assign the client to read psychoeducational chapters of books or treatment manuals on the development and treatment of eating disorders (e.g., *Overcoming Binge Eating* by Fairburn).

11. Keep a journal of food consumption. (15)

15. Assign the client to self-monitor and record food intake, thoughts, and feelings (or assign "A Reality Journal: Food, Weight, Thoughts, and Feelings" in *Adult Psychotherapy Homework Planner,* 2nd ed. by Jongsma, or "Daily Record of Dysfunctional Thoughts" in *Cognitive Therapy of Depression* by Beck, Rush, Shaw, and Emery); process the journal material to challenge maladaptive patterns of thinking and behaving, and replace them with adaptive alternatives.

12. Establish regular eating patterns by eating at regular intervals and consuming at least the minimum daily calories necessary to progressively gain weight. (16, 17, 18)

13. Attain and maintain balanced fluids and electrolytes as well as resumption of reproductive functions. (19, 20)

14. Identify and develop a hierarchy of high-risk situations for unhealthy eating or weight loss practices. (21, 22)

15. Identify, challenge, and replace self-talk and beliefs that promote the eating disorder. (15, 23, 24)

16. Establish a minimum daily caloric intake for the client and assist him/her in meal planning.

17. Establish healthy weight goals for the client per the Body Mass Index (BMI = pounds of body weight × 700/height in inches/height in inches; normal range is 19 to 24 and below 17 is medically critical), the Metropolitan Height and Weight Tables, or some other recognized standard.

18. Monitor the client's weight and give realistic feedback regarding body thinness.

19. Monitor the client's fluid intake and electrolyte balance; give realistic feedback regarding progress toward the goal of balance.

20. Refer the client back to the physician at regular intervals if fluids and electrolytes need monitoring due to poor nutritional habits.

21. Assess the nature of any external cues (e.g., persons, objects, and situations) and internal cues (thoughts, images, and impulses) that precipitate the client's uncontrolled eating and/or compensatory weight management behaviors.

22. Direct and assist the client in construction of a hierarchy of high-risk internal and external triggers for uncontrolled eating and/or compensatory weight management behaviors.

15. Assign the client to self-monitor and record food intake, thoughts, and feelings (or assign "A Reality Journal: Food, Weight, Thoughts,

and Feelings" in *Adult Psychotherapy Homework Planner,* 2nd ed. by Jongsma, or "Daily Record of Dysfunctional Thoughts" in *Cognitive Therapy of Depression* by Beck, Rush, Shaw, and Emery); process the journal material to challenge maladaptive patterns of thinking and behaving, and replace them with adaptive alternatives.

23. Assist the client in developing an awareness of his/her automatic thoughts and underlying assumptions, associated feelings, and actions that lead to maladaptive eating and weight control practices (e.g., poor self-image, distorted body image, perfectionism, fears of failure and/or rejection, fear of sexuality).

24. Do "behavioral experiments" in which the client's identified automatic thoughts are treated as hypotheses/predictions, more adaptive, reality-based alternative hypotheses/predictions are generated, and both are tested through homework exercises.

16. Participate in exposure exercises to build skills in managing urges to use maladaptive weight control practices. (25)

25. Conduct imaginal exposure and ritual prevention to the client's high-risk situations (e.g., purging, excessive exercising); select initial exposures that have a high likelihood of being a successful experience for the client; prepare and rehearse a plan for the session; do cognitive restructuring within and after the exposure; review/process the session with the client (e.g., exposure to eating high-carbohydrate foods while resisting the urge to self-induce vomiting).

17. Complete homework assignments involving behavioral experiments and/or exposure exercises. (26)

18. Discuss important people in your life, past and present, and describe the quality, good and bad, of those relationships. (27)

19. Learn and implement problem-solving and/or conflict resolution skills to resolve interpersonal problems. (28, 29, 30)

20. Implement relapse prevention strategies for managing possible future anxiety symptoms. (31, 32, 33, 34)

26. Assign the client a homework exercise in which he/she repeats the in-session behavioral experiment or exposure exercise between sessions and records responses; review the homework, doing cognitive restructuring, reinforcing success, and providing corrective feedback toward improvement.

27. Conduct Interpersonal Therapy, assessing the client's "interpersonal inventory" of important past and present relationships and evidence of themes that may be supporting the eating disorder (e.g., interpersonal disputes, role transitions, and/or interpersonal deficits).

28. Teach the client conflict resolution skills (e.g., empathy, active listening, "I messages," respectful communication, assertiveness without aggression, compromise); use modeling, role-playing, and behavior rehearsal to work through several current conflicts.

29. Help the client resolve interpersonal problems through the use of reassurance and support, clarification of cognitive and affective triggers that ignite conflicts, and active problem-solving.

30. In conjoint sessions, help the client resolve interpersonal conflicts.

31. Discuss with the client the distinction between a lapse and relapse, associating a lapse with an initial and reversible return of distress, urges, or to avoid and relapse with the decision to return to the cycle of maladaptive thoughts and actions (e.g., feeling anxious, binging, then purging).

32. Identify and rehearse with the client the management of future situations or circumstances in which lapses could occur. EB

33. Instruct the client to routinely use strategies learned in therapy (e.g., continued exposure to previous external or internal cues that arise) to prevent relapse. EB

34. Schedule periodic "maintenance" sessions to help the client maintain therapeutic gains and adjust to life without the eating disorder. EB

21. State a basis for positive identity that is not based on weight and appearance but on character, traits, relationships, and intrinsic value. (35)

35. Assist the client in identifying a basis for self-worth apart from body image by reviewing his/her talents, successes, positive traits, importance to others, and intrinsic spiritual value.

22. Attend an eating disorder group. (36)

36. Refer the client to a support group for eating disorders.

__. ______________________

__. ______________________

__. ______________________

__. ______________________

__. ______________________

__. ______________________

DIAGNOSTIC SUGGESTIONS

Axis I:	307.1	Anorexia Nervosa
	307.51	Bulimia Nervosa
	307.50	Eating Disorder NOS
	____	______________
	____	______________
Axis II:	301.6	Dependent Personality Disorder
	799.9	Diagnosis Deferred
	V71.09	No Diagnosis
	____	______________
	____	______________

EDUCATIONAL DEFICITS

BEHAVIORAL DEFINITIONS

1. Failure to complete requirements for high school diploma or GED certificate.
2. Possession of no marketable employment skills and need for vocational training.
3. Functional illiteracy.
4. History of difficulties, not involving behavior, in school or other learning situations.

—. ____
____

—. ____
____

—. ____
____

LONG-TERM GOALS

1. Recognize the need for high school completion or GED certificate and reenroll in the necessary courses.
2. Seek out vocational training to obtain marketable employment skill.
3. Increase literacy skills.
4. Receive high school diploma or GED certificate.
5. Establish the existence of a learning disability and begin the development of skills to overcome it.

—. ____
____

__. ____

____

__. ____

____

SHORT-TERM OBJECTIVES

1. Identify the factors that contributed to termination of education. (1, 2)

2. Verbally verify the need for a high school diploma or GED. (3, 4, 5, 6)

3. Complete an assessment to identify style of learning and to establish or rule out a specific learning disability. (7)

THERAPEUTIC INTERVENTIONS

1. Explore the client's attitude toward education and the family, peer, and/or school experiences that led to termination of education.

2. Gather an educational history from the client that includes family achievement history and difficulties he/she had with regard to specific subjects (e.g., reading, math).

3. Confront the client with his/her need for further education.

4. Assist the client in listing the negative effects that the lack of a GED certificate or high school diploma has had on his/her life.

5. Support and direct the client toward obtaining further academic training.

6. Reinforce and encourage the client in pursuing educational and/or vocational training by pointing out the social, monetary, and self-esteem advantages.

7. Administer testing or refer the client to an educational specialist to be tested for learning style, cognitive strengths, and to establish or rule out a learning disability.

4. Cooperate with a psychological assessment for symptoms of Attention Deficit Disorder (ADD) that may have interfered with educational achievement. (8)

8. Refer the client for or perform psychological assessment for Attention Deficit Disorder (see ADD–Adult chapter in this *Planner*).

5. Complete an evaluation for psychotropic medications. (9, 10, 11)

9. Refer the client for medication evaluation to treat his/her ADD.

10. Encourage the client to take the prescribed psychotropic medications, reporting as to their effectiveness and side effects.

11. Monitor the client's psychotropic medication prescription compliance, effectiveness, and side effects.

6. Implement the recommendations of evaluations. (12)

12. Encourage the client to implement the recommendations of the educational, psychological, and medical evaluations.

7. Identify the facts and feelings related to negative, critical education-related experiences endured from parents, teachers, or peers. (13, 14)

13. Ask the client to list the negative messages he/she has experienced in learning situations from teachers, parents, and peers, and to process this list with the therapist.

14. Facilitate the client's openness regarding shame or embarrassment surrounding lack of reading ability, educational achievement, or vocational skill.

8. Verbalize decreased anxiety and negativity associated with learning situations. (15, 16)

15. Give encouragement and verbal affirmation to the client as he/she works to increase his/her educational level.

16. Assist the client in developing strategies (e.g., deep breathing, muscle relaxation, positive self-talk) for coping with his/her own fears and anxieties in learning situations.

9. Identify own academic and motivational strengths. (17)

17. Assist the client in identifying his/her realistic academic and motivational strengths.

10. Verbalize positive self-talk regarding educational opportunities. (18)

18. Reframe the client's negative self-talk in light of testing results or overlooked accomplishments.

11. Agree to pursue educational assistance to attain reading skills. (19, 20)

19. Assess the client's reading deficits.

20. Refer the client to resources for learning to read. Monitor, and encourage the client's follow-through.

12. State commitment to obtain further academic or vocational training. (21)

21. Elicit a commitment from the client to pursue further academic or vocational training.

13. Make the necessary contacts to investigate enrollment in high school, GED, or vocational classes. (22, 23)

22. Provide the client with information regarding community resources available for adult education, GED, high school completion, and vocational skill training.

23. Assign the client to make preliminary contact with vocational and/or educational training agencies and report back regarding the experience.

14. Attend classes consistently to complete academic degree and/or vocational training course. (24)

24. Monitor and support the client's attendance at educational or vocational classes.

—. ______________________________
____

—. ______________________________
____

—. ______________________________
____

—. ______________________________
____

—. ______________________________
____

—. ______________________________
____

DIAGNOSTIC SUGGESTIONS

Axis I:	V62.3	Academic Problem
	V62.2	Occupational Problem
	315.2	Disorder of Written Expression
	315.00	Reading Disorder
	________	______________________________
	________	______________________________
Axis II:	V62.89	Borderline Intellectual Functioning
	317	Mild Mental Retardation
	________	______________________________
	________	______________________________

FAMILY CONFLICT

BEHAVIORAL DEFINITIONS

1. Constant or frequent conflict with parents and/or siblings.
2. A family that is not a stable source of positive influence or support, since family members have little or no contact with each other.
3. Ongoing conflict with parents, which is characterized by parents fostering dependence leading to feelings that the parents are overly involved.
4. Maintains a residence with parents and has been unable to live independently for more than a brief period.
5. Long period of noncommunication with parents, and description of self as the "black sheep."
6. Remarriage of two parties, both of whom bring children into the marriage from previous relationships.

—. ____

____

—. ____

____

—. ____

____

LONG-TERM GOALS

1. Resolve fear of rejection, low self-esteem, and/or oppositional defiance by resolving conflicts developed in the family or origin and understanding their connection to current life.
2. Begin the process of emancipating from parents in a healthy way by making arrangements for independent living.
3. Decrease the level of present conflict with parents while beginning to let go of or resolving past conflicts with them.

4. Achieve a reasonable level of family connectedness and harmony where members support, help, and are concerned for each other.
5. Become a reconstituted/blended family unit that is functional and whose members are bonded to each other.

—. ____

____

—. ____

____

—. ____

____

SHORT-TERM OBJECTIVES

1. Describe the conflicts and the causes of conflicts between self and parents. (1, 2)
2. Attend and participate in family therapy sessions where the focus is on controlled, reciprocal, respectful communication of thoughts and feelings. (3, 4)
3. Identify own as well as others' role in the family conflicts. (5, 6)

THERAPEUTIC INTERVENTIONS

1. Give verbal permission for the client to have and express own feelings, thoughts, and perspectives in order to foster a sense of autonomy from family.
2. Explore the nature of the client's family conflicts and their perceived causes.
3. Conduct family therapy sessions with the client and his/her parents to facilitate healthy communication, conflict resolution, and emancipation process.
4. Educate family members that resistance to change in styles of relating to one another is usually high and that change takes concerted effort by all members.
5. Confront the client when he/she is not taking responsibility for his/her role in the family conflict and reinforce the client for owning responsibility for his/her contribution to the conflict.

6. Ask the client to read material on resolving family conflict (e.g., *Making Peace with Your Parents* by Bloomfield and Felder); encourage and monitor the selection of concepts to begin using in conflict resolution.

4. Family members demonstrate increased openness by sharing thoughts and feelings about family dynamics, roles, and expectations. (7, 8)

7. Conduct a family session in which a process genogram is formed that is complete with members, patterns of interaction, rules, and secrets.

8. Facilitate each family member in expressing his/her concerns and expectations regarding becoming a more functional family unit.

5. Identify the role that chemical dependence behavior plays in triggering family conflict. (9)

9. Assess for the presence of chemical dependence in the client or family members; emphasize the need for chemical dependence treatment, if indicated, and arrange for such a focus (see Chemical Dependence and Chemical Dependence—Relapse chapters in this *Planner*).

6. Verbally describe an understanding of the role played by family relationship stress in triggering substance abuse or relapse. (10, 11)

10. Help the client to see the triggers for chemical dependence relapse in the family conflicts.

11. Ask the client to read material on the family aspects of chemical dependence (e.g., *It Will Never Happen to Me* by Black; *On the Family* by Bradshaw); process key family issues from the reading that are triggers for him/her.

7. Increase the number of positive family interactions by planning activities. (12, 13, 14)

12. Refer the family for an experiential weekend at a center for family education to build skills and confidence in working together. (Consider a physical confidence class with low or high ropes courses, etc.).

13. Ask the parents to read material on positive parenting methods (e.g., *Raising Self-Reliant Children* by Glenn and Nelsen; *Between Parent and Child* by Ginott; *Between Parent and Teenager* by Ginott); process key concepts gathered from their reading.
14. Assist the client in developing a list of positive family activities that promote harmony (e.g., bowling, fishing, playing table games, doing work projects). Schedule such activities into the family calendar.

8. Parents report how both are involved in the home and parenting process. (15, 16)

15. Elicit from the parents the role each takes in the parental team and his/her perspective on parenting.
16. Read and process in a family therapy session the fable "Raising Cain" or "Cinderella" (see *Friedman's Fables* by Friedman).

9. Identify ways in which the parental team can be strengthened. (17, 18, 19, 20)

17. Assist the parents in identifying areas that need strengthening in their "parental team," then work with them to strengthen these areas.
18. Refer the parents to a parenting group to help expand their understanding of children and to build discipline skills.
19. Direct the parents to attend a tough-love group for support and feedback on their situation.
20. Train the parents in the Barkley Method (see *Defiant Children* by Barkley) of understanding and managing defiant and oppositional behavior.

10. Parents report a decrease in the frequency of conflictual interactions with the child and between children. (13, 21, 22)

13. Ask the parents to read material on positive parenting methods (e.g., *Raising Self-Reliant Children* by Glenn and Nelsen; *Between Parent and Child* by Ginott; *Between Parent and Teenager* by Ginott); process key concepts gathered from their reading.

21. Assign the parents to read material on reducing sibling conflict (e.g., *Siblings Without Rivalry* by Faber and Mazlish); process key concepts and encourage implementation of interventions with their children.

22. Train the parents in a structured approach to discipline for young children (e.g., *1-2-3 Magic* by Phelan; *Parenting with Love and Logic* by Cline and Fay); monitor and readjust their implementation as necessary.

11. Report an increase in resolving conflicts with parent by talking calmly and assertively rather than aggressively and defensively. (23)

23. Use role-playing, role reversal, modeling, and behavioral rehearsal to help the client develop assertive ways to resolve conflict with parents.

12. Parents increase structure within the family. (24, 25)

24. Assist parents in developing rituals (e.g., dinner times, bedtime readings, weekly family activity times) that will provide structure and promote bonding.

25. Assist the parents in increasing structure within the family by setting times for eating meals together, limiting number of visitors, setting a lights-out time, establishing a phone call cutoff time, curfew time, "family meeting" time, and so on.

13. Each family member represents pictorially and then describes his/her role in the family. (26, 27)

26. Conduct a family session in which all members bring self-produced drawings of themselves in relationship to the family; ask each to describe what they've brought and then have the picture placed in an album.

27. Ask the family to make a collage of pictures cut out from magazines depicting "family" through their eyes and/or ask them to design a coat of arms that will signify the blended unit.

14. Family members report a desire for and vision of a new sense of connectedness. (28, 29, 30)

28. In a family session, assign the family the task of planning and going on an outing or activity; in the following session, process the experience with the family, giving positive reinforcement where appropriate.

29. Conduct a session with all new family members in which a genogram is constructed, gathering the history of both families and that visually shows how the new family connection will be.

30. Assign the parents to read the book *Changing Families* (Fassler, Lash, and Ives) at home with the family and report their impressions in family therapy sessions.

15. Identify factors that reinforce dependence on the family and discover how to overcome them. (31, 32)

31. For each factor that promotes the client's dependence on parents, develop a constructive plan to reduce that dependence.

32. Ask the client to make a list of ways he/she is dependent on parents.

16. Increase the level of independent functioning—that is, finding and keeping a job, saving money, socializing with friends, finding own housing, and so on. (33, 34, 35)

33. Confront the client's emotional dependence and avoidance of economic responsibility that promotes continuing pattern of living with parents.

34. Probe the client's fears surrounding emancipation.

35. Assist the client in developing a plan for healthy and responsible emancipation from parents that is, if possible, complete with their blessing.

—. ______________________

—. ______________________

—. ______________________

—. ______________________

—. ______________________

—. ______________________

DIAGNOSTIC SUGGESTIONS

Axis I:	300.4	Dysthymic Disorder
	300.00	Anxiety Disorder NOS
	312.34	Intermittent Explosive Disorder
	303.90	Alcohol Dependence
	304.20	Cocaine Dependence
	304.80	Polysubstance Dependence
	______	______________________
	______	______________________
Axis II:	301.7	Antisocial Personality Disorder
	301.6	Dependent Personality Disorder
	301.83	Borderline Personality Disorder
	301.9	Personality Disorder NOS
	______	______________________
	______	______________________

FEMALE SEXUAL DYSFUNCTION

BEHAVIORAL DEFINITIONS

1. Describes consistently very low or no pleasurable anticipation of or desire for sexual activity.
2. Strongly avoids and/or is repulsed by any and all sexual contact in spite of a relationship of mutual caring and respect.
3. Recurrently experiences a lack of the usual physiological response of sexual excitement and arousal (genital lubrication and swelling).
4. Reports a consistent lack of a subjective sense of enjoyment and pleasure during sexual activity.
5. Experiences a persistent delay in or absence of reaching orgasm after achieving arousal and in spite of sensitive sexual pleasuring by a caring partner.
6. Describes genital pain experienced before, during, or after sexual intercourse.
7. Reports consistent or recurring involuntary spasm of the vagina that prohibits penetration for sexual intercourse.

—. ______________________________

____

—. ______________________________

____

—. ______________________________

____

LONG-TERM GOALS

1. Increase desire for and enjoyment of sexual activity.
2. Attain and maintain physiological excitement response during sexual intercourse.

3. Reach orgasm with a reasonable amount of time, intensity, and focus to sexual stimulation.
4. Eliminate pain and achieve a presence of subjective pleasure before, during, and after sexual intercourse.
5. Eliminate vaginal spasms that prohibit penile penetration during sexual intercourse and achieve a sense of relaxed enjoyment of coital pleasure.

—. ____

____

—. ____

____

—. ____

____

SHORT-TERM OBJECTIVES

1. Provide a detailed sexual history that explores current problems and past experiences that have influenced sexual attitudes, feelings, and behavior. (1, 2, 3)

THERAPEUTIC INTERVENTIONS

1. Obtain a detailed sexual history that examines the client's current adult sexual functioning as well as childhood and adolescent sexual experiences level and sources of sexual knowledge, typical sexual practices and their frequency, medical history, drug and alcohol use, and lifestyle factors.
2. Assess the client's attitudes and fund of knowledge regarding sex, emotional responses to it, and self-talk that may be contributing to the dysfunction.
3. Explore the client's family-of-origin for factors that may be contributing to the dysfunction (e.g., negative attitudes regarding sexuality, feelings of inhibition, low self-esteem, guilt, fear, repulsion; or assign "Factors Influencing Negative Sexual Attitudes" in *Adult Psychotherapy Homework Planner,* 2nd ed. by Jongsma).

2. Discuss any feelings of and causes for depression. (4)

4. Assess the role of depression in possibly causing the client's sexual dysfunction and treat if depression appears causal (see Depression chapter in this *Planner*).

3. Participate in treatment of depressive feelings that may be causing sexual difficulties. (5)

5. Refer the client for antidepressant medication prescription to alleviate depression.

4. Honestly report substance abuse and cooperate with recommendations by the therapist for addressing it. (6)

6. Explore the client's use or abuse of mood-altering substances and their effect on sexual functioning; refer for focused substance abuse counseling.

5. Honestly and openly discuss the quality of the relationship including conflicts, unfulfilled needs, and anger. (7)

7. Assess the quality of the relationship including couple satisfaction, distress, attraction, communication, and sexual repertoire toward making a decision to focus treatment sexual problems or more broadly on the relationship (or assign "Positive and Negative Contributions to the Relationship" in *Adult Psychotherapy Homework Planner,* 2nd ed. by Jongsma).

EB 6. Participate in couples therapy as part of addressing sexual problems. (8)

8. If problem issues go beyond sexual dysfunction, conduct sex therapy in the context of couples therapy (see Intimate Relationship Conflicts chapter in this *Planner*). EB

EB 7. Cooperate with a physician's complete examination; discuss results with therapist. (9)

9. Refer the client to a physician for a complete exam to rule out any organic or medication-related basis for the sexual dysfunction (e.g., vascular, endocrine, medications). EB

EB indicates that the Objective/Intervention is consistent with those found in evidence-based treatments.

8. Cooperate with physician's recommendation for addressing a medical condition or medication that may be causing sexual problems. (10)

10. Encourage the client to follow physician's recommendations regarding treatment of a diagnosed medical condition or use of medication that may be causing the sexual problem.

9. Verbalize an understanding of the role that physical disease or medication has on sexual dysfunction. (11)

11. Discuss the contributory role that a diagnosed medical condition or medication use may be having on the client's sexual functioning.

10. Practice directed masturbation and sensate focus exercises alone and with partner and share feelings associated with activity. (12, 13)

12. Assign the client body exploration and awareness exercises that reduce inhibition and desensitize her to sexual aversion.

13. Direct the client in masturbatory exercises designed to maximize arousal; assign the client graduated steps of sexual pleasuring exercises with partner that reduce her performance anxiety and focus on experiencing bodily arousal sensations (or assign "Journaling the Response to Nondemand, Sexual Pleasuring [Sensate Focus]" in *Adult Psychotherapy Homework Planner,* 2nd ed. by Jongsma).

11. Report progress on graduated self-controlled vaginal penetration with a partner. (12, 14, 15)

12. Assign the client body exploration and awareness exercises that reduce inhibition and desensitize her to sexual aversion.

14. Direct the client's use of masturbation and/or vaginal dilator devices to reinforce relaxation and success surrounding vaginal penetration.

15. Direct the client's partner in sexual exercises that allow for client-controlled level of genital stimulation and gradually increased vaginal penetration.

12. Participate in sex therapy with a partner or individually if the partner is not available. (16)

16. Encourage couples sex therapy or treat individually if a partner is not available.

13. Demonstrate healthy acceptance and accurate knowledge of sexuality by freely learning and discussing accurate information regarding sexual functioning. (17, 18)

17. Disinhibit and educate the couple by encouraging them to talk freely and respectfully regarding her sexual body parts, sexual thoughts, feelings, attitudes, and behaviors.

18. Reinforce the client for talking freely, knowledgeably, and positively regarding her sexual thoughts, feelings, and behavior.

14. State an understanding of how family upbringing, including religious training, negatively influenced sexual thoughts, feelings, and behavior. (19, 20, 21)

19. Explore the role of the client's family of origin in teaching her negative attitudes regarding sexuality; process toward the goal of change.

20. Explore the role of the client's religious training in reinforcing her feelings of guilt and shame surrounding her sexual behavior and thoughts; process toward the goal of change.

21. Assist the client in developing insight into the role of unhealthy sexual attitudes and experiences of childhood in the development of current adult dysfunction; press for a commitment to try to put negative attitudes and experiences in the past while making a behavioral effort to become free from those influences.

15. Verbalize a resolution of feelings regarding sexual trauma or abuse experiences. (22, 23)

22. Probe the client's history for experiences of sexual trauma or abuse.

23. Process the client's emotions surrounding an emotional trauma in the sexual arena (see Sexual Abuse chapter in this *Planner*).

16. Verbalize an understanding of the influence of childhood sex role models. (24)

24. Explore sex role models the client has experienced in childhood or adolescence and how they have influenced the client's attitudes and behaviors.

17. Verbalize connection between previously failed intimate relationships and current fear. (25)

25. Explore the client's fears surrounding intimate relationships and whether there is evidence of repeated failure in this area.

18. Discuss feelings surrounding a secret affair and make a termination decision regarding one of the relationships. (26, 27)

26. Explore for any secret sexual affairs that may account for the client's sexual dysfunction with her partner.

27. Process a decision regarding the termination of one of the relationships that is leading to internal conflict over the dishonesty and disloyalty to a partner.

19. Openly acknowledge and discuss, if present, homosexual attraction. (28)

28. Explore for a homosexual interest that accounts for the client's heterosexual disinterest (or assign "Journal of Sexual Thoughts, Fantasies, Conflicts" in *Adult Psychotherapy Homework Planner,* 2nd ed. by Jongsma).

20. State a willingness to explore new ways to to approach sexual relations. (29, 30)

29. Direct conjoint sessions with the client and her partner that focus on conflict resolution, expression of feelings, and sex education.

30. Assign books (e.g., *Sexual Awareness* by McCarthy and McCarthy; *The Gift of Sex* by Penner and Penner; *For Yourself: The Fulfillment of Female Sexuality* by Barbach) that provide the client with accurate sexual information and/or outline sexual exercises that disinhibit and reinforce sexual sensate focus.

21. List conditions and factors that positively affect sexual arousal such as setting, time of day, atmosphere. (31)

31. Assign the couple to list conditions and factors that positively affect their sexual arousal; process the list toward creating an environment conducive to sexual arousal.

22. Identify and replace negative cognitive messages that trigger negative emotional reactions during sexual activity. (32, 33)

32. Probe automatic thoughts that trigger the client's negative emotions such as fear, shame, anger, or grief before, during, and after sexual activity.

33. Train the client in healthy alternative thoughts that will mediate pleasure, relaxation, and disinhibition.

23. Discuss low self-esteem issues that impede sexual functioning and verbalize positive self-image. (34)

34. Explore the client's fears of inadequacy as a sexual partner that led to sexual avoidance.

24. Communicate feelings of threat to partner that are based on perception of partner being too sexually aggressive or too critical. (35)

35. Explore the client's feelings of threat brought on by the perception of her partner as too sexually aggressive.

25. Verbalize a positive body image. (36, 37)

36. Assign the client to list assets of her body; confront unrealistic distortions and critical comments.

37. Explore the client's feelings regarding her body image, focusing on causes for negativism.

26. Implement new coital positions and settings for sexual activity that enhance pleasure and satisfaction. (30, 38)

30. Assign books (e.g., *Sexual Awareness* by McCarthy and McCarthy; *The Gift of Sex* by Penner and Penner; *For Yourself: The Fulfillment of Female Sexuality* by Barbach) that provide the client with accurate sexual information and/or outline sexual exercises that disinhibit and reinforce sexual sensate focus.

38. Suggest experimentation with coital positions and settings for sexual play that may increase the client's feelings of security, arousal, and satisfaction.

27. Engage in more assertive behaviors that allow for sharing sexual needs, feelings, and desires, behaving more sensuously and expressing pleasure. (39, 40)

39. Give the client permission for less inhibited, less constricted sexual behavior by assigning body-pleasuring exercises with partner.

40. Encourage the client to gradually explore the role of being more sexually assertive, sensuously provocative, and freely uninhibited in sexual play with partner.

28. Resolve conflicts or develop coping strategies that reduce stress interfering with sexual interest or performance. (41)

41. Probe stress in areas such as work, extended family, and social relationships that distract the client from sexual desire or performance (see Anxiety, Family Conflict, and Vocational Stress chapters in this *Planner*).

29. Verbalize increasing desire for and pleasure with sexual activity. (38, 40, 42)

38. Suggest experimentation with coital positions and settings for sexual play that may increase the client's feelings of security, arousal, and satisfaction.

40. Encourage the client to gradually explore the role of being more sexually assertive, sensuously provocative, and freely uninhibited in sexual play with partner.

42. Reinforce the client's expressions of desire for and pleasure with sexual activity.

__. ____________________

__. ____________________

__. ____________________

__. ____________________

__. ____________________

__. ____________________

DIAGNOSTIC SUGGESTIONS

Axis I:	302.71	Hypoactive Sexual Desire Disorder
	302.79	Sexual Aversion Disorder
	302.72	Female Sexual Arousal Disorder
	302.73	Female Orgasmic Disorder
	302.76	Dyspareunia
	306.51	Vaginismus
	995.53	Sexual Abuse of Child, Victim
	625.8	Female Hypoactive Sexual Desire Disorder Due to Axis III Disorder
	625.0	Female Dyspareunia Due to Axis III Disorder
	302.70	Sexual Dysfunction NOS
	________	________________________________
	________	________________________________

FINANCIAL STRESS

BEHAVIORAL DEFINITIONS

1. Indebtedness and overdue bills that exceed ability to meet monthly payments.
2. Loss of income due to unemployment.
3. Reduction in income due to change in employment status.
4. Conflict with spouse over management of money and the definition of necessary expenditures and savings goals.
5. A feeling of low self-esteem and hopelessness that is associated with the lack of sufficient income to cover the cost of living.
6. A long-term lack of discipline in money management that has led to excessive indebtedness.
7. An uncontrollable crisis (e.g., medical bills, job layoff) that has caused past-due bill balances to exceed ability to make payments.
8. Fear of losing housing because of an inability to meet monthly mortgage payments.
9. A pattern of impulsive spending that does not consider the eventual financial consequences.

__. ____

____

__. ____

____

__. ____

____

LONG-TERM GOALS

1. Establish a clear income and expense budget that will meet bill payment demands.

2. Contact creditors to develop a revised repayment plan for outstanding bills.
3. Gain a new sense of self-worth in which the substance of one's value is not attached to the capacity to do things or own things that cost money.
4. Understand personal needs, insecurities, and anxieties that make overspending possible.
5. Achieve an inner strength to control personal impulses, cravings, and desires that directly or indirectly increase debt irresponsibly.

—. ____

____

—. ____

____

—. ____

____

SHORT-TERM OBJECTIVES

1. Describe the details of the current financial situation. (1, 2, 3)
2. Isolate the sources and causes of the excessive indebtedness. (4)
3. Verbalize feelings of depression, hopelessness, and/or shame that are related to financial status. (5, 6)

THERAPEUTIC INTERVENTIONS

1. Provide the client a supportive, comforting environment by being empathetic, warm, and sensitive to the fact that the topic may elicit guilt, shame, and embarrassment.
2. Explore the client's current financial situation.
3. Assist the client in compiling a complete list of financial obligations.
4. Assist in identifying, without projection of blame or holding to excuses, the causes for the financial crisis through a review of the client's history of spending.
5. Probe the client's feelings of hopelessness or helplessness that may be associated with the financial crisis.
6. Assess the depth or seriousness of the client's despondency over the financial crisis.

4. Describe any suicidal impulses that may accompany financial stress. (6, 7)

6. Assess the depth or seriousness of the client's despondency over the financial crisis.

7. Assess the client's potential risk for suicidal behavior. If necessary, take steps to ensure the client's safety (see Suicidal Ideation chapter in this *Planner*).

5. Identify priorities that should control how money is spent. (8, 9)

8. Ask the client to list the priorities that he/she believes should give direction to how his/her money is spent; process those priorities.

9. Review the client's spending history to discover what priorities and values have misdirected spending.

6. Describe the family of origin pattern of money management and how that pattern may be impacting own credit crisis. (10)

10. Explore the client's family-of-origin patterns of earning, saving, and spending money, focusing on how those patterns are influencing his/her current financial decisions.

7. Meet with community agency personnel to apply for welfare assistance. (11, 12)

11. Review the client's need for filing for bankruptcy, applying for welfare, and/or obtaining credit counseling.

12. Direct the client to the proper church or community resources to seek welfare assistance and support him/her in beginning the humbling application process.

8. Write a budget that balances income with expenses. (13, 14)

13. If financial planning is needed, refer to a professional planner or ask partners to write a current budget and long-range savings and investment plan.

14. Review the client's budget as to reasonableness and completeness.

9. Attend a meeting with a credit counselor to gain assistance in budgeting and contacting creditors for establishment of a reasonable repayment plan. (15, 16)

15. Refer the client to a nonprofit, no-cost credit counseling service for the development of a budgetary plan of debt repayment.
16. Encourage the client's attendance at all credit counseling sessions and his/her discipline of self to control spending within budgetary guidelines.

10. Meet with an attorney to help reach a decision regarding filing for bankruptcy. (11, 17)

11. Review the client's need for filing for bankruptcy, applying for welfare, and/or obtaining credit counseling.
17. Refer the client to an attorney to discuss the feasibility and implications of filing for bankruptcy.

11. Identify personal traits that make undisciplined spending possible. (18, 19)

18. Probe the client for evidence of low self-esteem, need to impress others, loneliness, or depression that may accelerate unnecessary, unwarranted spending.
19. Assess the client for mood swings that are characteristic of Bipolar Disorder and could be responsible for careless spending due to the impaired judgment of manic phase.

12. Honestly describe any of own or family members' substance abuse problems that contribute to financial irresponsibility. (20, 21)

20. Probe the client for excessive alcohol or other drug use by asking questions from the CAGE or Michigan Alcohol Screening Test (MAST) screening instruments for substance abuse.
21. Explore the possibility of alcohol or drug use by the client's family members or significant other.

13. Verbalize a plan for seeking employment to raise level of income. (22, 23)

22. Review the client's income from employment and brainstorm ways to increase this (e.g., additional part-time employment, better-paying job, job training).

23. Assist the client in formulating a plan for a job search.

14. Set financial goals and make budgetary decisions with partner, allowing for equal input and balanced control over financial matters. (24, 25)

24. Encourage financial planning by the client that is done in conjunction with his/her partner.

25. Reinforce changes in managing money that reflect compromise, responsible planning, and respectful cooperation with the client's partner.

15. Keep weekly and monthly records of financial income and expenses. (26, 27)

26. Encourage the client to keep a weekly and monthly record of income and outflow; review his/her records weekly, and reinforce his/her responsible financial decision making.

27. Offer praise and ongoing encouragement of the client's progress toward debt resolution.

16. Use cognitive and behavioral strategies to control the impulse to make unnecessary and unaffordable purchases. (28, 29, 30, 31)

28. Role-play situations in which the client must resist the inner temptation to spend beyond reasonable limits, emphasizing positive self-talk that compliments self for being disciplined.

29. Role-play situations in which the client must resist external pressure to spend beyond what he/she can afford (e.g., friend's invitation to golf or go shopping, child's request for a toy), emphasizing being graciously assertive in refusing the request.

30. Teach the client the cognitive strategy of asking self before each purchase: Is this purchase absolutely necessary? Can we afford this? Do we have the cash to pay for this without incurring any further debt?

31. Urge the client to avoid all impulse buying by delaying every purchase until after 24 hours of thought and by buying only from a prewritten list of items to buy.

17. Report instances of successful control over impulse to spend on unnecessary expenses. (32, 33)

32. Reinforce with praise and encouragement all of the client's reports of resisting the urge to overspend.

33. Hold conjoint or family therapy session in which controlled spending is reinforced and continued cooperation is pledged by everyone.

__. ____________________

__. ____________________

__. ____________________

__. ____________________

__. ____________________

__. ____________________

DIAGNOSTIC SUGGESTIONS

Axis I:	309.0	Adjustment Disorder with Depressed Mood
	296.4x	Bipolar I Disorder, Manic
	296.89	Bipolar II Disorder
	296.xx	Major Depressive Disorder
	______	____________________
	______	____________________
Axis II:	301.83	Borderline Personality Disorder
	301.7	Antisocial Personality Disorder
	799.9	Diagnosis Deferred
	V71.09	No Diagnosis
	______	____________________
	______	____________________

GRIEF/LOSS UNRESOLVED

BEHAVIORAL DEFINITIONS

1. Thoughts dominated by loss coupled with poor concentration, tearful spells, and confusion about the future.
2. Serial losses in life (i.e., deaths, divorces, jobs) that led to depression and discouragement.
3. Strong emotional response exhibited when losses are discussed.
4. Lack of appetite, weight loss, and/or insomnia as well as other depression signs that occurred since the loss.
5. Feelings of guilt that not enough was done for the lost significant other, or an unreasonable belief of having contributed to the death of the significant other.
6. Avoidance of talking on anything more than a superficial level about the loss.
7. Loss of a positive support network due to a geographic move.

—. ____

____

—. ____

____

—. ____

____

LONG-TERM GOALS

1. Begin a healthy grieving process around the loss.
2. Develop an awareness of how the avoidance of grieving has affected life and begin the healing process.
3. Complete the process of letting go of the lost significant other.

4. Resolve the loss and begin renewing old relationships and initiating new contacts with others.

__. ____

____

__. ____

____

__. ____

____

SHORT-TERM OBJECTIVES

1. Tell in detail the story of the current loss that is triggering symptoms. (1, 2, 3)

2. Read books on the topic of grief to better understand the loss experience and to increase a sense of hope. (4, 5)

THERAPEUTIC INTERVENTIONS

1. Actively build the level of trust with the client in individual sessions through consistent eye contact, active listening, unconditional positive regard, and warm acceptance to help increase his/her ability to identify and express thoughts and feelings.

2. Using empathy and compassion, support and encourage the client to tell in detail the story of his/her recent loss.

3. Ask the client to elaborate in an autobiography the circumstances, feelings, and effects of the loss or losses in his/her life.

4. Ask the client to read books on grief and loss (e.g., *Getting to the Other Side of Grief: Overcoming the Loss of a Spouse* by Zonnebelt-Smeenge and De Vries; *How Can It Be All Right When Everything Is All Wrong* by Smedes; *How to Survive the Loss of a Love* by Colgrove, Bloomfield, and McWilliams; *When Bad Things Happen to Good People* by Kushner); process the content.

5. Ask the parents of a deceased child to read a book on coping with the loss (e.g., *The Bereaved Parent* by Schiff); process the key themes gleaned from the reading.

3. Identify what stages of grief have been experienced in the continuum of the grieving process. (6, 7, 8)

6. Ask the client to talk to several people about losses in their lives and how they felt and coped. Process the findings.

7. Educate the client on the stages of the grieving process and answer any questions he/she may have.

8. Assist the client in identifying the stages of grief that he/she has experienced and which stage he/she is presently working through.

4. Watch videos on the theme of grief and loss to compare own experience with that of the characters in the films. (9)

9. Ask the client to watch the films *Terms of Endearment, Dad, Ordinary People,* or a similar film that focuses on loss and grieving, then discuss how the characters cope with loss and express their grief.

5. Begin verbalizing feelings associated with the loss. (10, 11, 12)

10. Assign the client to keep a daily grief journal to be shared in therapy sessions.

11. Ask the client to bring pictures or mementos connected with his/her loss to a session and talk about them.

12. Assist the client in identifying and expressing feelings connected with his/her loss.

6. Attend a grief/loss support group. (13)

13. Ask the client to attend a grief/loss support group and report to the therapist how he/she felt about attending.

7. Identify how avoiding dealing with loss has negatively impacted life. (14)

14. Ask the client to list ways that avoidance of grieving has negatively impacted his/her life.

8. Identify how the use of substances has aided the avoidance

15. Assess the role that substance abuse has played as an escape for

of feelings associated with the loss. (15, 16)

the client from the pain or guilt of loss.

16. Arrange for chemical dependence treatment so that grief issues can be faced while the client is clean and sober. (see Chemical Dependence chapter in this *Planner*).

9. Acknowledge dependency on lost loved one and begin to refocus life on independent actions to meet emotional needs. (17, 18)

17. Assist the client in identifying how he/she depended upon the significant other, expressing and resolving the accompanying feelings of abandonment and of being left alone.

18. Explore the feelings of anger or guilt that surround the loss, helping the client understand the sources for such feelings.

10. Verbalize and resolve feelings of anger or guilt focused on self or deceased loved one that block the grieving process. (19, 20)

19. Encourage the client to forgive self and/or deceased to resolve his/her feelings of guilt or anger. Recommend books like *Forgive and Forget* (Smedes).

20. Support and assist the client in identifying and expressing angry feelings connected to his/her loss.

11. Identify causes for feelings of regret associated with actions toward or relationship with the deceased. (21)

21. Assign the client to make a list of all the regrets he/she has concerning the loss; process the list content.

12. Decrease statements and feelings of being responsible for the loss. (22)

22. Use a Rational Emotive Therapy (RET) approach to confront the client's statements of responsibility for the loss and compare them to factual reality-based statements.

13. Express thoughts and feelings about the deceased that went unexpressed while the deceased was alive. (23, 24, 25, 26)

23. Conduct an empty-chair exercise with the client where he/she focuses on expressing to the lost loved one imagined in the chair what he/she never said while that loved one was alive.

24. Assign the client to visit the grave of the lost loved one to "talk to" the deceased and ventilate his/her feelings.

25. Ask the client to write a letter to the lost person describing his/her fond memories, painful and regretful memories, and how he/she currently feels. Process the letter in session.

26. Assign the client to write to the deceased loved one with a special focus on his/her feelings associated with the last meaningful contact with that person.

14. Identify the positive characteristics of the deceased loved one, the positive aspects of the relationship with the deceased loved one, and how these things may be remembered. (27, 28)

27. Ask the client to list the most positive aspects of and memories about his/her relationship with the lost loved one.

28. Assist the client in developing rituals (e.g., placing memoriam in newspaper on anniversary of death, volunteering time to a favorite cause of the deceased person) that will celebrate the memorable aspects of the loved one and his/her life.

15. Attend and participate in a family therapy session focused on each member sharing his/her experience with grief. (29)

29. Conduct a family and/or group session with the client participating, where each member talks about his/her experience related to the loss.

16. Report decreased time spent each day focusing on the loss. (30, 31)

30. Develop a grieving ritual with an identified feeling state (e.g., dress in dark colors, preferably black, to indicate deep sorrow) which the client may focus on near the anniversary of the loss. Process what he/she received from the ritual.

31. Suggest that the client set aside a specific time-limited period each day to focus on mourning his/her loss. After each day's time is up the client will resume regular activities and put off grieving thoughts until the next scheduled time. For example, mourning times could include putting on dark clothing and/or sad music; clothing would be changed when the allotted time is up.

17. Develop and enact act(s) of penitence. (32)

32. Research with the client the activities, interests, commitments, loves, and passions of the lost loved one, then select a community-service-connected activity as an act of penitence for the feelings of having failed the departed one in some way. (Period of time should not be less than one month, with intensity and duration increasing with the depth of the perceived offense.)

18. Implement acts of spiritual faith as a source of comfort and hope. (33)

33. Encourage the client to rely upon his/her spiritual faith promises, activities (e.g., prayer, meditation, worship, music), and fellowship as sources of support.

__. ____________________________

__. ____________________________

__. ____________________________

__. ____________________________

__. ____________________________

__. ____________________________

DIAGNOSTIC SUGGESTIONS

Axis I:	296.2x	Major Depressive Disorder, Single Episode
	296.3x	Major Depressive Disorder, Recurrent

V62.82	Bereavement
309.0	Adjustment Disorder With Depressed Mood
309.3	Adjustment Disorder With Disturbance of Conduct
300.4	Dysthymic Disorder
______	______________________________
______	______________________________

IMPULSE CONTROL DISORDER

BEHAVIORAL DEFINITIONS

1. A tendency to act too quickly without careful deliberation, resulting in numerous negative consequences.
2. Loss of control over aggressive impulses resulting in assault, self-destructive behavior, or damage to property.
3. Desire to be satisfied almost immediately—decreased ability to delay pleasure or gratification.
4. A history of acting out in at least two areas that are potentially self-damaging (e.g., spending money, sexual activity, reckless driving, addictive behavior).
5. Overreactivity to mildly aversive or pleasure-oriented stimulation.
6. A sense of tension or affective arousal before engaging in the impulsive behavior (e.g., kleptomania, pyromania).
7. A sense of pleasure, gratification, or release at the time of committing the ego-dystonic, impulsive act.
8. Difficulty waiting for things—that is, restless standing in line, talking out over others in a group, and the like.

__. ____

____

__. ____

____

__. ____

____

LONG-TERM GOALS

1. Reduce the frequency of impulsive behavior and increase the frequency of behavior that is carefully thought out.

2. Reduce thoughts that trigger impulsive behavior and increase selftalk that controls behavior.
3. Learn to stop, listen, and think before acting.

__. ____

__. ____

__. ____

SHORT-TERM OBJECTIVES

1. Identify the impulsive behaviors that have been engaged in over the last six months. (1)
2. List the reasons or rewards that lead to continuation of an impulsive pattern. (2, 3)
3. List the negative consequences that accrue to self and others as a result of impulsive behavior. (4, 5, 6)

THERAPEUTIC INTERVENTIONS

1. Review the client's behavior pattern to assist him/her in clearly identifying, without minimization, denial, or projection of blame, his/her pattern of impulsivity.
2. Explore whether the client's impulsive behavior is triggered by anxiety and maintained by anxiety relief rewards.
3. Ask the client to make a list of the positive things he/she gets from impulsive actions and process it with the therapist.
4. Assign the client to write a list of the negative consequences that have occurred because of impulsivity.
5. Assist the client in making connections between his/her impulsivity and the negative consequences for himself/herself and others.
6. Confront the client's denial of responsibility for the impulsive behavior or the negative consequences.

4. Identify impulsive behavior's antecedents, mediators, and consequences. (7, 8)

7. Ask the client to keep a log of impulsive acts (time, place, feelings, thoughts, what was going on prior to the act, and what was the result); process log content to discover triggers and reinforcers.

8. Explore the client's past experiences to uncover his/her cognitive, emotional, and situational triggers to impulsive episodes.

5. Verbalize a clear connection between impulsive behavior and negative consequences to self and others. (5, 9)

5. Assist the client in making connections between his/her impulsivity and the negative consequences for himself/herself and others.

9. Reinforce the client's verbalized acceptance of responsibility for and connection between impulsive behavior and negative consequences.

6. Before acting on behavioral decisions, frequently review them with a trusted friend or family member for feedback regarding possible consequences. (10, 11)

10. Conduct a session with the client and his/her partner to develop a contract for receiving feedback prior to impulsive acts.

11. Brainstorm with the client who he/she could rely on for trusted feedback regarding action decisions; use role-play and modeling to teach how to ask for and accept this help.

7. Utilize cognitive methods to control trigger thoughts and reduce impulsive reactions to those trigger thoughts. (8, 12, 13)

8. Explore the client's past experiences to uncover his/her cognitive, emotional, and situational triggers to impulsive episodes.

12. Teach the client cognitive methods (thought stopping, thought substitution, reframing, etc.) for gaining and improving control over impulsive urges and actions.

13. Help the client to uncover dysfunctional thoughts that lead to impulsivity; then, replace each thought with a thought that is accurate, positive, self-enhancing, and adaptive.

8. Use relaxation exercises to control anxiety and reduce consequent impulsive behavior. (14)

14. Teach the client techniques such as progressive relaxation, self-hypnosis, or biofeedback; encourage him/her to relax whenever he/she feels uncomfortable.

9. Utilize behavioral strategies to manage anxiety. (15, 16)

15. Teach the use of positive behavioral alternatives to cope with anxiety (e.g., talking to someone about the stress, taking a time out to delay any reaction, calling a friend or family member, engaging in physical exercise).

16. Review the client's implementation of behavioral coping strategies to reduce urges and tension; reinforce success and redirect for failure.

10. Implement the assertive formula, "I feel . . . When you . . . I would prefer it if. . . ." (17, 18)

17. Using modeling, role playing, and behavior rehearsal, teach the client how to use the assertive formula, "I feel . . . When you . . . I would prefer it if . . ." in difficult situations.

18. Review and process the client's implementation of assertiveness and feelings about it as well as the consequences of it.

11. List instances where "stop, listen, think, and act" has been implemented, citing the positive consequences. (19, 20)

19. Using modeling, role-playing, and behavior rehearsal, teach the client how to use "stop, listen, and think" before acting in several current situations.

20. Review and process the client's use of "stop, listen, think, and act" in day-today living and identify the positive consequences.

12. Comply with the recommendations from a physician evaluation regarding the necessity for psychopharmacological intervention. (21, 22)

21. Refer the client to a physician for an evaluation for a psychotropic medication prescription.

22. Monitor the client for psychotropic medication prescription compliance, side effects, and effectiveness; consult with the prescribing physician at regular intervals.

13. Implement a reward system for replacing impulsive actions with reflection on consequences and choosing wise alternatives. (23, 24)

23. Assist the client in identifying rewards that would be effective in reinforcing himself/herself for suppressing impulsive behavior.

24. Assist the client and significant others in developing and putting into effect a reward system for deterring the client's impulsive actions.

14. Attend a self-help recovery group. (25)

25. Refer the client to a self-help recovery group (e.g., 12-step program, ADHD group, Rational Recovery, etc.) designed to help terminate self-destructive impulsivity; process his/her experience in the group.

__. ______________________________

__. ______________________________

__. ______________________________

__. ______________________________

__. ______________________________

__. ______________________________

DIAGNOSTIC SUGGESTIONS

Axis I:	312.34	Intermittent Explosive Disorder
	312.32	Kleptomania
	312.31	Pathological Gambling
	312.39	Trichotillomania
	312.30	Impulse Control Disorder NOS
	312.33	Pyromania
	310.1	Personality Change Due to Axis III Disorder
	______	____________________
	______	____________________
Axis II:	301.7	Antisocial Personality Disorder
	301.83	Borderline Personality Disorder
	799.9	Diagnosis Deferred
	V71.09	No Diagnosis
	______	____________________
	______	____________________

INTIMATE RELATIONSHIP CONFLICTS

BEHAVIORAL DEFINITIONS

1. Frequent or continual arguing with the partner.
2. Lack of communication with the partner.
3. A pattern of angry projection of responsibility for the conflicts onto the partner.
4. Marital separation.
5. Pending divorce.
6. Involvement in multiple intimate relationships at the same time.
7. Physical and/or verbal abuse in a relationship.
8. A pattern of superficial or no communication, infrequent or no sexual contact, excessive involvement in activities (work or recreation) that allows for avoidance of closeness to the partner.
9. A pattern of repeated broken, conflictual relationships due to personal deficiencies in problem-solving, maintaining a trust relationship, or choosing abusive or dysfunctional partners.

__. ____

____

__. ____

____

__. ____

____

LONG-TERM GOALS

1. Accept the termination of the relationship.
2. Develop the necessary skills for effective, open communication, mutually satisfying sexual intimacy, and enjoyable time for companionship within the relationship.

3. Increase awareness of own role in the relationship conflicts.
4. Learn to identify escalating behaviors that lead to abuse.
5. Make a commitment to one intimate relationship at a time.
6. Rebuild positive self-image after acceptance of the rejection associated with the broken relationship.

__. ______________________________

____

__. ______________________________

____

__. ______________________________

____

SHORT-TERM OBJECTIVES

1. Attend and actively participate in conjoint sessions with the partner. (1)

2. Complete psychological testing designed to assess and track marital satisfaction. (2)

3. (EBT) Identify the positive aspects of the relationship. (3)

4. (EBT) Identify problems in the relationship including one's own role in the problems. (4, 5)

THERAPEUTIC INTERVENTIONS

1. Facilitate conjoint sessions that focus on increasing the clients' communication and problem-solving skills.

2. Administer a measure of marital satisfaction to assess areas of satisfaction and dissatisfaction and/or to track treatment progress (e.g., The Dyadic Adjustment Scale by Spainer or Marital Satisfaction Inventory—Revised by Synder).

3. Assess the couple's positive behaviors that facilitate relationship building. (EBT)

4. Assess current, ongoing problem behaviors in the relationship, including possible abuse/neglect, substance use, and those involving communication, conflict-resolution, problem-

(EBT) indicates that the Objective/Intervention is consistent with those found in evidence-based treatments.

solving difficulties (if domestic violence is present, plan for safety and avoid early use of conjoint sessions; see "Physical Abuse" in *The Couples Psychotherapy Treatment Planner* by O'Leary, Heyman, and Jongsma). ♥

5. Assign the couple a between sessions task recording in journals the positive and negative things about the significant other and the relationship (or assign "Positive and Negative Contributions to the Relationship: Mine and Yours" in *Adult Psychotherapy Homework Planner,* 2nd ed. by Jongsma); ask the couple not to show their journal material to each other until the next session, when the material will be processed. ♥

♥ 5. Make a commitment to change specific behaviors that have been identified by self or the partner. (6)

6. Process the list of positive and problematic features of each partner and the relationship; ask couple to agree to work on changes he/she needs to make to improve the relationship, generating a list of targeted changes (or assign "How Can We Meet Each Other's Needs" in *Adult Psychotherapy Homework Planner,* 2nd ed. by Jongsma). ♥

♥ 6. Increase the frequency of the direct expression of honest, respectful, and positive feelings and thoughts within the relationship. (7, 8, 9)

7. Assist the couple in identifying conflicts that can be addressed using communication, conflict-resolution, and/or problem-solving skills (see "Behavioral Marital Therapy" by Holzworth-Munroe and Jacobson in *Handbook of Family Therapy* by Gurman and Knickerson [Eds.]). ♥

8. Use behavioral techniques (education, modeling, role-playing,

corrective feedback, and positive reinforcement) to teach communication skills including assertive communication, offering positive feedback, active listening, making positive requests of others for behavior change, and giving negative feedback in an honest and respectful manner. ▽EB

9. Assign the couple a homework exercise to use and record newly learned communication skills; process results in session, providing corrective feedback toward improvement. ▽EB

▽EB 7. Learn and implement problem-solving and conflict resolution skills. (7, 10, 11)

7. Assist the couple in identifying conflicts that can be addressed using communication, conflict-resolution, and/or problem-solving skills (see "Behavioral Marital Therapy" by Holzworth-Munroe and Jacobson in *Handbook of Family Therapy* by Gurman and Knickerson [Eds.]). ▽EB

10. Use behavioral techniques (education, modeling, role-playing, corrective feedback, and positive reinforcement) to teach the couple problem-solving and conflict resolution skills including defining the problem constructively and specifically, brainstorming options, evaluating options, compromise, choosing options and implementing a plan, evaluating the results. ▽EB

11. Assign the couple a homework exercise to use and record newly learned problem-solving and conflict resolution skills (or assign "Applying Problem-Solving to Interpersonal Conflict" in *Adult Psychotherapy Homework Planner,* 2nd ed. by Jongsma); process results in session. ▽EB

8. Identify any patterns of destructive and/or abusive behavior in the relationship. (12, 13)

12. Assess current patterns of destructive and/or abusive behavior for each partner, including those that existed in each family of origin.

13. Ask each partner to make a list of escalating behaviors that occur prior to abusive behavior.

9. Implement a "time out" signal that either partner may give to stop interaction that may escalate into abuse. (14, 15, 16)

14. Assist the partners in identifying a clear verbal or behavioral signal to be used by either partner to terminate interaction immediately if either fears impending abuse.

15. Solicit a firm agreement from both partners that the "time out" signal will be responded to favorably without debate.

16. Assign implementation and recording the use of the "time out" signal and other conflict resolution skills in daily interaction (or assign "Alternatives to Destructive Anger" in *Adult Psychotherapy Homework Planner,* 2nd ed. by Jongsma).

10. Identify and replace unrealistic expectations for the relationship. (17)

17. Identify irrational beliefs and unrealistic expectations regarding relationships and then assist the couple in adopting more realistic beliefs and expectations of each other and of the relationship.

11. Increase flexibility of expectations, willingness to compromise, and acceptance of irreconcilable differences. (18)

18. Teach both partners the key concepts of flexibility, compromise, sacrifice of wants, and acceptance of differences toward increased understanding, empathy, intimacy, and compassion for each other.

12. Increase time spent in enjoyable contact with the partner. (19)

19. Assist the client in identifying and planning rewarding social/recreational activities that can be shared with the partner (or assign "Identify and Schedule Pleasant

Activities" in *Adult Psychotherapy Homework Planner,* 2nd ed. by Jongsma).

13. Initiate verbal and physical affection behaviors toward the partner. (20)

20. Encourage increased use of verbal and physical affection, and address resistance surrounding initiating affectionate or sexual interactions with the partner.

14. Participate in an evaluation to identify or rule out sexual dysfunction. (21, 22)

21. Gather from each partner a thorough sexual history to determine areas of strength and to identify areas of dysfunction (see Female Sexual Dysfunction and Male Sexual Dysfunction chapters in this *Planner*).

22. Refer the client to a specialist for a diagnostic evaluation of sexual dysfunction (e.g., rule-out of organic and psychogenic factors), with recommendation for appropriate treatment (e.g., medication, sex therapy, surgery).

15. Commit to the establishment of healthy, mutually satisfying sexual attitudes and behavior that is not a reflection of destructive earlier experiences. (23, 24)

23. In a conjoint session identify sexual behavior, patterns, activities, and beliefs of each partner and the extended family (or assign "Factors Influencing Negative Sexual Attitudes" in *Adult Psychotherapy Homework Planner,* 2nd ed. by Jongsma).

24. Assist each partner in committing to attempt to develop healthy, mutually satisfying sexual beliefs, attitudes, and behavior that is independent of previous childhood, personal, or family training or experience.

16. Acknowledge the connection between substance abuse and the conflicts present within the relationship. (25)

25. Explore the role of substance abuse in precipitating conflict and/or abuse within the relationship.

17. Chemically dependent partner agrees to pursue treatment and seek clean and sober living. (26)

26. Solicit an agreement for substance abuse treatment for the chemically dependent partner (see Chemical Dependence chapter in this *Planner*).

18. Identify the message, cause, and consequences of the partner's infidelity. (27, 28)

27. Assist the couple in identifying the message behind the infidelity (see "Five Degrees for Affairs" in *Patterns of Infidelity and Their Treatment* by Brown).

28. Assign the clients to read *After the Affair* (Abrahms-Spring) and then process key concepts gathered from the reading in conjoint sessions with the therapist.

19. Verbalize acceptance of the loss of the relationship. (29, 30, 31)

29. Explore and clarify feelings associated with loss of the relationship.

30. Refer the client to a support group or divorce seminar to assist in resolving the loss and in adjusting to the new life.

31. Assign the client to read *How to Survive the Loss of a Love* (Colgrove, Bloomfield, and McWilliams) or *Surviving Separation and Divorce* (Oberlin); process key concepts.

20. Implement increased socialization activities to cope with loneliness. (32, 33)

32. Support the client in his/her adjustment to living alone and being single; encourage him/her in accepting some time in being alone and in making concrete plans for social contact.

33. Inform the client of opportunities within the community that assist him/her in building new social relationships.

—. ______________________________
____

—. ______________________________
____

__. ____________________ __. ____________________

__. ____________________ __. ____________________

DIAGNOSTIC SUGGESTIONS

Axis I:	312.34	Intermittent Explosive Disorder
	309.0	Adjustment Disorder With Depressed Mood
	309.24	Adjustment Disorder With Anxiety
	300.4	Dysthymic Disorder
	300.00	Anxiety Disorder NOS
	311	Depressive Disorder NOS
	309.81	Posttraumatic Stress Disorder
	____	__________
	____	__________
Axis II:	301.20	Schizoid Personality Disorder
	301.81	Narcissistic Personality Disorder
	301.9	Personality Disorder NOS
	____	__________
	____	__________

LEGAL CONFLICTS

BEHAVIORAL DEFINITIONS

1. Legal charges pending.
2. On parole or probation subsequent to legal charges.
3. Legal pressure has been central to the decision to enter treatment.
4. A history of criminal activity leading to numerous incarcerations.
5. Most arrests are related to alcohol or drug abuse.
6. Pending divorce accompanied by emotional turmoil.
7. Fear of loss of freedom due to current legal charges.

__. ____

____

__. ____

____

__. ____

____

LONG-TERM GOALS

1. Accept and responsibly respond to the mandates of court.
2. Understand how chemical dependence has contributed to legal problems and accept the need for recovery.
3. Accept responsibility for decisions and actions that have led to arrests and develop higher moral and ethical standards to govern behavior.
4. Internalize the need for treatment so as to change values, thoughts, feelings, and behavior to a more prosocial position.
5. Become a responsible citizen in good standing within the community.

__. ____

____

__. ____

____

__. ____

____

SHORT-TERM OBJECTIVES

1. Describe the behavior that led to current involvement with the court system. (1)

2. Obtain counsel and meet to make plans for resolving legal conflicts. (2)

3. Make regular contact with court officers to fulfill sentencing requirements. (3)

4. Verbalize the role drug and/or alcohol abuse has played in legal problems. (4, 5)

5. Maintain sobriety in accordance with rules of probation/parole. (6, 7)

THERAPEUTIC INTERVENTIONS

1. Explore the client's behavior that led to legal conflicts and assess whether it fits a pattern of antisocial behavior (see Antisocial Behavior chapter in this *Planner*).

2. Encourage and facilitate the client in meeting with an attorney to discuss plans for resolving legal issues.

3. Monitor and encourage the client to keep appointments with court officers.

4. Explore how chemical dependence may have contributed to the client's legal conflicts.

5. Confront the client's denial of chemical dependence by reviewing the various negative consequences of addiction that have occurred in his/her life.

6. Reinforce the client's need for a plan for recovery and sobriety as a means of improving judgment and control over behavior (see Chemical Dependence chapter in this *Planner*).

7. Monitor and reinforce the client's sobriety, using physiological measures to confirm, if advisable.

6. Verbalize and accept responsibility for the series of decisions and actions that eventually led to illegal activity. (8, 9)

8. Assist the client in clarification of values that allow him/her to act illegally.
9. Confront the client's denial and projection of responsibility onto others for his/her own illegal actions.

7. State values that affirm behavior within the boundaries of the law. (8, 10)

8. Assist the client in clarification of values that allow him/her to act illegally.
10. Teach the values associated with respecting legal boundaries and the rights of others as well as the consequences of crossing these boundaries.

8. Verbalize how the emotional state of anger, frustration, helplessness, or depression has contributed to illegal behavior. (11, 12)

11. Probe the client's negative emotional states that could contribute to his/her illegal behavior.
12. Refer the client for ongoing counseling to deal with emotional conflicts and antisocial impulses (see Antisocial Behavior, Anger Management, or Depression chapters in this *Planner*).

9. Identify the causes for the negative emotional state that was associated with illegal actions. (13, 14)

13. Explore causes for the client's underlying negative emotions that consciously or unconsciously fostered his/her criminal behavior.
14. Interpret the client's antisocial behavior that is linked to current or past emotional conflicts to foster insights and resolution.

10. Identify and replace cognitive distortions that foster antisocial behavior. (15, 16)

15. Assess and clarify the client's distorted cognitive belief structures that foster illegal behavior.
16. Restructure the client's distorted cognitions to those that foster keeping of legal boundaries and respecting the rights of others.

11. Attend an anger control group. (17)
12. Identify ways to meet life needs (i.e., social and financial) without resorting to illegal activities. (18, 19)
13. Attend class to learn how to successfully seek employment. (20)
14. Verbalize an understanding of the importance of honesty in earning the trust of others and esteem for self. (21)
15. Develop and implement a plan for restitution for illegal activity. (22, 23)

—. ______________________________

____

—. ______________________________

____

—. ______________________________

____

17. Refer the client to an impulse or anger management group.
18. Explore with the client ways he/she can meet social and financial needs without involvement with illegal activity (e.g., employment, further education or skill training, spiritual enrichment group).
19. Educate the client on the difference between antisocial and prosocial behaviors; assist him/her in writing a list of ways to show respect for the law, help others, and work regularly.
20. Refer the client to an ex-offender center for assistance in obtaining employment.
21. Help the client understand the importance of honesty in earning the trust of others and self-respect.
22. Assist the client in seeing the importance of restitution to self-worth; help him/her develop a plan to provide restitution for the results of his/her behavior.
23. Review the client's implementation of his/her restitution plan; reinforce success and redirect for failure.

—. ______________________________

____

—. ______________________________

____

—. ______________________________

____

DIAGNOSTIC SUGGESTIONS

Axis I:	304.30	Cannabis Dependence
	304.20	Cocaine Dependence
	303.90	Alcohol Dependence
	304.80	Polysubstance Dependence
	312.32	Kleptomania
	V71.01	Adult Antisocial Behavior
	309.3	Adjustment Disorder With Disturbance of Conduct
	______	______________________
	______	______________________
Axis II:	301.7	Antisocial Personality Disorder
	799.9	Diagnosis Deferred
	V71.09	No Diagnosis
	______	______________________
	______	______________________

LOW SELF-ESTEEM

BEHAVIORAL DEFINITIONS

1. Inability to accept compliments.
2. Makes self-disparaging remarks; sees self as unattractive, worthless, a loser, a burden, unimportant; takes blame easily.
3. Lack of pride in grooming.
4. Difficulty in saying no to others; assumes not being liked by others.
5. Fear of rejection of others, especially peer group.
6. Lack of any goals for life and setting of inappropriately low goals for self.
7. Inability to identify positive things about self.
8. Uncomfortable in social situations, especially larger groups.

__. ____

____

__. ____

____

__. ____

____

LONG-TERM GOALS

1. Elevate self-esteem.
2. Develop a consistent, positive self-image.
3. Demonstrate improved self-esteem through more pride in appearance, more assertiveness, greater eye contact, and identification of positive traits in self-talk messages.
4. Establish an inward sense of self-worth, confidence, and competence.

__. ____

____

__. ____

____

__. ____

____

SHORT-TERM OBJECTIVES

1. Acknowledge feeling less competent than most others. (1, 2)

2. Increase insight into the historical and current sources of low self-esteem. (3, 4)

3. Decrease the frequency of negative self-descriptive statements and increase frequency of positive self-descriptive statements. (5, 6, 7)

THERAPEUTIC INTERVENTIONS

1. Actively build the level of trust with the client in individual sessions through consistent eye contact, active listening, unconditional positive regard, and warm acceptance to help increase his/her ability to identify and express feelings.
2. Explore the client's assessment of himself/herself.
3. Help the client become aware of his/her fear of rejection and its connection with past rejection or abandonment experiences.
4. Discuss, emphasize, and interpret the client's incidents of abuse (emotional, physical, and sexual) and how they have impacted his/her feelings about himself/herself.
5. Confront and reframe the client's negative assessment of himself/herself.
6. Assist the client in becoming aware of how he/she expresses or acts out negative feelings about himself/herself.
7. Assist the client in developing self-talk as a way of boosting his/her confidence and positive self-image.

4. Identify negative self-talk messages used to reinforce low self-esteem. (8, 9)

8. Help the client identify his/her distorted, negative beliefs about self and the world.

9. Ask the client to complete and process an exercise in the book *Ten Days to Self Esteem!* (Burns).

5. Identify any secondary gain that is received by speaking negatively about self and refusing to take any risks. (10, 11)

10. Teach the client the meaning and power of secondary gain in maintaining negative behavior patterns.

11. Assist the client in identifying how self-disparagement and avoidance of risk taking could bring secondary gain (e.g., praise from others, others taking over responsibilities).

6. Decrease the verbalized fear of rejection while increasing statements of self-acceptance. (12, 13)

12. Ask the client to make one positive statement about self daily and record it on a chart or in a journal.

13. Verbally reinforce the client's use of positive statements of confidence and accomplishments.

7. Identify accomplishments that would improve self-image and verbalize a plan to achieve those goals. (14, 15)

14. Help the client analyze his/her goals to make sure they are realistic and attainable.

15. Assign self-esteem-building exercises from a workbook (e.g., *The Six Pillars of Self-Esteem* by Branden, or *Ten Days to Self Esteem!* by Burns); process the completed assignment.

8. Increase eye contact with others. (16, 17)

16. Assign the client to make eye contact with whomever he/she is speaking to; process the feelings associated with eye contact.

17. Confront the client when he/she is observed avoiding eye contact with others.

9. Take responsibility for daily grooming and personal hygiene. (18)

18. Monitor and give feedback to the client on his/her grooming and hygiene.

10. Identify positive traits and talents about self. (19, 20, 21)

19. Assign the client the exercise of identifying his/her positive physical characteristics in a mirror to help him/her become more comfortable with himself/herself.
20. Ask the client to keep a building list of positive traits and have him/her read list at beginning and end of each session.
21. Reinforce the client's positive self-descriptive statements.

11. Demonstrate an increased ability to identify and express personal feelings. (22, 23)

22. Assign the client to keep a journal of feelings on a daily basis.
23. Assist the client in identifying and labeling emotions.

12. Articulate a plan to be proactive in trying to get identified needs met. (24, 25, 26)

24. Assist the client in identifying and verbalizing his/her needs, met and unmet.
25. Conduct a conjoint or family therapy session in which the client is supported in expression of unmet needs.
26. Assist the client in developing a specific action plan to get each need met.

13. Positively acknowledge verbal compliments from others. (27)

27. Assign the client to be aware of and acknowledge graciously (without discounting) praise and compliments from others.

14. Increase the frequency of assertive behaviors. (28)

28. Train the client in assertiveness or refer him/her to a group that will educate and facilitate assertiveness skills via lectures and assignments.

15. Form realistic, appropriate, and attainable goals for self in all areas of life. (14, 29)

14. Help the client analyze his/her goals to make sure they are realistic and attainable.
29. Assign the client to make a list of goals for various areas of life and a plan for steps toward goal attainment.

16. Take verbal responsibility for accomplishments without discounting. (30)

30. Ask the client to list accomplishments; process the integration of these into his/her self-image.

17. Use positive self-talk messages to build self-esteem. (31, 32)

31. Assign the client to read *What to Say When You Talk to Yourself* (Helmstetter); process key ideas.

32. Reinforce the client's use of more realistic, positive messages to himself/herself in interpreting life events.

18. Increase the frequency of speaking up with confidence in social situations. (33, 34)

33. Use role-playing and behavioral rehearsal to improve the client's social skills in greeting people and carrying a conversation.

34. Recommend that the client read *Shyness* (Zimbardo); process the content.

__. ____________________

__. ____________________

__. ____________________

__. ____________________

__. ____________________

__. ____________________

DIAGNOSTIC SUGGESTIONS

Axis I:	300.23	Social Phobia
	300.4	Dysthymic Disorder
	296.xx	Major Depressive Disorder
	296.xx	Bipolar I Disorder
	296.89	Bipolar II Disorder
	_______	____________________
	_______	____________________

MALE SEXUAL DYSFUNCTION

BEHAVIORAL DEFINITIONS

1. Describes consistently very low or no pleasurable anticipation of or desire for sexual activity.
2. Strongly avoids and/or is repulsed by any and all sexual contact in spite of a relationship of mutual caring and respect.
3. Recurrently experiences a lack of the usual physiological response of sexual excitement and arousal (attaining and/or maintaining an erection).
4. Reports a consistent lack of a subjective sense of enjoyment and pleasure during sexual activity.
5. Experiences a persistent delay in or absence of reaching ejaculation after achieving arousal and in spite of sensitive sexual pleasuring by a caring partner.
6. Describes genital pain experienced before, during, or after sexual intercourse.

LONG-TERM GOALS

1. Increase desire for and enjoyment of sexual activity.
2. Attain and maintain physiological excitement response during sexual intercourse.
3. Reach ejaculation with a reasonable amount of time, intensity, and focus to sexual stimulation.

4. Eliminate pain and achieve a presence of subjective pleasure before, during, and after sexual intercourse.

__. ____

__. ____

__. ____

SHORT-TERM OBJECTIVES

1. Provide a detailed sexual history that explores current problems and past experiences that have influenced sexual attitudes, feelings, and behavior. (1, 2, 3)

2. Discuss any feelings of and causes for depression. (4)

THERAPEUTIC INTERVENTIONS

1. Obtain a detailed sexual history that examines the client's current adult sexual functioning as well as his childhood and adolescent sexual experiences; level and sources of sexual knowledge; typical sexual practices and their frequency; medical history; drug and alcohol use; and lifestyle factors.
2. Assess the client's attitudes and fund of knowledge regarding sex, emotional responses to it, and self-talk that may be contributing to the dysfunction.
3. Explore the client's family-of-origin for factors that may be contributing to the dysfunction (e.g., negative attitudes regarding sexuality, feelings of inhibition, low self-esteem, guilt, fear, repulsion; or assign "Factors Influencing Negative Sexual Attitudes" in *Adult Psychotherapy Homework Planner,* 2nd ed. by Jongsma).
4. Assess the role of depression in possibly causing the client's sexual dysfunction and treat if depression appears causal (see Depression chapter in this *Planner*).

3. Participate in treatment of depressive feelings that may be causing sexual difficulties. (5)
4. Honestly report substance abuse and cooperate with recommendations by the therapist for addressing it. (6)
5. Honestly and openly discuss the quality of the relationship including conflicts, unfulfilled needs, and anger. (7)
6. Participate in couples therapy as part of addressing sexual problems. (8) EBT
7. Cooperate with a physician's complete examination; discuss results with therapist. (9) EBT
8. Cooperate with physician's recommendation for addressing a medical condition or medication that may be causing sexual problems. (10) EBT

5. Refer the client for antidepressant medication prescription to alleviate depression.
6. Explore the client's use or abuse of mood-altering substances and their effect on sexual functioning; refer him for focused substance abuse counseling.
7. Assess the quality of the relationship including couple satisfaction, distress, attraction, communication, and sexual repertoire toward making a decision to focus treatment on sexual problems or more broadly on the relationship (or assign "Positive and Negative Contributions to the Relationship" in *Adult Psychotherapy Homework Planner,* 2nd ed. by Jongsma).
8. If problem issues go beyond sexual dysfunction, conduct sex therapy in the context of couples therapy (see Intimate Relationship Conflicts chapter in this *Planner*). EBT
9. Refer the client to a physician for a complete exam to rule out any organic or medication-related basis for the sexual dysfunction (e.g., vascular, endocrine, medications). EBT
10. Encourage the client to follow physician's recommendations regarding treatment of a diagnosed medical condition or use of medication that may be causing the sexual problem. EBT

EBT indicates that the Objective/Intervention is consistent with those found in evidence-based treatments.

▼ 9. Verbalize an understanding of the role that physical disease or medication has on sexual dysfunction. (11)

11. Discuss the contributory role that a diagnosed medical condition or medication use may be having on the client's sexual functioning. ▼

▼10. Take medication for impotence as ordered and report as to effectiveness and side effects. (12)

12. Refer the client to a physician for an evaluation regarding a prescription of medication to overcome impotence (e.g., Viagra). ▼

▼11. Practice directed masturbation and sensate focus exercises alone and with partner and share feelings associated with activity. (13, 14)

13. Assign the client body exploration and awareness exercises that reduce inhibition and desensitize him to sexual aversion. ▼

14. Direct the client in masturbatory exercises designed to maximize arousal; assign the client graduated steps of sexual pleasuring exercises with partner that reduce his performance anxiety and focus on experiencing bodily arousal sensations (or assign "Journaling the Response to Nondemand, Sexual Pleasuring [Sensate Focus]" in *Adult Psychotherapy Homework Planner,* 2nd ed. by Jongsma). ▼

▼12. Undergo desensitization (graduated exposure) to sexual exercises that have gradually increasing anxiety attached to them. (15, 16)

15. Direct and assist the client in construction of a hierarchy of anxiety-producing sexual situations associated with performance anxiety. ▼

16. Select initial in vivo or imaginal exposures that have a high likelihood of being a successful experience for the client and instruct him on attentional strategies (e.g., focus on partner, avoid spectatoring); review with the client and/or couple, moving up the hierarchy until associated anxiety has waned (or assign "Gradually Reducing Your Phobic Fear" in *Adult Psychotherapy Homework Planner,* 2nd ed. by Jongsma). ▼

13. Implement the squeeze technique during sexual intercourse and report on success in slowing premature ejaculation. (17)
14. Participate in sex therapy with a partner or individually if the partner is not available. (18)
15. Demonstrate healthy acceptance and accurate knowledge of sexuality by freely learning and discussing accurate information regarding sexual functioning. (19, 20)
16. State an understanding of how family upbringing, including religious training, negatively influenced sexual thoughts, feelings, and behavior. (21, 22, 23)

17. Instruct the client and partner in use of the squeeze technique to prevent premature ejaculation; use illustrations if needed (e.g., *The Illustrated Manual of Sex Therapy* by Kaplan); process the procedure and feelings about it, providing corrective feedback toward successful use.
18. Encourage couples sex therapy or treat individually if a partner is not available.
19. Disinhibit and educate the couple by encouraging them to talk freely and respectfully regarding his sexual body parts, sexual thoughts, feelings, attitudes, and behaviors.
20. Reinforce the client for talking freely, knowledgeably, and positively regarding his sexual thoughts, feelings, and behavior.
21. Explore the role of the client's family of origin in teaching his negative attitudes regarding sexuality; process toward the goal of change.
22. Explore the role of the client's religious training in reinforcing his feelings of guilt and shame surrounding his sexual behavior and thoughts; process toward the goal of change.
23. Assist the client in developing insight into the role of unhealthy sexual attitudes and experiences of childhood in the development of current adult dysfunction; press for a commitment to try to put negative attitudes and experiences in the past while making a behavioral effort to become free from those influences.

17. Verbalize a resolution of feelings regarding sexual trauma or abuse experiences. (24, 25)

24. Probe the client's history for experiences of sexual trauma or abuse.

25. Process the client's emotions surrounding an emotional trauma in the sexual arena (see Sexual Abuse chapter in this *Planner*).

18. Verbalize an understanding of the influence of childhood sex role models. (26)

26. Explore sex role models the client has experienced in childhood or adolescence and how they have influenced the client's attitudes and behaviors.

19. Verbalize connection between previously failed intimate relationships and current fear. (27)

27. Explore the client's fears surrounding intimate relationships and whether there is evidence of repeated failure in this area.

20. Discuss feelings surrounding a secret affair and make a termination decision regarding one of the relationships. (28, 29)

28. Explore for any secret sexual affairs that may account for the client's sexual dysfunction with his partner.

29. Process a decision regarding the termination of one of the relationships that is leading to internal conflict over the dishonesty and disloyalty to a partner.

21. Openly acknowledge and discuss, if present, homosexual attraction. (30)

30. Explore for a homosexual interest that accounts for the client's heterosexual disinterest (or assign "Journal of Sexual Thoughts, Fantasies, Conflicts" in *Adult Psychotherapy Homework Planner,* 2nd ed. by Jongsma).

22. State a willingness to explore new ways to approach sexual relations. (31, 32)

31. Direct conjoint sessions with the client and his partner that focus on conflict resolution, expression of feelings, and sex education.

32. Assign books (e.g., *Sexual Awareness* by McCarthy and McCarthy; *The Gift of Sex* by Penner and Penner; *The New Male Sexuality* by Zilbergeld) that provide the client with accurate sexual

information and/or outline sexual exercises that disinhibit and reinforce sexual sensate focus.

23. List conditions and factors that positively affect sexual arousal, such as setting, time of day, atmosphere. (33)

33. Assign the couple to list conditions and factors that positively affect their sexual arousal; process the list toward creating an environment conducive to sexual arousal.

24. Identify and replace negative cognitive messages that trigger negative emotional reactions during sexual activity. (34, 35)

34. Probe automatic thoughts that trigger the client's negative emotions such as fear, shame, anger, or grief before, during, and after sexual activity.

35. Train the client in healthy alternative thoughts that will mediate pleasure, relaxation, and disinhibition.

25. Discuss low self-esteem issues that impede sexual functioning and verbalize positive self-image. (36)

36. Explore the client's fears of inadequacy as a sexual partner that led to sexual avoidance.

26. Communicate feelings of threat to partner that are based on perception of partner being too sexually aggressive or too critical. (37)

37. Explore the client's feelings of threat brought on by the perception of his partner as too sexually aggressive.

27. Verbalize a positive body image. (38, 39)

38. Assign the client to list assets of his body; confront unrealistic distortions and critical comments.

39. Explore the client's feelings regarding his body image, focusing on causes for negativism.

28. Implement new coital positions and settings for sexual activity that enhance pleasure and satisfaction. (32, 40)

32. Assign books (e.g., *Sexual Awareness* by McCarthy and McCarthy; *The Gift of Sex* by Penner and Penner; *The New Male Sexuality* by Zilbergeld) that provide the client with accurate sexual information and/or outline sexual exercises that disinhibit and reinforce sexual sensate focus.

40. Suggest experimentation with coital positions and settings for sexual play that may increase the client's feelings of security, arousal, and satisfaction.

29. Engage in more assertive behaviors that allow for sharing sexual needs, feelings, and desires, behaving more sensuously and expressing pleasure. (41, 42)

41. Give the client permission for less inhibited, less constricted sexual behavior by assigning body-pleasuring exercises with partner.

42. Encourage the client to gradually explore the role of being more sexually assertive, sensuously provocative, and freely uninhibited in sexual play with partner.

30. Resolve conflicts or develop coping strategies that reduce stress interfering with sexual interest or performance. (43)

43. Probe stress in areas such as work, extended family, and social relationships that distract the client from sexual desire or performance (see Anxiety, Family Conflict, and Vocational Stress chapters in this *Planner*).

31. Verbalize increasing desire for and pleasure with sexual activity. (40, 42, 44)

40. Suggest experimentation with coital positions and settings for sexual play that may increase the client's feelings of security, arousal, and satisfaction.

42. Encourage the client to gradually explore the role of being more sexually assertive, sensuously provocative, and freely uninhibited in sexual play with partner.

44. Reinforce the client's expressions of desire for and pleasure with sexual activity.

__. ______________________________

____

__. ______________________________

____

__. ______________________________

____

__. ______________________________

____

__. ______________________ __. ______________________
______________________ ______________________

DIAGNOSTIC SUGGESTIONS

Axis I:	302.71	Hypoactive Sexual Desire Disorder
	302.79	Sexual Aversion Disorder
	302.72	Male Erectile Disorder
	302.74	Male Orgasmic Disorder
	302.76	Dyspareunia
	302.75	Premature Ejaculation
	608.89	Male Hypoactive Sexual Desire Disorder Due to Axis III Disorder
	607.84	Male Erectile Disorder Due to Axis III Disorder
	608.89	Male Dyspareunia Due to Axis III Disorder
	302.70	Sexual Dysfunction NOS
	995.53	Sexual Abuse of Child, Victim
	______	______________________
	______	______________________

MANIA OR HYPOMANIA

BEHAVIORAL DEFINITIONS

1. Demonstrates loquaciousness or pressured speech.
2. Reports flight of ideas or thoughts racing.
3. Verbalizes grandiose ideas and/or persecutory beliefs.
4. Shows evidence of a decreased need for sleep.
5. Reports little or no appetite.
6. Exhibits increased motor activity or agitation.
7. Displays a poor attention span and is easily distracted.
8. Loss of normal inhibition leads to impulsive, pleasure-oriented behavior without regard for painful consequences.
9. Engages in bizarre dress and grooming patterns.
10. Exhibits an expansive mood that can easily turn to impatience and irritable anger if goal-oriented behavior is blocked or confronted.
11. Lacks follow-through in projects, even though energy is very high, since behavior lacks discipline and goal-directedness.

__. ____

____

__. ____

____

__. ____

____

LONG-TERM GOALS

1. Reduce psychic energy and return to normal activity levels, good judgment, stable mood, and goal-directed behavior.
2. Reduce agitation, impulsivity, and pressured speech while achieving sensi-

tivity to the consequences of behavior and having more realistic expectations.
3. Talk about underlying feelings of low self-esteem or guilt and fears of rejection, dependency, and abandonment.
4. Achieve controlled behavior, moderated mood, and more deliberative speech and thought process through psychotherapy and medication.

__. ____

____

__. ____

____

__. ____

____

SHORT-TERM OBJECTIVES

1. Describe mood state, energy level, amount of control over thoughts, and sleeping pattern. (1, 2)
2. Differentiate between real and imagined losses, rejections, and abandonments. (3, 4, 5)
3. Verbalize grief, fear, and anger regarding real or imagined losses in life. (6, 7)

THERAPEUTIC INTERVENTIONS

1. Assess the client for classic signs of mania: pressured speech, impulsive behavior, euphoric mood, flight of ideas, reduced need for sleep, inflated self-esteem, and high energy.
2. Assess the client's stage of elation: hypomanic, manic, or psychotic.
3. Pledge to be there consistently to help, listen to, and support the client.
4. Explore the client's fears of abandonment by sources of love and nurturance.
5. Help the client differentiate between real and imagined, actual and exaggerated losses.
6. Probe real or perceived losses in the client's life.
7. Review ways for the client to replace the losses and put them in perspective.

4. Acknowledge the low self-esteem and fear of rejection that underlie the braggadocio. (8, 9)

8. Probe the causes for the client's low self-esteem and abandonment fears in the family-of-origin history.

9. Confront the client's grandiosity and demandingness gradually but firmly; emphasize his/her good qualities (or assign "What Are My Good Qualities" or "Acknowledging My Strengths" in *Adult Psychotherapy Homework Planner,* 2nd ed. by Jongsma).

EB 5. Cooperate with psychiatric evaluation as to the need for medication and/or hospitalization to stabilize mood and energy. (10, 11)

10. Arrange for or continue hospitalization if the client is judged to be potentially harmful to self or others, or unable to care for his/her own basic needs. EB

11. Arrange for a psychiatric evaluation of the client for pharmacotherapy (e.g., Lithium Carbonate, Depakote, Lamictil). EB

EB 6. Take psychotropic medications as directed. (12, 13)

12. Monitor the client's reaction to the psychotropic medication prescription (e.g., compliance, side effects, and effectiveness). EB

13. Continually evaluate the client's compliance with the psychotropic medication prescription. EB

EB 7. Achieve a level of symptom stability that allows for meaningful participation in psychotherapy. (14, 15)

14. Monitor the client's symptom improvement toward stabilization sufficient to allow participation in psychotherapy. EB

15. Conduct Family-Focused Treatment with the client and significant others, or adapt the model to individual therapy if family therapy is not possible

---

EB indicates that the Objective/Intervention is consistent with those found in evidence-based treatments.

(see *Bipolar Disorder: A Family-Focused Approach* by Miklowitz and Goldstein). ▼

▼ 8. Complete psychological testing to assess communication patterns within the family. (16)

16. Arrange for the administration of an objective assessment instrument for evaluating family communication patterns, particularly expressed emotion (e.g., *Perceived Criticism Scale* by Hooley and Teasdale); evaluate results and process feedback with the client and family. ▼

▼ 9. Verbalize an understanding of the causes for, symptoms of, and treatment of manic, hypomanic, mixed, and/or depressive episodes. (17, 18, 19)

17. Teach the client and family, using all modalities necessary, about the signs, symptoms, and phasic relapsing nature of the client's mood episodes; destigmatize and normalize. ▼

18. Teach the client a stress diathesis model of Bipolar Disorder that emphasizes the strong role of a biological predisposition to mood episodes that is vulnerable to stresses that are manageable. ▼

19. Provide the client with a rationale for treatment involving ongoing medication and psychosocial treatment to recognize, manage, and reduce biological and psychological vulnerabilities that could precipitate relapse. ▼

▼ 10. Identify sources of stress that increase the risk of relapse. (20)

20. Identify the client's sources of stress/triggers of potential relapse that will become the target of treatment (e.g., aversive communication, poor sleep hygiene, medication noncompliance). ▼

▼ 11. Verbalize acceptance of the need to take psychotropic medication and commit to prescription compliance with blood level monitoring. (21, 22, 23)

21. Educate the client about the importance of medication compliance; teach him/her the risk for relapse when medication is discontinued and work toward a commitment to prescription adherence. ▼

22. Assess factors (e.g., thoughts, feelings, stressors) that have precipitated the client's prescription noncompliance; develop a plan for recognizing and addressing them (or assign "Why I Dislike Taking My Medication" in *Adult Psychotherapy Homework Planner,* 2nd ed. by Jongsma). ▼

23. Educate and encourage the client to stay compliant with necessary labs involved in regulating his/her medication levels. ▼

▼12. Implement good sleep hygiene. (24)

24. Teach the client about the importance of good sleep hygiene (or assign "Sleep Pattern Record" in *Adult Psychotherapy Homework Planner,* 2nd ed. by Jongsma); assess and intervene accordingly (see Sleep Disturbance chapter in this *Planner*). ▼

▼13. Develop a "relapse drill" in which roles, responsibilities, and a course of action is agreed upon in the event that signs of relapse emerge. (25, 26)

25. Educate the client and family about the client's signs and symptoms of pending relapse. ▼

26. Help the client and family draw up a "relapse drill" detailing roles and responsibilities (e.g., who will call a meeting of the family to problem-solve potential relapse; who will call physician, schedule a serum level to be taken, or contact emergency services, if needed); problem-solve obstacles and work toward a commitment to adherence with the plan. ▼

▼14. Client and family commit to replacing aversive communication with positive, honest, and respectful communication. (27, 28, 29)

27. Assess and educate the client and family about the role of aversive communication (e.g., high expressed emotion) in family distress and risk for the client's manic relapse. ▼

28. Use behavioral techniques (education, modeling, role-playing, corrective feedback, and positive reinforcement) to teach communication skills, including offering positive feedback, active listening, making positive requests of others for behavior change, and giving negative feedback in an honest and respectful manner. ♥

29. Assign the client and family homework exercises to use and record use of newly learned communication skills; process results in session. ♥

♥15. Client and family implement a problem-solving approach to addressing current conflicts. (30, 31, 32)

30. Assist the client and family in identifying conflicts that can be addressed with problem-solving techniques. ♥

31. Use behavioral techniques (education, modeling, role-playing, corrective feedback, and positive reinforcement) to teach the client and family problem-solving skills, including defining the problem constructively and specifically, brainstorming options, evaluating options, choosing options and implementing a plan, evaluating the results, and reevaluating the plan. ♥

32. Assign the client and family homework exercises to use and record use of newly learned problem-solving skills (or assign "Plan Before Acting" in *Adult Psychotherapy Homework Planner,* 2nd ed. by Jongsma); process results in session. ♥

16. Terminate self-destructive behaviors, such as promiscuity, substance abuse, and the expression of overt hostility or aggression. (33, 34, 35, 36)

33. Repeatedly focus on the negative consequences of the client's behavior to reduce his/her thoughtless impulsivity (or assign "Recognizing the Negative Consequences of Impulsive Behavior" or "Impulsive Behavior Journal" in *Adult Psychotherapy Homework Planner,* 2nd ed. by Jongsma).

34. Facilitate the client's impulse control by using role-playing, behavioral rehearsal, and role reversal to increase his/her sensitivity to consequences of his/her behavior.

35. Calmly listen to the client's expressions of hostility while setting limits on his/her aggressive or impulsive behavior.

36. Set limits on the client's manipulation or acting out by making clear rules and establishing clear consequences for breaking rules.

17. Speak more slowly and be more subject-focused. (37, 38)

37. Provide structure and focus for the client's thoughts and actions by regulating the direction of conversation and establishing plans for behavior.

38. Verbally reinforce the client's slower speech and more deliberate thought process.

18. Be less agitated and distracted—that is, able to sit quietly and calmly for 30 minutes. (39)

39. Reinforce increased control over hyperactivity and help the client set goals and limits on agitation; model and role-play increased behavioral control.

19. Report more control over impulses and thoughts, and a slower thinking process. (40, 41)

40. Monitor the client's energy level and reinforce increased control over behavior, pressured speech, and expression of ideas.

41. Reinforce the client's reports of behavior that is more focused on goal attainment and less distractible. ▽

▽20. Participate in periodic "maintenance" sessions. (42)

42. Hold periodic "maintenance" sessions within the first few months after therapy to facilitate the client's positive changes; problem-solve obstacles to improvement. ▽

21. Increase understanding of bipolar illness by reading a book on the disorder. (43)

43. Ask the client to read a book on Bipolar Disorder (e.g., *The Bipolar Disorder Survival Guide* by Miklowitz). ▽

__. ____________________

__. ____________________

__. ____________________

__. ____________________

__. ____________________

__. ____________________

DIAGNOSTIC SUGGESTIONS

Axis I:	296.xx	Bipolar I Disorder
	296.89	Bipolar II Disorder
	301.13	Cyclothymic Disorder
	295.70	Schizoaffective Disorder
	296.80	Bipolar Disorder NOS
	310.1	Personality Change Due to Axis III Disorder
	______	____________________
	______	____________________

MEDICAL ISSUES

BEHAVIORAL DEFINITIONS

1. A diagnosis of a chronic illness that is not life threatening but necessitates changes in living.
2. A diagnosis of an acute, serious illness that is life threatening.
3. A diagnosis of a chronic illness that eventually will lead to an early death.
4. Sad affect, social withdrawal, anxiety, loss of interest in activities, and low energy.
5. Suicidal ideation.
6. Denial of the seriousness of the medical condition.
7. Refusal to cooperate with recommended medical treatments.
8. A positive test for human immunodeficiency virus (HIV).
9. Acquired immune deficiency syndrome (AIDS).
10. Medical complications secondary to chemical dependence.
11. Psychological or behavioral factors that influence the course of the medical condition.
12. History of neglecting physical health.

—. ____
____

—. ____
____

—. ____
____

LONG-TERM GOALS

1. Medically stabilize physical condition.
2. Work through the grieving process and face with peace the reality of own death.

3. Accept emotional support from those who care, without pushing them away in anger.
4. Live life to the fullest extent possible, even though remaining time may be limited.
5. Cooperate with the medical treatment regimen without passive-aggressive or active resistance.
6. Become as knowledgeable as possible about the diagnosed condition and about living as normally as possible.
7. Reduce fear, anxiety, and worry associated with the medical condition.
8. Accept the illness, and adapt life to the necessary limitations.
9. Accept the role of psychological or behavioral factors in development of medical condition and focus on resolution of these factors.

__. ____

____

__. ____

____

__. ____

____

SHORT-TERM OBJECTIVES

1. Describe history, symptoms, and treatment of the medical condition. (1, 2)
2. Identify feelings associated with the medical condition. (3)
3. Family members share with each other feelings that are triggered by the client's medical condition. (4)

THERAPEUTIC INTERVENTIONS

1. Gather a history of the facts regarding the client's medical condition, including symptoms, treatment, and prognosis.
2. With the client's informed consent, contact treating physician and family members for additional medical information regarding the client's diagnosis, treatment, and prognosis.
3. Assist the client in identifying, sorting through, and verbalizing the various feelings generated by his/her medical condition.
4. Meet with family members to facilitate their clarifying and sharing possible feelings of guilt, anger, helplessness, and/or sibling

attention jealousy associated with the client's medical condition.

4. Identify the losses or limitations that have been experienced due to the medical condition. (5)

5. Ask the client to list the changes, losses, or limitations that have resulted from the medical condition.

5. Verbalize an increased understanding of the steps to grieving the losses brought on by the medical condition. (6, 7)

6. Educate the client on the stages of the grieving process and answer any questions that he/she may have.

7. Suggest that the client read a book on grief and loss (e.g., *Good Grief* by Westberg; *How Can It Be Right When Everything Is All Wrong?* by Smedes; *When Bad Things Happen to Good People* by Kushner).

6. Verbalize feelings associated with the losses related to the medical condition. (3, 8)

3. Assist the client in identifying, sorting through, and verbalizing the various feelings generated by his/her medical condition.

8. Assign the client to keep a daily grief journal to be shared in therapy sessions.

7. Decrease time spent focusing on the negative aspects of the medical condition. (9, 10)

9. Suggest that the client set aside a specific time-limited period each day to focus on mourning his/her medical condition. After each day's time period has elapsed, the client will resume regular activities and put off grieving thoughts until the next scheduled time. For example, mourning times could include putting on dark clothing and/or sad music; the clothing would be changed when the allotted time has ended.

10. Challenge the client to focus his/her thoughts on the positive aspects of life rather than on the losses associated with his/her medical condition; reinforce instances of such a positive focus.

8. Implement faith-based activities as a source of comfort and hope. (11)

11. Encourage the client to rely upon his/her spiritual faith promises, activities (e.g., prayer, meditation, worship, music), and fellowship as sources of support.

9. Verbalize acceptance of the reality of the medical condition and the need for treatment. (12, 13, 14, 15)

12. Gently confront the client's denial of the seriousness of his/her condition and need for compliance with medical treatment procedures; reinforce the client's acceptance of his/her medical condition and compliance with treatment.

13. Explore and process the client's fears associated with medical treatment, deterioration of physical health, and subsequent death.

14. Normalize the client's feelings of grief, sadness, or anxiety associated with medical condition; encourage verbal expression of these emotions to significant others and medical personnel.

15. Assess the client for and treat his/her depression and anxiety (see Depression and Anxiety chapters in this *Planner*).

10. Attend a support group of others diagnosed with a similar illness. (16)

16. Refer the client to a support group of others living with a similar medical condition.

11. Partner and family members attend a support group. (17)

17. Refer family members to a community-based support group associated with the client's medical condition.

12. Comply with the medication regimen and necessary medical procedures, reporting any side effects or problems to physicians or therapists. (2, 18, 19, 20)

2. With the client's informed consent, contact treating physician and family members for additional medical information regarding the client's diagnosis, treatment, and prognosis.

18. Monitor and reinforce the client's compliance with medical treatment regimen.
19. Explore and address the client's misconceptions, fears, and situational factors that interfere with medical treatment compliance.
20. Confront any manipulative, passive-aggressive, and denial mechanisms that block the client's compliance with the medical treatment regimen.

13. Engage in social, productive, and recreational activities that are possible in spite of medical condition. (21, 22)

21. Sort out with the client activities that he/she can still enjoy either alone or with others.
22. Solicit a commitment from the client to increase his/her activity level by engaging in enjoyable and challenging activities; reinforce such engagement.

14. Implement behavioral stress-reduction skills to terminate exacerbation of medical condition due to tension. (23, 24, 25)

23. To reduce tension and stress, teach the client deep muscle relaxation and deep-breathing methods along with positive imagery.
24. Utilize electromyograph (EMG) biofeedback to monitor, increase, and reinforce the client's depth of relaxation.
25. Develop and encourage a routine of physical exercise for the client.

15. Identify and replace negative self-talk and catastrophizing that is associated with the medical condition. (26, 27)

26. Assist the client in identifying the cognitive distortions and negative automatic thoughts that contribute to his/her negative attitude and hopeless feelings associated with the medical condition.
27. Generate with the client a list of positive, realistic self-talk that can replace the cognitive distortions and catastrophizing regarding his/her medical condition and its treatment.

16. Implement positive imagery as a means of triggering peace of mind and reducing tension. (28, 29)

28. Teach the client the use of positive, relaxing, healing imagery to reduce stress and promote peace of mind.

29. Encourage the client to rely on faith-based promises of God's love, presence, caring, and support to bring peace of mind.

17. Verbalize increased factual understanding of medical condition. (30, 31)

30. Provide the client with accurate information regarding the symptoms, causes, treatment, and prognosis for his/her medical condition.

31. Refer the client and his/her family to reading material and reliable Internet resources for accurate information regarding the medical condition.

18. Identify the sources of emotional support that have been beneficial and additional sources that could be tapped. (32, 33)

32. Probe and evaluate the client's and family members' resources of emotional support.

33. Encourage the client and his/her family members to reach out for support from church leaders, extended family, hospital social services, community support groups, and God.

19. Client's partner and family members verbalize their fears regarding the client's severely disabled life or possible death. (34)

34. Draw out from the client's partner and family members their unspoken fears about his/her possible death; empathize with their feelings of panic, helpless frustration, and anxiety. Reassure them of God's presence as the giver and supporter of life.

20. Maintain a life of sobriety that supports recovery from medical condition. (35, 36)

35. Explore and assess the role of chemical abuse on the client's medical condition.

36. Recommend that the client pursue treatment for his/her chemical dependence (see Chemical Dependence chapter in this *Planner*).

21. Acknowledge any high-risk behaviors associated with sexually transmitted disease (STD). (37)

37. Assess the client's behavior for the presence of high-risk behaviors (e.g., IV drug use, unprotected sex, gay lifestyle, promiscuity) related to STD and HIV.

22. Accept the presence of an STD or HIV and follow through with medical treatment. (38, 39)

38. Refer the client to public health or a physician for STD and/or HIV testing, education, and treatment.

39. Encourage and monitor the client's follow-through on pursuing medical treatment for STD and HIV at a specialized treatment program, if necessary.

23. Identify sources of emotional distress that could have a negative impact on physical health. (40, 41)

40. Teach the client how lifestyle and emotional distress can have negative impacts on medical condition; review his/her lifestyle and emotional status to identify negative factors for physical health.

41. Assign the client to make a list of lifestyle changes he/she could make to help maintain physical health; process list.

__. ____________________________

__. ____________________________

__. ____________________________

__. ____________________________

__. ____________________________

__. ____________________________

DIAGNOSTIC SUGGESTIONS

Axis I:	316	Psychological Symptoms Affecting Axis III Disorder
	309.0	Adjustment Disorder With Depressed Mood
	309.24	Adjustment Disorder With Anxiety
	309.28	Adjustment Disorder With Mixed Anxiety and Depressed Mood

	309.3	Adjustment Disorder With Disturbance of Conduct
	309.4	Adjustment Disorder With Mixed Disturbance of Emotions and Conduct
	296.xx	Major Depressive Disorder
	311	Depressive Disorder NOS
	300.02	Generalized Anxiety Disorder
	300.00	Anxiety Disorder NOS
	______	____________________
	______	____________________
Axis II:	799.9	Diagnosis Deferred
	V71.09	No Diagnosis or Condition
	______	____________________
	______	____________________

OBSESSIVE-COMPULSIVE DISORDER (OCD)

BEHAVIORAL DEFINITIONS

1. Intrusive, recurrent, and unwanted thoughts, images, or impulses that distress and/or interfere with the client's daily routine, job performance, or social relationships.
2. Failed attempts to ignore or control these thoughts or impulses or neutralize them with other thoughts and actions.
3. Recognition that obsessive thoughts are a product of his/her own mind.
4. Repetitive and/or excessive mental or behavioral actions are done to neutralize or prevent discomfort or some dreaded outcome.
5. Recognition of repetitive behaviors as excessive and unreasonable.

—. ____

____

—. ____

____

—. ____

____

LONG-TERM GOALS

1. Reduce the frequency, intensity, and duration of obsessions.
2. Reduce time involved with or interference from obsessions and compulsions.
3. Function daily at a consistent level with minimal interference from obsessions and compulsions.
4. Resolve key life conflicts and the emotional stress that fuels obsessive-compulsive behavior patterns.

5. Let go of key thoughts, beliefs, and past life events in order to maximize time free from obsessions and compulsions.

—. ______________________________

—. ______________________________

—. ______________________________

SHORT-TERM OBJECTIVES

1. Describe the history and nature of obsessions and compulsions. (1, 2)
2. Complete psychological tests designed to assess and track the nature and severity of obsessions and compulsions. (3)
3. ♥ Cooperate with an evaluation by a physician for psychotropic medication. (4, 5)

THERAPEUTIC INTERVENTIONS

1. Establish rapport with the client toward building a therapeutic alliance.
2. Assess the client's frequency, intensity, duration, and history of obsessions and compulsions (e.g., *The Anxiety Disorders Interview Schedule for the DSM-IV* by DiNardo, Brown, and Barlow).
3. Administer a measure of OCD to further assess its depth and breadth (e.g., *The Yale-Brown Obsessive-Compulsive Scale* by Goodman and colleagues, 1989a, 1989b).
4. Arrange for an evaluation for a prescription of psychotropic medications (e.g., serotonergic medications). ♥
5. Monitor the client for prescription compliance, side effects, and overall effectiveness of the medication; consult with the prescribing physician at regular intervals. ♥

♥ indicates that the Objective/Intervention is consistent with those found in evidence-based treatments.

4. Participate in small group exposure and ritual prevention therapy for obsessions and compulsions. (6)

6. Enroll the client in intensive (e.g., daily) or nonintensive (e.g., weekly) small (closed enrollment) group exposure and ritual prevention therapy for OCD (see *Obsessive-Compulsive Disorder* by Foa and Franklin).

5. Verbalize an understanding of the rationale for treatment of OCD. (7, 8)

7. Assign the client to read psychoeducational chapters of books or treatment manuals on the rationale for exposure and ritual prevention therapy and/or cognitive restructuring for OCD (e.g., *Mastery of Obsessive-Compulsive Disorder* by Kozak and Foa; *Stop Obsessing* by Foa and Wilson).

8. Discuss how treatment serves as an arena to desensitize learned fear, reality test obsessional fears and underlying beliefs, and build confidence in managing fears without compulsions (see *Mastery of Obsessive-Compulsive Disorder* by Kozak and Foa).

6. Identify and replace biased, fearful self-talk and beliefs. (9)

9. Explore the client's schema and self-talk that mediate his/her obsessional fears and compulsive behavior, and assist him/her in generating thoughts that correct for the biases (see *Mastery of Obsessive-Compulsive Disorder* by Kozak and Foa; *Obsessive-Compulsive Disorder* by Salkovskis and Kirk).

7. Undergo repeated imaginal exposure to feared external and/or internal cues. (10, 11, 12)

10. Assess the nature of any external cues (e.g., persons, objects, situations) and internal cues (thoughts, images, impulses) that precipitate the client's obsessions and compulsions.

11. Direct and assist the client in construction of a hierarchy of feared internal and external fear cues.

12. Select initial imaginal exposures to the internal and/or external OCD cues that have a high likelihood of being a successful experience for the client: do cognitive restructuring within and after the exposure (see *Mastery of Obsessive-Compulsive Disorder* by Kozak and Foa; *Treatment of Obsessive-Compulsive Disorder* by McGinn and Sanderson). ♥

♥ 8. Complete homework assignments involving in vivo exposure to feared external and/or internal cues. (13)

13. Assign the client a homework exercise in which he/she repeats the exposure to the internal and/or external OCD cues using restructured cognitions between sessions and records responses (or assign "Reducing the Strength of Compulsive Behaviors" in *Adult Psychotherapy Homework Planner,* 2nd ed. by Jongsma); review during next session, reinforcing success and providing corrective feedback toward improvement (see *Mastery of Obsessive-Compulsive Disorder* by Kozak and Foa). ♥

♥ 9. Implement relapse prevention strategies for managing possible future anxiety symptoms. (14, 15, 16, 17)

14. Discuss with the client the distinction between a lapse and relapse, associating a lapse with an initial and reversible return of symptoms, fear, or urges to avoid and relapse with the decision to return to fearful and avoidant patterns. ♥

15. Identify and rehearse with the client the management of future situations or circumstances in which lapses could occur. ♥

16. Instruct the client to routinely use strategies learned in therapy (e.g., continued exposure to previously feared external or internal cues that arise) to prevent relapse into obsessive-compulsive patterns. ♥

17. Schedule periodic "maintenance" sessions to help the client maintain therapeutic gains and adjust to life without OCD (see Hiss, Foa, and Kozak, 1994, for a description of relapse prevention strategies for OCD).

10. Implement the use of the thought-stopping technique to reduce the frequency of obsessive thoughts. (18, 19)

18. Teach the client to interrupt obsessive thoughts using the thought-stopping technique of shouting STOP to himself/herself silently while picturing a red traffic signal and then thinking about a calming scene.

19. Assign the client to implement the thought-stopping technique on a daily basis between sessions (or assign "Making Use of the Thought-Stopping Technique" in *Adult Psychotherapy Homework Planner,* 2nd ed. by Jongsma); review implementation, reinforcing success and redirecting for failure.

11. Identify key life conflicts that raise anxiety. (20, 21, 22)

20. Explore the client's life circumstances to help identify key unresolved conflicts.

21. Read with the client the fable "The Friendly Forest" or "Round in Circles" from *Friedman's Fables* (Friedman), and then process using discussion questions.

22. Assign the client to read or read to him/her the story "The Little Clock That Couldn't Tell Time" or "The Little Centipede Who Didn't Know How to Walk" from *Stories for the Third Ear* (Wallas); process the stories as they are applied to the client's current life.

12. Verbalize and clarify feelings connected to key life conflicts. (23)

23. Encourage, support, and assist the client in identifying and expressing feelings related to key unresolved life issues.

13. Implement the Ericksonian task designed to interfere with OCD. (24)

24. Develop and assign an Ericksonian task (e.g., if obsessed with a loss, give the client the task to visit, send a card, or bring flowers to someone who has lost someone) to the client that is centered around the obsession or compulsion and assess the results with the client.

14. Engage in a strategic ordeal to overcome OCD impulses. (25)

25. Create and sell a strategic ordeal that offers a guaranteed cure to the client for the obsession or compulsion. (Note that Haley emphasizes that the "cure" offers an intervention to achieve a goal and is not a promise to cure the client at the beginning of the therapy. See *Ordeal Therapy* by Haley.)

15. Develop and implement a daily ritual that interrupts the current pattern of compulsions. (26)

26. Help the client create and implement a ritual (e.g., find a job that the client finds necessary but very unpleasant, and have him/her do this job each time he/she finds thoughts becoming obsessive); follow up with the client on the outcome of its implementation and make necessary adjustments.

—. ____________________________
____

—. ____________________________
____

—. ____________________________
____

—. ____________________________
____

—. ____________________________
____

—. ____________________________
____

DIAGNOSTIC SUGGESTIONS

Axis I:	300.3	Obsessive-Compulsive Disorder
	300.00	Anxiety Disorder NOS
	296.xx	Major Depressive Disorder
	______	____________________
	______	____________________
Axis II:	301.4	Obsessive-Compulsive Personality Disorder
	______	____________________
	______	____________________

PANIC/AGORAPHOBIA

BEHAVIORAL DEFINITIONS

1. Complains of unexpected, sudden, debilitating panic symptoms (e.g., shallow breathing, sweating, heart racing or pounding, dizziness, depersonalization or derealization, trembling, chest tightness, fear of dying or losing control, nausea) that have occurred repeatedly, resulting in persisting concern about having additional attacks.
2. Demonstrates marked avoidance of activities or environments due to fear of triggering intense panic symptoms, resulting in interference with normal routine.
3. Acknowledges a persistence of fear in spite of the recognition that the fear is unreasonable.
4. Increasingly isolates self due to fear of traveling or leaving a "safe environment," such as home.
5. Avoids public places or environments with large groups of people, such as malls or big stores.
6. Displays no evidence of agoraphobia.

—. ____

____

—. ____

____

—. ____

____

LONG-TERM GOALS

1. Reduce the frequency, intensity, and duration of panic attacks.
2. Reduce the fear that panic symptoms will recur without the ability to manage them.

3. Reduce the fear of triggering panic and eliminate avoidance of activities and environments thought to trigger panic.
4. Increase comfort in freely leaving home and being in a public environment.

—. ____

____

—. ____

____

—. ____

____

SHORT-TERM OBJECTIVES

1. Describe the history and nature of the panic symptoms. (1, 2)

THERAPEUTIC INTERVENTIONS

1. Assess the client's frequency, intensity, duration, and history of panic symptoms, fear, and avoidance (e.g., *The Anxiety Disorders Interview Schedule for the DSM-IV* by DiNardo, Brown, and Barlow).
2. Assess the nature of any stimulus, thoughts, or situations that precipitate the client's panic (or assign "Monitoring My Panic Attack Experiences" in *Adult Psychotherapy Homework Planner,* 2nd ed. by Jongsma).

2. Complete psychological tests designed to assess the depth of agoraphobia and anxiety sensitivity. (3, 4)

3. Administer a fear survey to further assess the depth and breadth of agoraphobic responses (e.g., *The Mobility Inventory for Agoraphobia* by Chambless, Caputo, and Gracely).
4. Administer a measure of fear of anxiety symptoms to further assess its depth and breadth (e.g., *The Anxiety Sensitivity Index* by Reiss, Peterson, and Gursky).

3. Cooperate with an evaluation by a physician for psychotropic medication. (5, 6) ▼

5. Arrange for an evaluation for a prescription of psychotropic medications to alleviate the client's symptoms. ▼

6. Monitor the client for prescription compliance, side effects, and overall effectiveness of the medication; consult with the prescribing physician at regular intervals. ▼

4. Verbalize an accurate understanding of panic attacks and agoraphobia and their treatment. (7, 8) ▼

7. Discuss how panic attacks are "false alarms" of danger, not medically dangerous, not a sign of weakness or craziness, common, but often lead to unnecessary avoidance. ▼

8. Assign the client to read psychoeducational chapters of books or treatment manuals on panic disorders and agoraphobia (e.g., *Mastery of Your Anxiety and Panic* by Barlow and Craske; *Don't Panic: Taking Control of Anxiety Attacks* by Wilson; *Living with Fear* by Marks). ▼

5. Verbalize an understanding of the rationale for treatment of panic. (9) ▼

9. Discuss how exposure serves as an arena to desensitize learned fear, build confidence, and feel safer by building a new history of success experiences. ▼

6. Implement calming and coping strategies to reduce overall anxiety and to manage panic symptoms. (10, 11) ▼

10. Teach the client progressive muscle relaxation as a daily exercise for general relaxation and train him/her in the use of coping strategies (e.g., staying focused on behavioral goals, muscular relaxation, evenly paced diaphragmatic breathing, positive self-talk) to manage symptom attacks. ▼

▼ indicates that the Objective/Intervention is consistent with those found in evidence-based treatments.

11. Teach the client to keep focus on external stimuli and behavioral responsibilities during panic rather than being preoccupied with internal focus on physiological changes. ♥

♥ 7. Practice positive self-talk that builds confidence in the ability to endure anxiety symptoms without serious consequences. (12, 13)

12. Consistently reassure the client of no connection between panic symptoms and heart attack, loss of control over behavior, or serious mental illness ("going crazy"). ♥

13. Use modeling and behavioral rehearsal to train the client in positive self-talk that reassures him/her of the ability to endure anxiety symptoms without serious consequences. ♥

♥ 8. Identify, challenge, and replace biased, fearful self-talk with reality-based, positive self-talk. (14, 15)

14. Explore the client's schema and self-talk that mediate his/her fear response, challenge the biases; assist him/her in replacing the distorted messages with self-talk that does not overestimate the likelihood of catastrophic outcomes nor underestimate the ability to cope with panic symptoms. ♥

15. Assign the client a homework exercise in which he/she identifies fearful self-talk and creates reality-based alternatives (or assign "Journal and Replace Self-Defeating Thoughts" in *Adult Psychotherapy Homework Planner,* 2nd ed. by Jongsma); review and reinforce success, providing corrective feedback for failure (see *10 Simple Solutions to Panic* by Antony and McCabe; *Mastery of Your Anxiety and Panic* by Barlow and Craske). ♥

9. Undergo gradual repeated exposure to feared physical sensations until they are no longer frightening to experience. (16, 17)

16. Teach the client a sensation exposure technique in which he/she generates feared physical sensations through exercise (e.g., breathes rapidly until slightly lightheaded, spins in chair briefly until slightly dizzy), then uses coping strategies (e.g., staying focused on behavioral goals, muscular relaxation, evenly paced diaphragmatic breathing, positive self-talk) to calm himself/herself down; repeat exercise until anxiety wanes (see *10 Simple Solutions to Panic* by Antony and McCabe; *Mastery of Your Anxiety and Panic—Therapist Guide* by Craske, Barlow, and Meadows).

17. Assign the client a homework exercise in which he/she does sensation exposures and records (e.g., *Mastery of Your Anxiety and Panic* by Barlow and Craske; *10 Simple Solutions to Panic* by Antony and McCabe); review and reinforce success, providing corrective feedback for failure.

10. Undergo gradual repeated exposure to feared or avoided situations in which a symptom attack and its negative consequences are feared. (18, 19, 20)

18. Direct and assist the client in construction of a hierarchy of anxiety-producing situations associated with the phobic response.

19. Select initial exposures that have a high likelihood of being a successful experience for the client; develop a plan for managing the symptoms and rehearse the plan in imagination.

20. Assign the client a homework exercise in which he/she does situational exposures and records responses (e.g., "Gradually Reducing Your Phobic Fear" in *Adult Psychotherapy Homework*

Planner, 2nd ed. by Jongsma; *Mastery of Your Anxiety and Panic* by Barlow and Craske; *10 Simple Solutions to Panic* by Antony and McCabe); review and reinforce success, providing corrective feedback for failure. EB

EB 11. Implement relapse prevention strategies for managing possible future anxiety symptoms. (21, 22, 23, 24)

21. Discuss with the client the distinction between a lapse and relapse, associating a lapse with an initial and reversible return of symptoms, fear, or urges to avoid and relapse with the decision to return to fearful and avoidant patterns. EB

22. Identify and rehearse with the client the management of future situations or circumstances in which lapses could occur. EB

23. Instruct the client to routinely use strategies learned in therapy (e.g., cognitive restructuring, exposure), building them into his/her life as much as possible. EB

24. Develop a "coping card" on which coping strategies and other important information (e.g., "Pace your breathing," "Focus on the task at hand," "You can manage it," and "It will go away") are written for the client's later use. EB

12. Verbalize the costs and benefits of remaining fearful and avoidant. (25)

25. Probe for the presence of secondary gain that reinforces the client's panic symptoms through escape or avoidance mechanisms; challenge the client to remain in feared situations and to use coping skills to endure.

13. Verbalize the separate realities of the irrationally feared object or situation and the

26. Clarify and differentiate between the client's current irrational fear and past emotional pain.

emotionally painful experience from the past that has been evoked by the phobic stimulus. (26, 27)

14. Commit self to not allowing panic symptoms to take control of life and lead to a consistent avoidance of normal responsibilities. (28)

15. Return for a follow-up session to track progress, reinforce gains, and problem-solve barriers. (29)

__. ____________________

__. ____________________

__. ____________________

27. Encourage the client's sharing of feelings associated with past traumas through active listening, positive regard, and questioning.

28. Support the client in following through with work, family, and social activities rather than escaping or avoiding them to focus on panic.

29. Schedule a "booster session" for the client for 1 to 3 months after therapy ends.

__. ____________________

__. ____________________

__. ____________________

DIAGNOSTIC SUGGESTIONS

Axis I:	300.01	Panic Disorder Without Agoraphobia
	300.21	Panic Disorder With Agoraphobia
	300.22	Agoraphobia Without Panic Disorder
	______	____________________
	______	____________________

PARANOID IDEATION

BEHAVIORAL DEFINITIONS

1. Extreme or consistent distrust of others generally or someone specifically, without sufficient basis.
2. Expectation of being exploited or harmed by others.
3. Misinterpretation of benign events as having threatening personal significance.
4. Hypersensitivity to hints of personal critical judgment by others.
5. Inclination to keep distance from others out of fear of being hurt or taken advantage of.
6. Tendency to be easily offended and quick to anger; defensiveness is common.
7. A pattern of being suspicious of the loyalty or fidelity of spouse or significant other without reason.
8. Level of mistrust is obsessional to the point of disrupting daily functioning.

—. ____

____

—. ____

____

—. ____

____

LONG-TERM GOALS

1. Show more trust in others by speaking positively of them and reporting comfort in socializing.
2. Interact with others without defensiveness or anger.

3. Verbalize trust of significant other and eliminate accusations of disloyalty.
4. Report reduced vigilance and suspicion around others as well as more relaxed, trusting, and open interaction.
5. Concentrate on important matters without interference from suspicious obsessions.
6. Function appropriately at work, in social activities, and in the community with only minimal interference from distrustful obsessions.

__. ____

____

__. ____

____

__. ____

____

SHORT-TERM OBJECTIVES

1. Demonstrate a level of trust with therapist by disclosing feelings and beliefs. (1, 2)
2. Identify those people or agencies that are distrusted and why. (3, 4)
3. Identify feelings of vulnerability. (5, 6, 7)

THERAPEUTIC INTERVENTIONS

1. Actively build level of trust with the client through consistent eye contact, active listening, unconditional positive regard, and warm acceptance to help increase his/her ability to identify and express feelings.
2. Demonstrate a calm, tolerant demeanor in sessions to decrease the client's fear of others.
3. Explore the nature and extent of the client's paranoia, probing for delusional components.
4. Explore the client's basis for fears; assess his/her degree of irrationality and ability to acknowledge that he/she is thinking irrationally.
5. Probe the client's fears of personal inadequacy and vulnerability.

6. Interpret the client's fears of his/her own anger as the basis for his/her mistrust of others.

7. Explore historical sources of the client's feelings of vulnerability in family-of-origin experiences.

4. Identify and replace core belief that others are untrustworthy and malicious. (4, 8)

4. Explore the client's basis for fears; assess his/her degree of irrationality and ability to acknowledge that he/she is thinking irrationally.

8. Review the client's social interactions and explore his/her distorted cognitive beliefs operative during interactions; replace those core beliefs that are distorted and that trigger paranoid feelings.

5. Comply with a psychiatric evaluation and take psychotropic medication prescribed. (9, 10, 11)

9. Assess the necessity of the use of antipsychotic medication to counteract the client's altered thought processes (see Psychoticism chapter in this *Planner*).

10. Arrange for the client to be evaluated by a physician for a psychotropic medication prescription.

11. Monitor the client's psychotropic medication prescription for compliance, effectiveness, and side effects; report to the prescribing physician and confront the client if he/she is not taking medication as prescribed.

6. Complete a psychological evaluation to assess the depth of paranoia. (12)

12. Arrange for a psychological evaluation to assess the client for possible psychotic process; give feedback as to results.

7. Comply with a neuropsychological evaluation to rule out the possibility of organic etiology. (13)

13. Refer the client for or perform neuropsychological evaluation; if organic factors are found refer him/her to a neurologist for consultation.

8. Acknowledge that the belief about others being threatening is based more on subjective interpretation than on objective data. (4, 8, 14, 15)

4. Explore the client's basis for fears; assess his/her degree of irrationality and ability to acknowledge that he/she is thinking irrationally.

8. Review the client's social interactions and explore his/her distorted cognitive beliefs operative during interactions; replace those core beliefs that are distorted and that trigger paranoid feelings.

14. Assist the client in seeing the pattern of distrusting others as being related to his/her own fears of inadequacy.

15. Ask the client to complete a cost-benefit analysis (see *The Feeling Good Handbook* by Burns) around his/her specific fears; process the exercise.

9. Verbalize trust in significant other and feel relaxed when not in his/her presence. (16, 17)

16. Conduct conjoint sessions to assess and reinforce the client's verbalizations of trust toward significant other.

17. Provide alternative explanations for significant other's behavior that counters the client's pattern of assumption of other's malicious intent.

10. Increase social interaction without fear or suspicion being reported. (18, 19)

18. Encourage the client to check out his/her beliefs regarding others by assertively verifying conclusions with others.

19. Use role-playing, behavioral rehearsal, and role reversal to increase the client's empathy for others and his/her understanding of the impact that his/her distrustful, defensive behavior has on others.

__. ______________________ __. ______________________

______________________ ______________________

__. ______________________ __. ______________________

______________________ ______________________

__. ______________________ __. ______________________

______________________ ______________________

DIAGNOSTIC SUGGESTIONS

Axis I:	300.23	Social Phobia
	310.1	Personality Change Due to Axis III Disorder
	295.30	Schizophrenia, Paranoid Type
	297.1	Delusional Disorder
	______	______________________
	______	______________________
Axis II:	301.0	Paranoid Personality Disorder
	310.22	Schizotypal Personality Disorder
	______	______________________
	______	______________________

PARENTING

BEHAVIORAL DEFINITIONS

1. Express feelings of inadequacy in setting effective limits with their child.
2. Report difficulty in managing the challenging problem behavior of their child.
3. Frequently struggle to control their emotional reactions to their child's misbehavior.
4. Exhibit increasing conflict between spouses over how to parent/discipline their child.
5. Demonstrate a pattern of lax supervision and inadequate limit setting.
6. Regularly overindulge their child's wishes and demands.
7. Display a pattern of harsh, rigid, and demeaning behavior toward their child.
8. Show a pattern of physically and emotionally abusive parenting.
9. Lack knowledge regarding reasonable expectations for a child's behavior at a given developmental level.
10. Have exhausted their ideas and resources in attempting to deal with their child's behavior.

—. ____

____

—. ____

____

—. ____

____

LONG-TERM GOALS

1. Achieve a level of competent, effective parenting.
2. Effectively manage challenging problem behavior of the child.

3. Reach a realistic view and approach to parenting, given the child's developmental level.
4. Terminate ineffective and/or abusive parenting and implement positive, effective techniques.
5. Strengthen the parental team by resolving marital conflicts.
6. Achieve a level of greater family connectedness.

—. ____

____

—. ____

____

—. ____

____

SHORT-TERM OBJECTIVES

1. Provide information on the marital relationship, child behavior expectations, and style of parenting. (1)
2. Identify specific marital conflicts and work toward their resolution. (2, 3)
3. Complete recommended evaluation instruments and receive the results. (4, 5, 6)

THERAPEUTIC INTERVENTIONS

1. Engage the parents through the use of empathy and normalization of their struggles with parenting and obtain information on their marital relationship, child behavior expectations, and parenting style.
2. Analyze the data received from the parents about their relationship and parenting and establish or rule out the presence of marital conflicts.
3. Conduct or refer the parents to marital/relationship therapy to resolve the conflicts that are preventing them from being effective parents.
4. Administer or arrange for the parents to complete assessment instruments to evaluate their parenting strengths and weaknesses (e.g., the Parenting Stress Index [PSI] or the Parent-Child Relationship Inventory [PCRI]).

5. Share results of assessment instruments with the parents and identify issues to begin working on to strengthen the parenting team.
6. Use testing results to identify parental strengths and begin to build the confidence and effectiveness level of the parental team.

4. Express feelings of frustration, helplessness, and inadequacy that each experiences in the parenting role. (7, 8, 9)

7. Create a compassionate, empathetic environment where the parents become comfortable enough to let their guard down and express the frustrations of parenting.
8. Educate the parents on the full scope of parenting by using humor and normalization.
9. Help the parents reduce their unrealistic expectations of their parenting performance.

5. Identify unresolved childhood issues that affect parenting and work toward their resolution. (10, 11)

10. Explore each parent's story of his/her childhood to identify any unresolved issues that are present and to identify how these issues are now affecting the ability to effectively parent.
11. Assist the parents in working through issues from childhood that are unresolved.

6. Decrease reactivity to the child's behaviors. (12, 13, 14)

12. Evaluate the level of the parental team's reactivity to the child's behavior and then help them to learn to respond in a more modulated, thoughtful, planned manner.
13. Help the parents become aware of the "hot buttons" they have that the child can push to get a quick negative response and how this overreactive response reduces their effectiveness as parents.
14. Role-play reactive situations with the parents to help them learn to

thoughtfully respond instead of automatically reacting to their child's demands or negative behaviors.

7. Identify the child's personality/temperament type that causes challenges and develop specific strategies to more effectively deal with that personality/temperament type. (15, 16, 17)

15. Have the parents read *The Challenging Child* (Greenspan) and then identify which type of difficult behavior pattern their child exhibits; encourage implementation of several of the parenting methods suggested for that type of child.

16. Expand the parents' repertoire of intervention options by having them read material on parenting difficult children (e.g., *The Difficult Child* by Turecki and Tonner; *The Explosive Child* by Greene; *How to Handle a Hard-to-Handle Kid* by Edwards).

17. Support, empower, monitor, and encourage the parents in implementing new strategies for parenting their child, giving feedback and redirection as needed.

EBT 8. Verbalize an understanding of the impact of their reaction on their child's behavior. (18, 19)

18. Use a Parent Management Training approach beginning with teaching the parents how parent and child behavioral interactions can encourage or discourage positive or negative behavior and that changing key elements of those interactions (e.g., prompting and reinforcing positive behaviors) can be used to promote positive change (e.g., *Parenting the Strong-willed Child* by Forehand and Long). EBT

EBT indicates that the Objective/Intervention is consistent with those found in evidence-based treatments.

19. Teach the parents how to specifically define and identify problem behaviors, identify their reactions to the behavior, determine whether the reaction encourages or discourages the behavior; generate alternative constructive reactive behaviors. ▽

▽ 9. Implement parenting practices that have been proven to be effective. (20, 21, 22)

20. Teach the parents how to implement key parenting practices consistently, including establishing realistic age-appropriate rules for acceptable and unacceptable behavior, prompting of positive behavior in the environment, use of positive reinforcement to encourage behavior (e.g., praise), use of clear direct instruction, time out and other loss-of-privilege practices for problem behavior, negotiation, and renegotiation (usually with older children and adolescents). ▽

21. Assign the parents home exercises in which they implement and record results of implementation exercises; review in session, providing corrective feedback toward improved, appropriate, and consistent use of skills. ▽

22. Ask the parents to read parent-training manuals (e.g., *Parenting through Change* by Forgatch) or watch videotapes demonstrating effective parenting techniques (see Webster-Stratton, 1994). ▽

10. Verbalize a sense of increased skill, effectiveness, and confidence in parenting. (17, 23, 24, 25)

17. Support, empower, monitor, and encourage the parents in implementing new strategies for parenting their child, giving feedback and redirection as needed.

23. Train the parents or refer them to structured training in effective parenting methods (e.g., *1-2-3 Magic* by Phelan; *Parenting with Love and Logic* by Cline and Fay).
24. Educate the parents on the numerous key differences between boys and girls, such as rate of development, perspectives, impulse control, and anger, and how to handle these differences in the parenting process.
25. Have the children complete the "Parent Report Card" (Berg-Gross) and then give feedback to the parents; support areas of parenting strength and identify weaknesses that need to be bolstered.

11. Partners express verbal support of each other in the parenting process. (26, 27)

26. Assist the parental team in identifying areas of parenting weaknesses; help the parents improve their skills and boost their confidence and follow-through.
27. Help the parents identify and implement specific ways they can support each other as parents and in realizing the ways children work to keep the parents from cooperating in order to get their way.

12. Decrease outside pressures, demands, and distractions that drain energy and time from the family. (28, 29)

28. Give the parents permission to not involve their child and themselves in too numerous activities, organizations, or sports.
29. Ask the parents to provide a weekly schedule of their entire family's activities and then evaluate the schedule with them, looking for which activities are valuable and which can possibly be eliminated to create a more focused and relaxed time to parent.

13. Develop skills to talk openly and effectively with the children. (30, 31)

30. Use modeling and role-play to teach the parents to listen more than talk to their child and to use open-ended questions that encourage openness, sharing, and ongoing dialogue.

31. Ask the parents to read material on parent-child communication (e.g., *How to Talk So Kids Will Listen and Listen So Kids Will Talk* by Faber and Mazlish; *Parent Effectiveness Training* by Gordon); help them implement the new communication style in daily dialogue with their children and to see the positive responses each child had to it.

14. Parents verbalize a termination of their perfectionist expectations of the child. (32, 33)

32. Point out to the parents any unreasonable and perfectionist expectations of their child they hold and help them to modify these expectations.

33. Help the parents identify the negative consequences/outcomes that perfectionist expectations have on a child and on the relationship between the parents and the child.

15. Verbalize an increased awareness and understanding of the unique issues and trials of parenting adolescents. (34, 35, 36)

34. Provide the parents with a balanced view of the impact that adolescent peers have on their child.

35. Teach the parents the concept that adolescence is a time in which the parents need to "ride the adolescent rapids" (see *Turning Points* by Pittman; *Preparing for Adolescence: How to Survive the Coming Years of Change* by Dobson) until both survive.

36. Assist the parents in coping with the issues and reducing their fears regarding negative peer groups, negative peer influences, and losing their influence to these groups.

16. Increase the gradual letting go of their adolescent in constructive, affirmative ways. (37)

37. Guide the parents in identifying and implementing constructive, affirmative ways they can allow and support the healthy separation of their adolescent.

17. Parents and child report an increased feeling of connectedness between them. (38, 39)

38. Assist the parents in removing and resolving any barriers that prevent or limit connectedness between family members and in identifying activities that will promote connectedness (e.g., games, one-to-one time).

39. Plant the thought with the parents that just "hanging out at home" or being around/available is what quality time is about.

—. ______________________________

—. ______________________________

—. ______________________________

—. ______________________________

—. ______________________________

—. ______________________________

DIAGNOSTIC SUGGESTIONS

Axis I:	309.3	Adjustment Disorder With Disturbance of Conduct
	309.4	Adjustment Disorder With Mixed Disturbances of Emotions and Conduct
	V61.21	Neglect of Child
	V61.20	Parent-Child Relational Problem
	V61.10	Partner Relational Problem
	V61.21	Physical Abuse of Child
	V61.21	Sexual Abuse of Child

	313.81	Oppositional Defiant Disorder
	312.9	Disruptive Behavior Disorder NOS
	312.8	Conduct Disorder, Adolescent-Onset Type
	314.01	Attention-Deficit/Hyperactivity Disorder, Combined Type
	_______	____________________
	_______	____________________
Axis II:	301.7	Antisocial Personality Disorder
	301.6	Dependent Personality Disorder
	301.81	Narcissistic Personality Disorder
	799.9	Diagnosis Deferred
	V71.09	No Diagnosis on Axis II
	_______	____________________
	_______	____________________

PHASE OF LIFE PROBLEMS

BEHAVIORAL DEFINITIONS

1. Difficulty adjusting to the accountability and interdependence of a new marriage.
2. Anxiety and depression related to the demands of being a new parent.
3. Grief related to children emancipating from the family ("empty nest stress").
4. Restlessness and feelings of lost identity and meaning due to retirement.
5. Feelings of isolation, sadness, and boredom related to quitting employment to be a full-time homemaker and parent.
6. Frustration and anxiety related to providing oversight and caretaking to an aging, ailing, and dependent parent.

—. ____

____

—. ____

____

—. ____

____

LONG-TERM GOALS

1. Resolve conflicted feelings and adapt to the new life circumstances.
2. Reorient life view to recognize the advantages of the current situation.
3. Find satisfaction in serving, nurturing, and supporting significant others who are dependent and needy.
4. Balance life activities between consideration of others and development of own interests.

__. ____

____

__. ____

____

__. ____

____

SHORT-TERM OBJECTIVES

1. Describe the circumstances of life that are contributing to stress, anxiety, or lack of fulfillment. (1, 2, 3)

THERAPEUTIC INTERVENTIONS

1. Explore the client's current life circumstances that are causing frustration, anxiety, depression, or lack of fulfillment.
2. Assign the client to write a list of those circumstances that are causing concern and how or why each is contributing to his/her dissatisfaction.
3. Assist the client in listing those desirable things that are missing from his/her life that could increase his/her sense of fulfillment.

2. Identify values that guide life's decisions and determine fulfillment. (4, 5)

4. Assist the client in clarifying and prioritizing his/her values.
5. Assign the client to read books on values clarification (e.g., *Values Clarification* by Simon, Howe, and Kirschenbaum; *In Search of Values: 31 Strategies for Finding Out What Really Matters Most to You* by Simon); process the content and list values that he/she holds as important.

3. Implement new activities that increase a sense of satisfaction. (6, 7)

6. Develop a plan with the client to include activities that will increase his/her satisfaction, fulfill his/her values, and improve the quality of his/her life.

7. Review the client's attempts to modify his/her life to include self-satisfying activities; reinforce success and redirect for failure.

4. Identify and implement changes that will reduce feelings of being overwhelmed by caretaking responsibilities. (8, 9)

8. Brainstorm with the client possible sources of support or respite (e.g., parent support group, engaging spouse in more child care, respite care for elderly parent, sharing parent-care responsibilities with a sibling, utilizing home health-care resources, taking a parenting class) from the responsibilities that are overwhelming him/her.

9. Encourage the client to implement the changes that will reduce the burden of responsibility felt; monitor progress, reinforcing success and redirecting for failure.

5. Implement increased assertiveness to take control of conflicts. (10, 11, 12)

10. Use role-playing, modeling, and behavior rehearsal to teach the client assertiveness skills that can be applied to reducing conflict or dissatisfaction.

11. Refer the client to an assertiveness training class.

12. Encourage the client to read books on assertiveness and boundary setting (e.g., *Asserting Yourself* by Bower and Bower; *When I Say No, I Feel Guilty* by Smith; *Your Perfect Right* by Alberti and Emmons; *Boundaries: Where You End and I Begin* by Katherine); process the content and its application to the client's daily life.

6. Apply problem-solving skills to current circumstances. (13, 14)

13. Teach the client problem-resolution skills (e.g., defining the problem clearly, brainstorming multiple solutions, listing the pros

and cons of each solution, seeking input from others, selecting and implementing a plan of action, evaluating outcome, and readjusting plan as necessary).

14. Use modeling and role-playing with the client to apply the problem-solving approach to his/her current circumstances; encourage implementation of action plan, reinforcing success and redirecting for failure.

7. Increase communication with significant others regarding current life stress factors. (15, 16)

15. Teach the client communication skills (e.g., "I messages," active listening, eye contact) to apply to his/her current life stress factors.

16. Invite the client's partner and/or other family members for conjoint sessions to address the client's concerns; encourage open communication and group problem solving.

8. Identify five advantages of current life situation. (17)

17. Assist the client in identifying at least five advantages to his/her current life circumstance that may have been overlooked or discounted (e.g., opportunity to make own decisions, opportunity for intimacy and sharing with a partner, a time for developing personal interests or meeting the needs of a significant other).

9. Implement changes in time and effort allocation to restore balance to life. (18)

18. Assist the client in identifying areas of life that need modification in order to restore balance in his/her life (e.g., adequate exercise, proper nutrition and sleep, socialization and reaction activities, spiritual development, conjoint activities with partner as well as individual activities and interests, service to others as well as self-indulgence); develop a plan of implementation.

10. Increase activities that reinforce a positive self-identity. (19, 20)

19. Assist the client in clarifying his/her identity and meaning in life by listing his/her strengths, positive traits and talents, potential ways to contribute to society, and areas of interest and ability that have not yet been developed.

20. Develop an action plan with the client to increase activities that give meaning and expand his/her sense of identity at a time of transition in life phases (e.g., single to married, employed to homemaker, childless to parent, employed to retired); monitor implementation.

11. Increase social contacts to reduce sense of isolation. (21, 22)

21. Explore opportunities for the client to overcome his/her sense of isolation (e.g., joining a community recreational or educational group, becoming active in church or synagogue activities, taking formal education classes, enrolling in an exercise group, joining a hobby support group); encourage implementation of these activities.

22. Use role-playing and modeling to teach the client social skills needed to reach out to build new relationships (e.g., starting conversations, introducing self, asking questions of others about themselves, smiling and being friendly, inviting new acquaintances to his/her home, initiating a social engagement or activity with a new acquaintance).

12. Share emotional struggles related to current adjustment stress. (23, 24)

23. Explore the client's feelings, coping mechanisms, and support system as he/she tries to adjust to the current life stress factors; assess for depth of depression, anxiety, or grief and recommend treatment focused on these

problems if warranted (see Depression, Anxiety, and Grief chapters in this *Planner*).

24. Assess the client for suicide potential if feelings of depression, helplessness, and isolation are present; initiate suicide prevention precautions, if necessary (see Suicidal Ideation chapter in this *Planner*).

13. Significant others offer support to reduce the client's stress. (25)

25. Hold family therapy sessions in which significant others are given the opportunity to support the client and offer suggestions for reducing his/her stress; challenge the client to share his/her needs assertively and challenge significant others to take responsibility for support (e.g., partner to increasing parenting involvement, partner to support the client's need for affirmation and stimulation outside the home, family members to take more responsibility for elderly parent's care).

__. ____________________

__. ____________________

__. ____________________

__. ____________________

__. ____________________

__. ____________________

DIAGNOSTIC SUGGESTIONS

Axis I:	V62.89	Phase of Life Problem
	313.82	Identity Problem
	V61.1	Partner Relational Problem
	V61.20	Parent-Child Relational Problem
	309.0	Adjustment Disorder With Depressed Mood

	309.28	Adjustment Disorder With Mixed Anxiety and Depressed Mood
	309.24	Adjustment Disorder With Anxiety
	_______	___________________________
	_______	___________________________
Axis II:	799.9	Diagnosis Deferred
	V71.09	No Diagnosis
	_______	___________________________
	_______	___________________________

PHOBIA

BEHAVIORAL DEFINITIONS

1. Describes a persistent and unreasonable fear of a specific object or situation that promotes avoidance behaviors because an encounter with the phobic stimulus provokes an immediate anxiety response.
2. Avoids the phobic stimulus/feared environment or endures it with distress, resulting in interference of normal routines.
3. Acknowledges a persistence of fear despite recognition that the fear is unreasonable.
4. Demonstrates no evidence of a panic disorder.

—. ____

____

—. ____

____

—. ____

____

LONG-TERM GOALS

1. Reduce fear of the specific stimulus object or situation that previously provoked phobic anxiety.
2. Reduce phobic avoidance of the specific object or situation, leading to comfort and independence in moving around in public environment.
3. Eliminate interference in normal routines and remove distress from feared object or situation.

—. ____

____

—. ____

___ . ____

SHORT-TERM OBJECTIVES

1. Describe the history and nature of the phobia(s), complete with impact on functioning and attempt to overcome it. (1, 2)

2. Complete psychological tests designed to assess features of the phobia. (3)

3. Cooperate with an evaluation by a physician for psychotropic medication. (4, 5) (EB)

THERAPEUTIC INTERVENTIONS

1. Explore and identify the objects or situations that precipitate the client's phobic fear.

2. Assess the client's fear and avoidance, including the focus of fear, types of avoidance (e.g., distraction, escape, dependence on others), development, and disability (e.g., *The Anxiety Disorders Interview Schedule for the DSM-IV* by DiNardo, Brown, and Barlow).

3. Administer a client-report measure (e.g., from *Measures for Specific Phobia* by Antony) to further assess the depth and breadth of phobic responses.

4. Arrange for an evaluation for a prescription of psychotropic medications if the client requests it or if the client is likely to be noncompliant with gradual exposure. (EB)

5. Monitor the client for prescription compliance, side effects, and overall effectiveness of the medication; consult with the prescribing physician at regular intervals. (EB)

(EB) indicates that the Objective/Intervention is consistent with those found in evidence-based treatments.

4. Verbalize an accurate understanding of information about phobias and their treatment. (6, 7, 8)

6. Discuss how phobias are very common, a natural but irrational expression of our fight or flight response, are not a sign of weakness, but cause unnecessary distress and disability.

7. Discuss how phobic fear is maintained by a "phobic cycle" of unwarranted fear and avoidance that precludes positive, corrective experiences with the feared object or situation, and how treatment breaks the cycle by encouraging these experiences (see *Mastery of Your Specific Phobia—Therapist Guide* by Craske, Antony and Barlow; *Specific Phobias* by Bruce and Sanderson).

8. Assign the client to read psychoeducational chapters of books or treatment manuals on specific phobias (e.g., *Mastery of Your Specific Phobia—Client Manual* by Antony, Craske, and Barlow; *The Anxiety and Phobia Workbook* by Bourne; *Living with Fear* by Marks).

5. Verbalize an understanding of the cognitive, physiological, and behavioral components of anxiety and its treatment. (9, 10)

9. Discuss how phobias involve perceiving unrealistic threats, bodily expressions of fear, and avoidance of what is threatening that interact to maintain the problem (see *Mastery of Your Specific Phobia—Therapist Guide* by Craske, Antony, and Barlow; *Specific Phobias* by Bruce and Sanderson).

10. Discuss how exposure serves as an arena to desensitize learned fear, build confidence, and feel safer by building a new history of success experiences (see *Mastery of Your Specific Phobia—Therapist Guide* by Craske, Antony, and Barlow; *Specific Phobias* by Bruce and Sanderson).

6. Learn and implement calming skills to reduce and manage anxiety symptoms that may emerge during encounters with phobic objects or situations. (11, 12, 13)

11. Teach the client anxiety management skills (e.g., staying focused on behavioral goals, muscular relaxation, evenly paced diaphragmatic breathing, positive self-talk) to address anxiety symptoms that may emerge during encounters with phobic objects or situations.

12. Assign the client a homework exercise in which he/she practices daily calming skills; review and reinforce success, providing corrective feedback for failure.

13. Use biofeedback techniques to facilitate the client's success at learning calming skills.

7. Learn and implement applied tension skills. (14, 15)

14. Teach the client applied tension in which he/she tenses neck and upper torso muscles to curtail blood flow out of the brain to help prevent fainting during encounters with phobic objects or situations involving blood, injection, or injury (see "Applied tension, exposure in vivo, and tension-only in the treatment of blood phobia" in *Behaviour Research and Therapy* by Ost, Fellenius, and Sterner).

15. Assign the client a homework exercise in which he/she practices daily applied tension skills; review and reinforce success, providing corrective feedback for failure. ▽

▽ 8. Identify, challenge, and replace biased, fearful self-talk with positive, realistic, and empowering self-talk. (16, 17, 18)

16. Explore the client's schema and self-talk that mediate his/her fear response; challenge the biases; assist him/her in replacing the distorted messages with reality-based, positive self-talk. ▽

17. Assign the client a homework exercise in which he/she identifies fearful self-talk and creates reality-based alternatives (or assign "Journal and Replace Self-Defeating Thoughts" in *Adult Psychotherapy Homework Planner,* 2nd ed. by Jongsma); review and reinforce success, providing corrective feedback for failure. ▽

18. Use behavioral techniques (e.g., modeling, corrective feedback, imaginal rehearsal, social reinforcement) to train the client in positive self-talk that prepares him/her to endure anxiety symptoms without serious consequences. ▽

▽ 9. Undergo repeated exposure to feared or avoided phobic objects or situations. (19, 20, 21)

19. Direct and assist the client in construction of a hierarchy of anxiety-producing situations associated with the phobic response. ▽

20. Select initial exposures that have a high likelihood of being a successful experience for the client; develop a plan for managing the symptoms and rehearse the plan. ▽

21. Assign the client a homework exercise in which he/she does situational exposures and records responses (see "Gradually Reducing Your Phobic Fear" in *Adult Psychotherapy Homework Planner,* 2nd ed. by Jongsma; *Mastery of Your Specific Phobia—Client Manual* by Antony, Craske, and Barlow; *Living with Fear* by Marks); review and reinforce success or provide corrective feedback toward improvement. ▼

▼10. Implement relapse prevention strategies for managing possible future anxiety symptoms. (22, 23, 24, 25)

22. Discuss with the client the distinction between a lapse and relapse, associating a lapse with a temporary and reversible return of symptoms, fear, or urges to avoid and relapse with the decision to return to fearful and avoidant patterns. ▼

23. Identify and rehearse with the client the management of future situations or circumstances in which lapses could occur. ▼

24. Instruct the client to routinely use strategies learned in therapy (e.g., cognitive restructuring, exposure), building them into his/her life as much as possible. ▼

25. Develop a "coping card" on which coping strategies and other important information (e.g., "You're safe," "Pace your breathing," "Focus on the task at hand," "You can manage it," "Stay in the situation," and "Let the anxiety pass") are written for the client's later use. ▼

11. Verbalize the costs and benefits of remaining fearful and avoidant. (26)

12. Verbalize the separate realities of the irrationally feared object or situation and the emotionally painful experience from the past that has been evoked by the phobic stimulus. (27, 28)

13. Commit self to not allowing phobic fear to take control of life and lead to a consistent avoidance of normal responsibilities and activities. (29, 30)

14. Return for a follow-up session to track progress, reinforce gains, and problem-solve barriers. (31)

__. ______________________________

__. ______________________________

__. ______________________________

26. Probe for the presence of secondary gain that reinforces the client's phobic actions through escape or avoidance mechanisms.

27. Clarify and differentiate between the client's current irrational fear and past emotional pain.

28. Encourage the client's sharing of feelings associated with past traumas through active listening, positive regard, and questioning.

29. Support the client in following through with work, family, and social activities rather than escaping or avoiding them.

30. Ask the client to list several ways his/her life will be more satisfying or fulfilling as he/she manages his/her symptoms of panic and continues normal responsibilities.

31. Schedule a "booster session" for the client for 1 to 3 months after therapy ends.

__. ______________________________

__. ______________________________

__. ______________________________

DIAGNOSTIC SUGGESTION

Axis I: 300.29 Specific Phobia

______ ______________________________

______ ______________________________

POSTTRAUMATIC STRESS DISORDER (PTSD)

BEHAVIORAL DEFINITIONS

SYMPTOMS

1. Exposure to actual or threatened death or serious injury that resulted in an intense emotional response of fear, helplessness, or horror.
2. Intrusive, distressing thoughts or images that recall the traumatic event.
3. Disturbing dreams associated with the traumatic event.
4. A sense that the event is reoccurring, as in illusions or flashbacks.
5. Intense distress when exposed to reminders of the traumatic event.
6. Physiological reactivity when exposed to internal or external cues that symbolize the traumatic event.
7. Avoidance of thoughts, feelings, or conversations about the traumatic event.
8. Avoidance of activity, places, or people associated with the traumatic event.
9. Inability to recall some important aspect of the traumatic event.
10. Lack of interest and participation in significant activities.
11. A sense of detachment from others.
12. Inability to experience the full range of emotions, including love.
13. A pessimistic, fatalistic attitude regarding the future.
14. Sleep disturbance.
15. Irritability.
16. Lack of concentration.
17. Hypervigilance.
18. Exaggerated startle response.
19. Sad or guilty affect and other signs of depression.
20. Alcohol and/or drug abuse.
21. Suicidal thoughts.
22. A pattern of interpersonal conflict, especially in intimate relationships.
23. Verbally and/or physically violent threats of behavior.
24. Inability to maintain employment due to supervisor/coworker conflict of anxiety symptoms.
25. Symptoms have been present for more than 1 month.

—. ____

____

—. ____

____

—. ____

____

LONG-TERM GOALS

1. Reduce the negative impact that the traumatic event has had on many aspects of life and return to the pre-trauma level of functioning.
2. Develop and implement effective coping skills to carry out normal responsibilities and participate constructively in relationships.
3. Recall the traumatic event without becoming overwhelmed with negative thoughts, feelings, or urges.
4. Terminate the destructive behaviors that serve to maintain escape and denial while implementing behaviors that promote healing, acceptance of the past events, and responsible living.

—. ____

____

—. ____

____

—. ____

____

SHORT-TERM OBJECTIVES

1. Describe the history and nature of PTSD symptoms. (1, 2)

THERAPEUTIC INTERVENTIONS

1. Establish rapport with the client toward building a therapeutic alliance.
2. Assess the client's frequency, intensity, duration, and history of PTSD symptoms and their impact on functioning (or assign "How the Trauma Affects Me" in *Adult Psychotherapy Homework Planner,* 2nd ed. by Jongsma; see also

The Anxiety Disorders Interview Schedule for the DSM-IV by DiNardo, Brown, and Barlow).

2. Complete psychological tests designed to assess and or track the nature and severity of PTSD symptoms. (3)

3. Administer or refer the client for administration of psychological testing to assess for the presence of strength of PTSD symptoms (e.g., Minnesota Multiphasic Personality Inventory–2 [MMPI-2], Impact of Events Scale, PTSD Symptom Scale, or Mississippi Scale for Combat Related PTSD).

3. Describe the traumatic event in as much detail as possible. (4)

4. Gently and sensitively explore the client's recollection of the facts of the traumatic incident and his/her emotional reactions at the time (or assign "Share the Painful Memory" in *Adult Psychotherapy Homework Planner,* 2nd ed. by Jongsma).

4. Verbalize the symptoms of depression, including any suicidal ideation. (5)

5. Assess the client's depth of depression and suicide potential and treat appropriately, taking the necessary safety precautions as indicated (see Depression and Suicidal Ideation chapters in this *Planner*).

5. Provide honest and complete information for a chemical dependence biopsychosocial history. (6, 7, 8)

6. Assess the client for the presence of chemical dependence associated with the trauma.

7. Use the biopsychosocial history to help the client understand the familial, emotional, and social factors that contributed to the development of chemical dependence.

8. Refer the client for treatment for chemical dependence (see Chemical Dependence chapter in this *Planner*).

EB 6. Cooperate with an evaluation by a physician for psychotropic medication. (9, 10)

9. Assess the client's need for medication (e.g., selective serotonin reuptake inhibitors) and arrange for prescription if appropriate. EB

10. Monitor and evaluate the client's psychotropic medication prescription compliance and the effectiveness of the medication on his/her level of functioning. EB

EB 7. Verbalize an accurate understanding PTSD and how it develops. (11, 12)

11. Discuss how PTSD results from exposure to trauma, resulting in intrusive recollections, unwarranted fears, anxiety, and a vulnerability to other negative emotions such as shame, anger, and guilt. EB

12. Assign the client to read psychoeducational chapters of books or treatment manuals on PTSD that explain its features and development (e.g., *Coping with Trauma* by Allen). EB

EB 8. Verbalize an understanding of the rationale for treatment of PTSD. (13, 14)

13. Discuss how coping skills, cognitive restructuring, and exposure help build confidence, desensitize and overcome fears, and see one's self, others, and the world in a less fearful and/or depressing way. EB

14. Assign the client to read about stress inoculation, cognitive restructuring, and/or exposure-based therapy in chapters of books or treatment manuals on PTSD (e.g., *Reclaiming Your Life After Rape* by Rothbaum and Foa; *I Can't Get Over It* by Matsakis). EB

EB indicates that the Objective/Intervention is consistent with those found in evidence-based treatments.

9. Learn and implement calming and coping strategies to manage challenging situations related to trauma. (15, 16)

15. Teach the client strategies from stress inoculation training such as relaxation, breathing control, covert modeling (i.e., imagining the successful use of the strategies) and/or role-playing (i.e., with therapist or trusted other) for managing fears until a sense of mastery is evident (see *A Clinical Handbook for Treating PTSD* by Meichenbaum).

16. Explore the client's schema and self-talk that mediate trauma-related fears; challenge negative biases and assist him/her in generating appraisals that correct for the biases and build confidence.

10. Identify, challenge, and replace biased, fearful self-talk with reality-based, positive self-talk. (16, 17)

16. Explore the client's schema and self-talk that mediate trauma-related fears; challenge negative biases and assist him/her in generating appraisals that correct for the biases and build confidence.

17. Assign the client a homework exercise in which he/she identifies fearful self-talk and creates reality-based alternatives; review and reinforce success, providing corrective feedback for failure (see "Negative Thoughts Trigger Negative Feelings" in *Adult Psychotherapy Homework Planner,* 2nd ed. by Jongsma; *Reclaiming Your Life After Rape* by Rothbaum and Foa).

11. Participate in imaginal and in vivo exposure to trauma-related memories until talking or thinking about the trauma does not cause marked distress. (18, 19, 20)

18. Direct and assist the client in constructing a fear and avoidance hierarchy of feared and avoided trauma-related stimuli.

19. Assign the client a homework exercise in which he/she does an exposure exercise and records

responses (see "Gradually Reducing Your Phobic Fear" in *Adult Psychotherapy Homework Planner,* 2nd ed. by Jongsma; *Posttraumatic Stress Disorder* by Resick and Calhoun); review and reinforce progress, problem-solve obstacles.

20. Have the client undergo imaginal exposure to the trauma by having him/her describe a traumatic experience at an increasing but client-chosen level of detail; repeat until associated anxiety reduces and stabilizes. Record the session; have the client listen to it between sessions (see *Posttraumatic Stress Disorder* by Resick and Calhoun); review and reinforce progress, problem-solve obstacles.

12. Learn and implement thought stopping to manage intrusive unwanted thoughts. (21)

21. Teach the client thought-stopping in which he/she internally voices the word "Stop" and/or imagines something representing the concept of stopping (e.g., a stop sign or light) immediately upon noticing unwanted trauma or otherwise negative unwanted thoughts (or assign "Making Use of the Thought-Stopping Technique" in *Adult Psychotherapy Homework Planner,* 2nd ed. by Jongsma).

Pt. will

13. Learn and implement guided self-dialogue to manage thoughts, feelings, and urges brought on by encounters with trauma-related stimuli. (22)

22. Teach the client guided self-dialogue procedure in which he/she learns to recognize maladaptive self-talk, challenge its biases, cope with engendered feelings, overcome avoidance, and reinforce his/her accomplishments (see *Posttraumatic Stress Disorder* by Resick and Calhoun); review and reinforce progress, problem-solve obstacles.

14. Implement relapse prevention strategies for managing possible future trauma-related symptoms. (23, 24, 25, 26)

15. Cooperate with eye movement desensitization and reprocessing (EMDR) technique to reduce emotional reaction to the traumatic event. (27)

16. Acknowledge the need to implement anger control techniques; learn and implement anger management techniques. (28, 29)

23. Discuss with the client the distinction between a lapse and relapse, associating a lapse with an initial and reversible return of symptoms, fear, or urges to avoid and relapse with the decision to return to fearful and avoidant patterns.

24. Identify and rehearse with the client the management of future situations or circumstances in which lapses could occur.

25. Instruct the client to routinely use strategies learned in therapy (e.g., using cognitive restructuring, social skills, and exposure) while building social interactions and relationships.

26. Develop a "coping card" or other reminder on which coping strategies and other important information (e.g., "Pace your breathing," "Focus on the task at hand," "You can manage it," and "It will go away") are recorded for the client's later use.

27. Utilize EMDR technique to reduce the client's emotional reactivity to the traumatic event.

28. Assess the client for instances of poor anger management that have led to threats or actual violence that caused damage to property and/or injury to people.

29. Teach the client anger management techniques (see Anger Management chapter in this *Planner*).

17. Implement a regular exercise regimen as a stress release technique. (30, 31)

30. Develop and encourage a routine of physical exercise for the client.

31. Recommend that the client read and implement programs from *Exercising Your Way to Better Mental Health* (Leith).

18. Sleep without being disturbed by dreams of the trauma. (32)

32. Monitor the client's sleep pattern and encourage use of relaxation, positive imagery, and sleep hygiene as aids to sleep (see Sleep Disturbance chapter in this *Planner*).

19. Participate in conjoint and/or family therapy sessions. (33)

33. Conduct family and conjoint sessions to facilitate healing of hurt caused by the client's symptoms of PTSD.

20. Participate in group therapy sessions focused on PTSD. (34)

34. Refer the client to or conduct group therapy sessions where the focus is on sharing traumatic events and their effects with other PTSD survivors.

21. Verbalize an understanding of the negative impact PTSD has had on vocational functioning. (35)

35. Explore the client's vocational history and treat his/her vocational issues as appropriate (see Vocational Stress chapter in this *Planner*).

22. Verbalize hopeful and positive statements regarding the future. (36)

36. Reinforce the client's positive, reality-based cognitive messages that enhance self-confidence and increase adaptive action.

__. ____________________________

__. ____________________________

__. ____________________________

__. ____________________________

__. ____________________________

__. ____________________________

DIAGNOSTIC SUGGESTIONS

Axis I:	309.81	Posttraumatic Stress Disorder
	300.14	Dissociative Identity Disorder
	300.6	Depersonalization Disorder
	300.15	Dissociative Disorder NOS
	995.54	Physical Abuse of Child, Victim
	995.81	Physical Abuse of Adult, Victim
	995.53	Sexual Abuse of Child, Victim
	995.83	Sexual Abuse of Adult, Victim
	308.3	Acute Stress Disorder
	304.80	Polysubstance Dependence
	305.00	Alcohol Abuse
	303.90	Alcohol Dependence
	304.30	Cannabis Dependence
	304.20	Cocaine Dependence
	304.00	Opioid Dependence
	296.xx	Major Depressive Disorder
	______	____________________
	______	____________________
Axis II:	301.83	Borderline Personality Disorder
	301.9	Personality Disorder NOS
	______	____________________
	______	____________________

PSYCHOTICISM

BEHAVIORAL DEFINITIONS

1. Bizarre content of thought (delusions of grandeur, persecution, reference, influence, control, somatic sensations, or infidelity).
2. Illogical form of thought/speech (loose association of ideas in speech, incoherence; illogical thinking; vague, abstract, or repetitive speech; neologisms, perseverations, clanging).
3. Perception disturbance (auditory, visual, or olfactory hallucinations).
4. Disturbed affect (blunted, none, flattened, or inappropriate).
5. Lost sense of self (loss of ego boundaries, lack of identity, blatant confusion).
6. Volition diminished (inadequate interest, drive, or ability to follow a course of action to its logical conclusion; pronounced ambivalence or cessation of goal-directed activity).
7. Relationship withdrawal (withdrawal from involvement with external world and preoccupation with egocentric ideas and fantasies, alienation feelings).
8. Psychomotor abnormalities (marked decrease in reactivity to environment; various catatonic patterns such as stupor, rigidity, excitement, posturing, or negativism; unusual mannerisms or grimacing).
9. Extreme agitation, including a high degree of irritability, anger, unpredictability, or impulsive physical acting out.
10. Bizarre dress or grooming.

__. ____

____

__. ____

____

__. ____

____

LONG-TERM GOALS

1. Control or eliminate active psychotic symptoms so that supervised functioning is positive and medication is taken consistently.
2. Eliminate acute, reactive, psychotic symptoms and return to normal functioning in affect, thinking, and relating.
3. Increase goal-directed behaviors.
4. Focus thoughts on reality.
5. Normalize speech patterns, which can be evidenced by coherent statements, attentions to social cues, and remaining on task.

—. ____

____

—. ____

____

—. ____

____

SHORT-TERM OBJECTIVES

1. Describe the type and history of the psychotic symptoms. (1, 2, 3)
2. Client or significant other provides family history of serious mental illness. (4)
3. Accept and understand that distressing symptoms are due to mental illness. (5, 6)

THERAPEUTIC INTERVENTIONS

1. Demonstrate acceptance to the client through calm, nurturing manner; good eye contact; and active listening.
2. Assess the pervasiveness of the client's thought disorder through clinical interview and/or psychological testing.
3. Determine whether the client's psychosis is of a brief reactive nature or long-term with prodromal and reactive elements.
4. Explore the client's family history for serious mental illness.
5. Provide supportive therapy to alleviate the client's fears and reduce feelings of alienation.

6. Explain to the client the nature of the psychotic process, its biochemical components, and the confusing effect on rational thought.

4. Take antipsychotic medications consistently with or without supervision. (7, 8)

7. Refer the client for an immediate evaluation by a psychiatrist regarding his/her psychotic symptoms and a possible prescription for antipsychotic medication.

8. Monitor the client for psychotropic medication prescription compliance, effectiveness, and side effects; redirect if the client is noncompliant.

5. Accept the need for a supervised living environment. (9, 10)

9. Arrange for the client to remain in a stable, supervised situation (e.g., crisis adult foster care placement or a friend's/family member's home).

10. Make arrangements for involuntary commitment to an inpatient psychiatric facility if the client is assessed to be unable to care for his/her basic needs or is potentially harmful to himself/herself or others.

6. Describe recent perceived severe stressors that may have precipitated the acute psychotic break. (11, 12, 13)

11. Probe causes for the client's reactive psychosis.

12. Explore the client's feelings surrounding the stressors that triggered his/her psychotic episodes.

13. Assist the client in reducing threat in the environment (e.g., finding a safer place to live, arranging for regular visits from caseworker, arranging for family members to call more frequently).

7. Report diminishing or absence of hallucinations and/or delusions. (7, 8, 14, 15, 16)

7. Refer the client for an immediate evaluation by a psychiatrist regarding his/her psychotic symptoms and a possible prescription for antipsychotic medication.

8. Monitor the client for psychotropic medication prescription compliance, effectiveness, and side effects; redirect if the client is noncompliant.

14. Assist the client in restructuring his/her irrational beliefs by reviewing reality-based evidence and his/her misinterpretation.

15. Encourage the client to focus on the reality of the external world versus his/her distorted fantasy.

16. Differentiate for the client the source of stimuli between self-generated messages and the reality of the external world.

8. Begin to show limited social functioning by responding appropriately to friendly encounters. (14, 17)

14. Assist the client in restructuring his/her irrational beliefs by reviewing reality-based evidence and his/her misinterpretation.

17. Reinforce the client's socially and emotionally appropriate responses to others.

9. Think more clearly as demonstrated by logical, coherent speech. (7, 18, 19)

7. Refer the client for an immediate evaluation by a psychiatrist regarding his/her psychotic symptoms and a possible prescription for antipsychotic medication.

18. Gently confront the client's illogical thoughts and speech to refocus disordered thinking.

19. Reinforce the client's clarity and rationality of thought and speech.

10. Verbalize an understanding of the underlying needs, conflicts, and emotions that support the irrational beliefs. (14, 20)

14. Assist the client in restructuring his/her irrational beliefs by reviewing reality-based evidence and his/her misinterpretation.

20. Probe the client's underlying needs and feelings (e.g., inadequacy, rejection, anxiety, guilt) that trigger irrational thought.

11. Family members increase their positive support of the client to reduce changes of acute exacerbation of psychotic episodes. (21, 22)

21. Arrange family therapy sessions to educate regarding the client's illness, treatment, and prognosis.

22. Assist the family in avoiding double-bind messages that increase anxiety and psychotic symptoms in the client.

12. Family members share their feelings of guilt, frustration, and fear associated with the client's mental illness. (23, 24)

23. Encourage the family members to share their feelings of frustration, guilt, fear, or depression surrounding the client's mental illness and behavior patterns.

24. Refer the family members to a community-based support group designed for the families of psychotic patients.

13. Gradually return to premorbid level of functioning and accept responsibility of caring for own basic needs, including medication regimen. (8, 25)

8. Monitor the client for psychotropic medication prescription compliance, effectiveness, and side effects; redirect if the client is noncompliant.

25. Monitor the client's daily level of functioning (i.e., reality orientation, personal hygiene, social interactions, and affect appropriateness) and give feedback that either redirects or reinforces the client's progress.

__. ____________________________

__. ____________________________

__. ____________________________

__. ____________________________

__. ____________________________

__. ____________________________

DIAGNOSTIC SUGGESTIONS

Axis I:	297.1	Delusional Disorder
	298.8	Brief Psychotic Disorder

295.xx	Schizophrenia
295.30	Schizophrenia, Paranoid Type
295.70	Schizoaffective Disorder
295.40	Schizophreniform Disorder
296.xx	Bipolar I Disorder
296.89	Bipolar II Disorder
296.xx	Major Depressive Disorder
310.1	Personality Change Due to Axis III Disorder
________	________________________________
________	________________________________

SEXUAL ABUSE

BEHAVIORAL DEFINITIONS

1. Vague memories of inappropriate childhood sexual contact that can be corroborated by significant others.
2. Self-report of being sexually abused with clear, detailed memories.
3. Inability to recall years of childhood.
4. Extreme difficulty becoming intimate with others.
5. Inability to enjoy sexual contact with a desired partner.
6. Unexplainable feelings of anger, rage, or fear when coming into contact with a close family relative.
7. Pervasive pattern of promiscuity or the sexualization of relationships.

__. ____

____

__. ____

____

__. ____

____

LONG-TERM GOALS

1. Resolve the issue of being sexually abused with an increased capacity for intimacy in relationships.
2. Begin the healing process from sexual abuse with resultant enjoyment of appropriate sexual contact.
3. Work successfully through the issues related to being sexually abused with consequent understanding and control of feelings.
4. Recognize and accept the sexual abuse without inappropriate sexualization of relationships.
5. Establish whether sexual abuse occurred.

6. Begin the process of moving away from being a victim of sexual abuse and toward becoming a survivor of sexual abuse.

—. ____

____

—. ____

____

—. ____

____

SHORT-TERM OBJECTIVES

1. Tell the story of the nature, frequency, and duration of the abuse. (1, 2, 3)
2. Identify a support system of key individuals who will be encouraging and helpful in aiding the process of resolving the issue. (4, 5)
3. Verbalize an increased knowledge of sexual abuse and its effect. (6, 7)

THERAPEUTIC INTERVENTIONS

1. Actively build the level of trust with the client in individual sessions through consistent eye contact, unconditional positive regard, and warm acceptance to help increase his/her ability to identify and express feelings.
2. Gently explore the client's sexual abuse experience without pressing early for unnecessary details.
3. Ask the client to draw a diagram of the house in which he/she was raised, complete with where everyone slept.
4. Help the client identify those individuals who would be compassionate and encourage him/her to enlist their support.
5. Encourage the client to attend a support group for survivors of sexual abuse.
6. Assign the client to read material on sexual abuse (e.g., *The Courage to Heal* by Bass and Davis; *Betrayal of Innocence* by Forward and Buck; *Outgrowing the Pain* by Gil); process key concepts.

7. Assign and process a written exercise from *The Courage to Heal Workbook* (Davis).

4. Identify and express the feelings connected to the abuse. (8, 9)

8. Explore, encourage, and support the client in verbally expressing and clarifying feelings associated with the abuse.
9. Encourage the client to be open in talking of the abuse without shame or embarrassment as if he/she was responsible for the abuse.

5. Decrease the secrecy in the family by informing key non-abusive members regarding the abuse. (10, 11, 12)

10. Guide the client in an empty chair conversation exercise with a key figure connected to the abuse (e.g., perpetrator, sibling, parent) telling them of the sexual abuse and its effects.
11. Hold conjoint session where the client tells his/her spouse of the abuse.
12. Facilitate family session with the client, assisting and supporting him/her in revealing the abuse to parent(s).

6. Describe how sex abuse experience is part of a family pattern of broken boundaries through physical contact or verbal suggestiveness. (13)

13. Develop with the client a genogram and assist in illuminating key family patterns of broken boundaries related to sex and intimacy.

7. Verbalize the ways the sexual abuse has had an impact on life. (14, 15)

14. Ask the client to make a list of the ways sexual abuse has impacted his/her life; process the list content.
15. Develop with the client a symptom line connected to the abuse.

8. Clarify memories of the abuse. (16, 17)

16. Refer or conduct hypnosis with the client to further uncover or clarify the nature and extent of the abuse.

17. Facilitate the client's recall of the details of the abuse by asking him/her to keep a journal and talk and think about the incident(s). Caution him/her against embellishment based on book, video, or drama material, and be very careful not to lead the client into only confirming therapist-held suspicions.

9. Decrease statements of shame, being responsible for the abuse, or being a victim, while increasing statements that reflect personal empowerment. (18, 19, 20, 21)

18. Assign the client to read material on overcoming shame (e.g., *Healing the Shame That Binds You* by Bradshaw; *Shame* by Kaufman; *Facing Shame* by Fossum and Mason); process key concepts.

19. Encourage, support, and assist the client in identifying, expressing, and processing any feelings of guilt related to feelings of physical pleasure, emotional fulfillment, or responsibility connected with the events.

20. Confront and process with the client any statements that reflect taking responsibility for the abuse or indicating he/she is a victim; assist the client in feeling empowered by working through the issues and letting go of the abuse.

21. Assign the client to complete a cost-benefit exercise (see *Ten Days to Self- Esteem!* by Burns), or a similar exercise, on being a victim versus a survivor or on holding on versus forgiving; process completed exercises.

10. Identify the positive benefits for self of being able to forgive all those involved with the abuse. (22, 23, 24)

22. Read and process the story from *Stories for the Third Ear* (Wallas) titled "The Seedling" (a story for a client who has been abused as a child).

23. Assist the client in removing any barriers that prevent him/her from being able to identify the benefits of forgiving those responsible for the abuse.

24. Recommend that the client read *Forgive and Forget* (Smedes).

11. Express feelings to and about the perpetrator, including the impact the abuse has had both at the time of occurrence and currently. (25, 26, 27)

25. Assign the client to write an angry letter to the perpetrator; process the letter within the session.

26. Prepare the client for a face-to-face meeting with the perpetrator of the abuse by processing the feelings that arise around the event and role-playing the meeting.

27. Hold a conjoint session where the client confronts the perpetrator of the abuse; afterward, process his/her feelings and thoughts related to the experience.

12. Increase level of forgiveness of self, perpetrator, and others connected with the abuse. (28)

28. Assign the client to write a forgiveness letter and/or complete a forgiveness exercise (see *Forgiving* by Simon and Simon) and to process each with therapist.

13. Increase level of trust of others as shown by more socialization and greater intimacy tolerance. (29, 30)

29. Teach the client the share-check method of building trust in relationships (i.e., share only a little of self and then check to be sure that the shared data is treated respectfully, kindly, and confidentially; as proof of trustworthiness is verified, share more freely).

30. Use role-playing and modeling to teach the client how to establish reasonable personal boundaries that are neither too porous nor too restrictive.

14. Report increased ability to accept and initiate appropriate physical contact with others. (31, 32)

31. Encourage the client to give and receive appropriate touches; help him/her define what is appropriate.

32. Ask the client to practice one or two times a week initiating appropriate touching or a touching activity (i.e., giving a back rub to spouse, receiving a professional massage, hugging a friend, etc.).

15. Verbally identify self as a survivor of sexual abuse. (33, 34)

33. Reinforce with the client the benefits of seeing himself/herself as a survivor rather than the victim and work to remove any barriers that remain in the way of him/her doing so.

34. Give positive verbal reinforcement when the client identifies himself/herself as a survivor.

__. ______________________________

__. ______________________________

__. ______________________________

__. ______________________________

__. ______________________________

__. ______________________________

DIAGNOSTIC SUGGESTIONS

Axis I:	303.90	Alcohol Dependence
	304.80	Polysubstance Dependence
	300.4	Dysthymic Disorder
	296.xx	Major Depressive Disorder
	300.02	Generalized Anxiety Disorder
	300.14	Dissociative Identity Disorder
	300.15	Dissociative Disorder NOS
	995.53	Sexual Abuse of Child, Victim
	995.83	Sexual Abuse of Adult, Victim
	______	______________________
	______	______________________
Axis II:	301.82	Avoidant Personality Disorder
	301.6	Dependent Personality Disorder
	______	______________________
	______	______________________

SEXUAL IDENTITY CONFUSION—ADULT*

BEHAVIORAL DEFINITIONS

1. Uncertainty about basic sexual orientation.
2. Difficulty in enjoying sexual activities with opposite-sex partner because of low arousal.
3. Sexual fantasies and desires about same-sex partners, which causes distress.
4. Sexual activity with person of same sex that has caused confusion, guilt, and anxiety.
5. Depressed mood, diminished interest in activities.
6. Marital conflicts caused by uncertainty about sexual orientation.
7. Feelings of guilt, shame, and/or worthlessness.
8. Concealing sexual identity from significant others (e.g., friends, family, spouse).

__. ____

____

__. ____

____

__. ____

____

LONG-TERM GOALS

1. Identify sexual identity and engage in a wide range of relationships that are supportive of that identity.

---

*Most of the content of this chapter (with only slight revisions) originates from J. M. Evosevich and M. Avriette, *The Gay and Lesbian Psychotherapy Treatment Planner* (New York: John Wiley & Sons, 2000). Copyright © 2000 by J. M. Evosevich and M. Avriette. Reprinted with permission.

2. Reduce overall frequency and intensity of the anxiety associated with sexual identity so that daily functioning is not impaired.
3. Disclose sexual orientation to significant others.
4. Return to previous level of emotional, psychological, and social functioning.
5. Eliminate all feelings of depression (e.g., depressed mood, guilt, worthlessness).

—. ____

____

—. ____

____

—. ____

____

SHORT-TERM OBJECTIVES

1. Describe fear, anxiety, and distress about confusion over sexual identity. (1)
2. Identify sexual experiences that have been a source of excitement, satisfaction, and emotional gratification. (2, 3, 4, 5)

THERAPEUTIC INTERVENTIONS

1. Actively build trust with the client and encourage his/her expression of fear, anxiety, and distress over sexual identity confusion.
2. Assess the client's current sexual functioning by asking him/her about previous sexual history, fantasies, and thoughts.
3. Assist the client in identifying sexual experiences that have been a source of excitement, satisfaction, and emotional gratification.
4. To assist the client in increasing his/her awareness of sexual attractions and conflicts, assign him/her to write a journal describing sexual thoughts, fantasies, and conflicts that occur throughout the week.
5. Have the client rate his/her sexual attraction to both men and women on a scale of 1 to 10 (with 10 being extremely attracted and 1 being not at all attracted).

3. Verbalize an understanding of how cultural, racial, and/or ethnic identity factors contribute to confusion about sexual identity. (6)

    6. Explore with the client how cultural, racial, and/or ethnic factors contribute to confusion about homosexual behavior and/or identity.

4. Write a "future" biography detailing life as a heterosexual and as a homosexual to assist in identifying primary orientation. (7)

    7. Assign the client the homework of writing a "future" biography describing his/her life 20 years in the future, once as a heterosexual, another as a homosexual; read and process in session (e.g., ask him/her which life was more satisfying, which life had more regret).

5. Verbalize an understanding of the range of sexual identities possible. (8, 9)

    8. Educate the client about the range of sexual identities possible (i.e., heterosexual, homosexual, bisexual).

    9. Have the client read *The Invention of Heterosexuality* (Katz); process the client's thoughts and feelings about its content.

6. Identify the negative emotions experienced by hiding sexuality. (10, 11)

    10. Explore the client's negative emotions (e.g., shame, guilt, anxiety, loneliness) related to hiding/denying his/her sexuality.

    11. Explore the client's religious convictions and how these may conflict with identifying himself/herself as homosexual and cause feelings of shame or guilt (see Spiritual Confusion chapter in this *Planner*).

7. Verbalize an understanding of safer-sex practices. (12)

    12. Teach the client the details of safer-sex guidelines and encourage him/her to include them in all future sexual activity.

8. Verbalize an increased understanding of homosexuality. (8, 13, 14)

    8. Educate the client about the range of sexual identities possible (i.e., heterosexual, homosexual, bisexual).

13. Assign the client homework to identify 10 myths about homosexuals and assist him/her in replacing them with more realistic, positive beliefs.

14. Assign the client to read books that provide accurate, positive messages about homosexuality (e.g., *Is It a Choice?* by Marcus; *Outing Yourself* by Signorile; *Coming Out: An Act of Love* by Eichberg).

9. List the advantages and disadvantages of disclosing sexual orientation to significant people in life. (15)

15. Assign the client to list advantages and disadvantages of disclosing sexual orientation to significant others; process the list content.

10. Watch films/videos that depict lesbian women/gay men in positive ways. (16)

16. Ask the client to watch movies/videos that depict lesbians/gay men as healthy and happy (e.g., *Desert Hearts; In and Out; Jeffrey; When Night is Falling*); process his/her reactions to the films.

11. Attend a support group for those who want to disclose themselves as homosexual. (17)

17. Refer the client to a comingout support group (e.g., at Gay and Lesbian Community Service Center or AIDS Project).

12. Identify gay/lesbian people to socialize with or to obtain support from. (18, 19, 20)

18. Assign the client to read lesbian/gay magazines and newspapers (e.g., *The Advocate*).

19. Encourage the client to gather information and support from the Internet (e.g., coming-out bulletin boards on AOL, lesbian/gay organizations' web sites).

20. Encourage the client to identify gay men or lesbians to interact with by reviewing people he/she has met in support groups, at work, and so on, and encourage him/her to initiate social activities.

13. Develop a plan detailing when, where, how, and to whom sexual orientation is to be disclosed. (21, 22)

21. Have the client role-play disclosure of sexual orientation to significant others (e.g., family, friends, coworkers; see Family Conflict chapter in this *Planner*).

22. Assign the client homework to write a detailed plan to disclose his/her sexual orientation, including to whom it will be disclosed, where, when, and possible questions and reactions recipient(s) might have.

14. Identify one friend who is likely to have a positive reaction to homosexuality disclosure. (23, 24)

23. Encourage the client to identify one friend who is likely to be accepting of his/her homosexuality.

24. Suggest the client have casual talks with a friend about lesbian/gay rights, or some item in the news related to lesbians and gay men to "test the water" before disclosing sexual orientation to that friend.

15. Reveal sexual orientation to significant others according to written plan. (25, 26)

25. Encourage the client to disclose sexual orientation to friends/family according to the written plan.

26. Probe the client about reactions of significant others to disclosure of homosexuality (e.g., acceptance, rejection, shock); provide encouragement and positive feedback.

__. ______________________________

__. ______________________________

__. ______________________________

__. ______________________________

__. ______________________________

__. ______________________________

DIAGNOSTIC SUGGESTIONS

Axis I:	309.0	Adjustment Disorder With Depressed Mood
	309.28	Adjustment Disorder With Mixed Anxiety and Depressed Mood
	300.00	Anxiety Disorder NOS
	309.24	Adjustment Disorder With Anxiety
	300.4	Dysthymic Disorder
	302.85	Gender Identity Disorder in Adolescents or Adults
	300.02	Generalized Anxiety Disorder
	313.82	Identity Problem
	296.2x	Major Depressive Disorder, Single Episode
	296.3x	Major Depressive Disorder, Recurrent
	302.9	Sexual Disorder NOS
	______	______________________
	______	______________________
Axis II:	301.82	Avoidant Personality Disorder
	301.83	Borderline Personality Disorder
	301.81	Narcissistic Personality Disorder
	______	______________________
	______	______________________

SLEEP DISTURBANCE

BEHAVIORAL DEFINITIONS

1. Complains of difficulty falling asleep
2. Complains of difficulty remaining asleep.
3. Reports sleeping adequately, but not feeling refreshed or rested after waking.
4. Exhibits daytime sleepiness or falling asleep too easily during daytime.
5. Insomnia or hypersomnia complaints due to a reversal of the normal sleep-wake schedule.
6. Reports distress resulting from repeated awakening with detailed recall of extremely frightening dreams involving threats to self.
7. Experiences abrupt awakening with a panicky scream followed by intense anxiety and autonomic arousal, no detailed dream recall, and confusion or disorientation.
8. Others report repeated incidents of sleepwalking accompanied by amnesia for the episode.

__. ____

____

__. ____

____

__. ____

____

LONG-TERM GOALS

1. Restore restful sleep pattern.
2. Feel refreshed and energetic during wakeful hours.
3. Terminate anxiety-producing dreams that cause awakening.

4. End abrupt awakening in terror and return to peaceful, restful sleep pattern.
5. Restore restful sleep with reduction of sleepwalking incidents.

__. ____

____

__. ____

____

__. ____

____

SHORT-TERM OBJECTIVES

THERAPEUTIC INTERVENTIONS

1. Describe the history and details of sleep pattern. (1, 2)

1. Assess the exact nature of sleep pattern, including bedtime routine, activities associated with the bed, activity level while awake, nutritional habits including stimulant use, napping practice, actual sleep time, rhythm of time for being awake versus sleeping, and so on.
2. Assign the client to keep a journal of sleep patterns, stressors, thoughts, feelings, and activities associated with going to bed, and other relevant client-specific factors possibly associated with sleep problems; process the material for details of the sleep-wake cycle.

2. Share history of substance abuse or medication use. (3)

3. Assess the contribution of the client's medication or substance abuse to his/her sleep disorder; refer him/her for chemical dependence treatment, if indicated (see Chemical Dependence chapter in this *Planner*).

3. Verbalize depressive or anxious feelings and share possible causes. (4)

4. Assess the role of depression or anxiety as the cause of the client's sleep disturbance (see Depression or Anxiety chapters in this *Planner*).

4. Keep physician appointment to assess organic contributions to sleep disorder and the need for psychotropic medications. (5) (EB)

5. Refer the client to a physician to rule out physical or pharmacological causes for sleep disturbance and to consider sleep lab studies and/or need for a prescription of psychotropic medications. (EB)

5. Take psychotropic medication as prescribed to assess the effect on sleep. (6) (EB)

6. Monitor the client for psychotropic medication prescription compliance, effectiveness, and side effects. (EB)

6. Learn and implement stimulus control strategies to establish a consistent sleep-wake rhythm. (7, 8, 9, 10) (EB)

7. Discuss with the client the rationale for stimulus control strategies to establish a consistent sleep-wake cycle (see *Behavioral Treatments for Insomnia* by Bootzin and Nicassio). (EB)

8. Teach the client stimulus control techniques (e.g., lie down to sleep only when sleepy; do not use the bed for activities like T.V., reading, listening to music, but only for sleep or sexual activity; get out of bed if sleep doesn't arrive soon after retiring; lie back down when sleepy; set alarm to the same wake-up time every morning regardless of sleep time or quality; do not nap during the day); assign consistent implementation. (EB)

9. Instruct the client to move activities associated with arousal and activation from the bedtime ritual to other times during the day (e.g., reading stimulating content, reviewing day's events, planning for next day, watching disturbing television). (EB)

10. Monitor the client's sleep patterns and compliance with stimulus

---

(EB) indicates that the Objective/Intervention is consistent with those found in evidence-based treatments.

control instructions; problem-solve obstacles and reinforce successful, consistent implementation. ▽

▽ 7. Practice good sleep hygiene. (11)

11. Instruct the client in sleep hygiene practices such as restricting excessive liquid intake, spicy late night snacks, or heavy evening meals; exercising regularly, but not within 3–4 hours of bedtime; minimizing or avoiding caffeine, alcohol, tobacco, and stimulant intake (or assign "Sleep Pattern Record" in *Adult Psychotherapy Homework Planner,* 2nd ed. by Jongsma). ▽

▽ 8. Learn and implement calming skills for use at bedtime. (12, 13)

12. Teach the client relaxation skills (e.g., progressive muscle, guided imagery, slow diaphragmatic breathing); teach the client how to apply these skills to facilitate relaxation and sleep at bedtime. ▽

13. Refer the client for or conduct biofeedback training to strengthen the client's successful relaxation response. ▽

▽ 9. Identify, challenge, and replace self-talk associated with sleep disturbance with positive, realistic, and reassuring self-talk. (14, 15)

14. Explore the client's schema and self-talk that mediate his/her emotional responses counterproductive to sleep (e.g., fears, worries of sleeplessness), challenge the biases; assist him/her in replacing the distorted messages with reality-based alternatives and positive self-talk that will increase the likelihood of establishing a sound sleep pattern. ▽

15. Assign the client a homework exercise in which he/she identifies targeted self-talk and creates reality-based alternatives (or assign "Negative Thoughts Trigger Negative Feelings" in *Adult*

Psychotherapy Homework Planner, 2nd ed. by Jongsma); review and reinforce success, providing corrective feedback toward improvement. EB

EB 10. Implement a thought-stopping technique to dismiss thoughts counterproductive to sleep. (16)

16. Assign the client to implement the thought-stopping technique on a daily basis and at night between sessions (or assign "Making Use of the Thought-Stopping Technique" in *Adult Psychotherapy Homework Planner,* 2nd ed. by Jongsma); review implementation, reinforcing success and redirecting for failure. EB

EB 11. Learn and implement relapse prevention practices. (17, 18, 19, 20, 21)

17. Discuss with the client the distinction between a lapse and relapse, associating a lapse with an occasional and reversible slip into old habits and relapse with the decision to return to old habits that risk sleep disturbance (e.g., poor sleep hygiene, poor stimulus control practices). EB
18. Identify and rehearse with the client the management of future lapses. EB
19. Instruct the client to routinely use strategies learned in therapy (e.g., good sleep hygiene and stimulus control) to prevent relapse into habits associated with sleep disturbance. EB
20. Develop a "coping card" or other reminder where relapse prevention practices are recorded for the client's later use. EB
21. Schedule periodic "maintenance sessions" to help the client maintain therapeutic gains. EB

12. Identify current stressors that may be interfering with sleep. (22, 23)

22. Explore the client's current life circumstances for causes of stress and/or anxiety that may be interfering with his/her sleep.

23. Probe the client for the presence and nature of disturbing dreams and their relationship to his/her life stress; if needed, assign him/her to keep a dream journal to be processed in future appointments.

13. Verbalize a plan to deal with stressors proactively. (24)

24. Assist the client in formulating a plan to modify his/her life situation to reduce stress and anxiety; monitor the plan implementation, reinforcing success and redirecting for failure.

14. Discuss experiences of emotional traumas that may disturb sleep. (25)

25. Explore recent traumatic events that may be interfering with the client's sleep.

15. Discuss fears regarding relinquishing control. (26)

26. Probe the client's fears related to letting go of control.

16. Disclose fears of death that may contribute to sleep disturbance. (27)

27. Probe a fear of death that may contribute to the client's sleep disturbance.

17. Share childhood traumatic experiences associated with sleep experience. (28, 29)

28. Explore traumas of the client's childhood that surround the sleep experience.

29. Probe the client for the presence and nature of disturbing dreams and explore their possible relationship to present or past trauma.

18. Reveal sexual abuse incidents that continue to be disturbing. (29, 30)

29. Probe the client for the presence and nature of disturbing dreams and explore their possible relationship to present or past trauma.

30. Explore for possible sexual abuse to the client that has not been revealed (see Sexual Abuse chapter in this *Planner*).

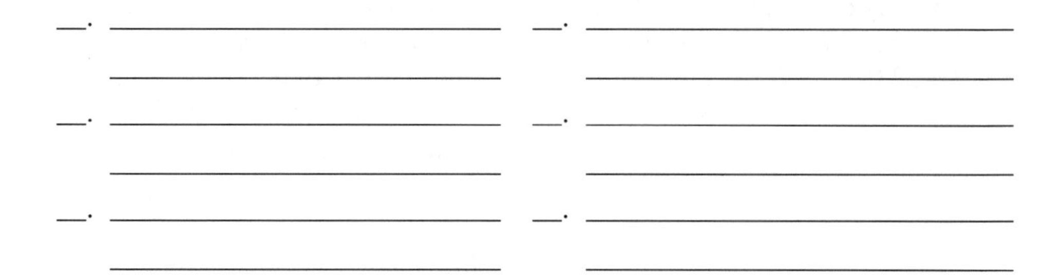

DIAGNOSTIC SUGGESTIONS

Axis I:	307.42	Primary Insomnia
	307.44	Primary Hypersomnia
	307.45	Circadian Rhythm Sleep Disorder
	307.47	Nightmare Disorder
	307.46	Sleep Terror Disorder
	307.46	Sleepwalking Disorder
	309.81	Posttraumatic Stress Disorder
	296.xx	Major Depressive Disorder
	300.4	Dysthymic Disorder
	______	____________________
	______	____________________

SOCIAL DISCOMFORT

BEHAVIORAL DEFINITIONS

1. Overall pattern of social anxiety, shyness, or timidity that presents itself in most social situations.
2. Hypersensitivity to the criticism or disapproval of others.
3. No close friends or confidants outside of first-degree relatives.
4. Avoidance of situations that require a degree of interpersonal contact.
5. Reluctant involvement in social situations out of fear of saying or doing something foolish or of becoming emotional in front of others.
6. Debilitating performance anxiety and/or avoidance of required social performance demands.
7. Increased heart rate, sweating, dry mouth, muscle tension, and shakiness in social situations.

—. ____

____

—. ____

____

—. ____

____

LONG-TERM GOALS

1. Interact socially without undue fear or anxiety.
2. Participate in social performance requirements without undue fear or anxiety.
3. Develop the essential social skills that will enhance the quality of relationship life.
4. Develop the ability to form relationships that will enhance recovery support system.

5. Reach a personal balance between solitary time and interpersonal interaction with others.

__. ____

____

__. ____

____

__. ____

____

SHORT-TERM OBJECTIVES

1. Describe the history and nature of social fears and avoidance. (1, 2, 3)
2. Complete psychological tests designed to assess the nature and severity of social anxiety and avoidance. (4)
3. ▼ Cooperate with an evaluation by a physician for psychotropic medication. (5, 6)

THERAPEUTIC INTERVENTIONS

1. Establish rapport with the client toward building a therapeutic alliance.
2. Assess the client's frequency, intensity, duration, and history of panic symptoms, fear, and avoidance (e.g., *The Anxiety Disorders Interview Schedule for the DSM-IV* by DiNardo, Brown, and Barlow).
3. Assess the nature of any stimulus, thoughts, or situations that precipitate the client's social fear and/or avoidance.
4. Administer a measure of social anxiety to further assess the depth and breadth of social fears and avoidance (e.g., *The Social Interaction Anxiety Scale and/or Social Phobia Scale* by Mattick and Clarke).
5. Arrange for an evaluation for a prescription of psychotropic medications. ▼

▼ indicates that the Objective/Intervention is consistent with those found in evidence-based treatments.

6. Monitor the client for prescription compliance, side effects, and overall effectiveness of the medication; consult with the prescribing physician at regular intervals. ▽

▽ 4. Participate in a small group therapy for social anxiety. (7)

7. Enroll clients in a small (closed enrollment) group for social anxiety (see "Shyness" in *The Group Therapy Treatment Planner,* 2nd ed. by Paleg and Jongsma; "Social Anxiety Disorder" by Turk, Heimberg, and Hope in *Clinical Handbook of Psychological Disorders* by Barlow [Ed.]). ▽

▽ 5. Verbalize an accurate understanding of the vicious cycle of social anxiety and avoidance. (8, 9)

8. Discuss how social anxiety derives from cognitive biases that overestimate negative evaluation by others, undervalue the self, distress, and often lead to unnecessary avoidance. ▽

9. Assign the client to read psychoeducational chapters of books or treatment manuals on social anxiety that explain the cycle of social anxiety and avoidance and the rationale for treatment (e.g., *Overcoming Shyness and Social Phobia* by Rapee; *Overcoming Social Anxiety and Shyness* by Butler; *The Shyness and Social Anxiety Workbook* by Antony and Swinson). ▽

▽ 6. Verbalize an understanding of the rationale for treatment of panic. (10)

10. Discuss how cognitive restructuring and exposure serve as an arena to desensitize learned fear, build social skills and confidence, and reality test biased thoughts. ▽

▽ 7. Learn and implement calming and coping strategies to manage anxiety symptoms during moments of social anxiety. (11)

11. Teach the client relaxation and attentional focusing skills (e.g., staying focused externally and on behavioral goals, muscular

relaxation, evenly paced diaphragmatic breathing, ride the wave of anxiety) to manage social anxiety symptoms. ▼

▼ 8. Identify, challenge, and replace biased, fearful self-talk with reality-based, positive self-talk. (12, 13)

12. Explore the client's schema and self-talk that mediate his/her social fear response, challenge the biases (or assign "Journal and Replace Self-Defeating Thoughts" in *Adult Psychotherapy Homework Planner,* 2nd ed. by Jongsma); assist him/her in generating appraisals that correct for the biases and build confidence. ▼

13. Assign the client a homework exercise in which he/she identifies fearful self-talk and creates reality-based alternatives; review and reinforce success, providing corrective feedback for failure (see "Restoring Socialization Comfort" in *Adult Psychotherapy Homework Planner,* 2nd ed. by Jongsma; *The Shyness and Social Anxiety Workbook* by Antony and Swinson; *Overcoming Shyness and Social Phobia* by Rapee). ▼

▼ 9. Undergo gradual repeated exposure to feared social situations within therapy. (14, 15)

14. Direct and assist the client in construction of a hierarchy of anxiety-producing situations associated with the phobic response. ▼

15. Select initial in vivo or role-played exposures that have a high likelihood of being a successful experience for the client; do cognitive restructuring within and after the exposure, use behavioral strategies (e.g., modeling, rehearsal, social reinforcement) to facilitate the exposure (see "Social Anxiety Disorder" by Turk, Heimberg, and Hope in *Clinical Handbook of Psychological Disorders* by Barlow [Ed.]). ▼

10. Undergo gradual repeated exposure to feared social situations in daily life. (14, 15, 16)

14. Direct and assist the client in construction of a hierarchy of anxiety-producing situations associated with the phobic response.

15. Select initial in vivo or role-played exposures that have a high likelihood of being a successful experience for the client; do cognitive restructuring within and after the exposure, use behavioral strategies (e.g., modeling, rehearsal, social reinforcement) to facilitate the exposure (see "Social Anxiety Disorder" by Turk, Heimberg, and Hope in *Clinical Handbook of Psychological Disorders* by Barlow [Ed.]).

16. Assign the client a homework exercise in which he/she does an exposure exercise and records responses (or assign "Gradually Reducing Your Phobic Fear" in *Adult Psychotherapy Homework Planner,* 2nd ed. by Jongsma; also see *The Shyness and Social Anxiety Workbook* by Antony and Swinson; *Overcoming Shyness and Social Phobia* by Rapee); review and reinforce success, providing corrective feedback toward improvement.

11. Learn and implement social skills to reduce anxiety and build confidence in social interactions. (17, 18)

17. Use instruction, modeling, and role-playing to build the client's general social and/or communication skills (see *Social Effectiveness Therapy* by Turner, Beidel, and Cooley).

18. Assign the client to read about general social and/or communication skills in books or treatment manuals on building social skills (e.g., *Your Perfect Right* by Alberti and Emmons; *Conversationally Speaking* by Garner).

12. Implement relapse prevention strategies for managing possible future anxiety symptoms. (19, 20, 21, 22)

19. Discuss with the client the distinction between a lapse and relapse, associating a lapse with an initial and reversible return of symptoms, fear, or urges to avoid and relapse with the decision to return to fearful and avoidant patterns.

20. Identify and rehearse with the client the management of future situations or circumstances in which lapses could occur.

21. Instruct the client to routinely use strategies learned in therapy (e.g., using cognitive restructuring, social skills, and exposure) while building social interactions and relationships.

22. Develop a "coping card" on which coping strategies and other important information (e.g., "Pace your breathing," "Focus on the task at hand," "You can manage it," and "It will go away") are written for the client's later use.

13. Explore past experiences that may be the source of low self-esteem and social anxiety currently. (23, 24)

23. Probe childhood experiences of criticism, abandonment, or abuse that would foster low self-esteem and shame, process these.

24. Assign the client to read the books *Healing the Shame That Binds You* (Bradshaw) and *Facing Shame* (Fossum and Mason), and process key ideas.

14. Verbally describe the defense mechanisms used to avoid close relationships. (25)

25. Assist the client in identifying defense mechanisms that that keep others at a distance and prevent him/her from developing trusting relationships; identify ways to minimize defensiveness.

15. Explore beliefs and communication patterns that cause social anxiety and isolation. (26, 27)

26. Utilize a transactional analysis (TA) approach to undercover and identify the client's beliefs and fears. Then use the TA approach to alter beliefs and actions.

27. Assign the client to read a book on improving social relationships using transactional analysis (e.g., *Achieving Emotional Literacy* by Steiner).

16. Return for a follow-up session to track progress, reinforce gains, and problem-solve barriers. (28)

28. Schedule a follow-up or "booster session" for the client for 1 to 3 months after therapy ends.

—. ____________________________
____

—. ____________________________
____

—. ____________________________
____

—. ____________________________
____

—. ____________________________
____

—. ____________________________
____

DIAGNOSTIC SUGGESTIONS

Axis I:	300.23	Social Phobia
	300.4	Dysthymic Disorder
	296.xx	Major Depressive Disorder
	300.7	Body Dysmorphic Disorder
	_______	____________________________
	_______	____________________________
Axis II:	301.82	Avoidant Personality Disorder
	301.0	Paranoid Personality Disorder
	310.22	Schizotypal Personality Disorder
	_______	____________________________
	_______	____________________________

SOMATIZATION

BEHAVIORAL DEFINITIONS

1. Complains of a physical malady that seems to be caused by a psychosocial stressor triggering a psychological conflict.
2. Preoccupied with the fear of having serious physical disease, without any medical basis for concern.
3. Exhibits a multitude of physical complaints that have no organic foundation but have led to life changes (e.g., seeing doctors often, taking prescriptions, withdrawing from responsibilities).
4. Preoccupied with chronic pain beyond what is expected for a physical malady or in spite of no known organic cause.
5. Complains of one or more physical problems (usually vague) that have no known organic basis, resulting in impairment in life functioning in excess of what is expected.
6. Preoccupied with pain in one or more anatomical sites with both psychological factors and a medical condition as a basis for the pain.
7. Preoccupied with an imagined physical defect in appearance or a vastly exaggerated concern about a minimal defect (Body Dysmorphic Disorder).

__. ____

____

__. ____

____

__. ____

____

LONG-TERM GOALS

1. Reduce frequency of physical complaints and improve the level of independent functioning.

2. Reduce verbalizations focusing on pain while increasing productive activities.
3. Accept body appearance as normal even with insignificant flaws.
4. Accept self as relatively healthy with no known medical illness or defects.
5. Improve physical functioning due to development of adequate coping mechanisms for stress management.

__. ____

____

__. ____

____

__. ____

____

SHORT-TERM OBJECTIVES

1. Verbalize negative feelings regarding body and discuss self-prediction of catastrophized consequences of perceived body abnormality. (1)
2. Discuss causes for emotional stress in life that underlie the focus on physical complaints. (2, 3, 4)
3. Identify family patterns that exist around exaggerated focus on physical maladies. (5)
4. Verbalize the secondary gain that results from physical complaints. (6)
5. Identify causes for anger. (7)

THERAPEUTIC INTERVENTIONS

1. Build a level of trust and understanding with client by listening to his/her initial complaints without rejection or confrontation.
2. Refocus the client's discussion from physical complaints to emotional conflicts and expression of feelings.
3. Explore the client's sources of emotional pain—feelings of fear, inadequacy, rejection, or abuse.
4. Assist the client in acceptance of connection between physical focus and avoidance of facing emotional conflicts.
5. Explore the client's family history for modeling and reinforcement of physical complaints.
6. Assist the client in developing insight into the secondary gain received from physical illness, complaints, and the like.
7. Explore for causes for the client's anger.

6. Express angry feelings assertively and directly. (8, 9, 10)

8. Using role-playing and behavioral rehearsal, teach the client assertive, respectful expression of angry feelings.

9. Train the client in assertiveness or refer him/her to an assertiveness training class.

10. Reinforce the client's assertiveness as a means of him/her attaining healthy need satisfaction in contrast to whining helplessness.

7. Identify the connection between negative body image and general low self-esteem. (11, 12)

11. Probe the client for causes for low self-esteem and fears of inadequacy in his/her childhood experiences.

12. Teach the client the connection between low self-esteem and preoccupation with body image.

8. Increase social and productive activities rather than being preoccupied with self and physical complaints. (13, 14)

13. Assign the client to develop a list of pleasurable activities that can serve as rewards and diversions from bodily focus.

14. Assign diversion activities that take the client's focus off himself/herself and redirect it toward hobbies, social activities, assisting others, completing projects, or returning to work.

9. Implement the use of relaxation skills and exercise to reduce tension in response to stress. (15, 16)

15. Train the client in relaxation techniques using biofeedback, deep breathing, and positive imagery techniques.

16. Assign the client to a daily exercise routine.

10. Decrease physical complaints, doctor visits, and reliance on medication while increasing verbal assessment of self as able to function normally and productively. (17, 18, 19)

17. Challenge the client to endure pain and carry on with responsibilities so as to build self-esteem and a sense of contribution.

18. Structure specific times each day for the client to think about, talk about, and write down his/her

physical problems while outside of those times the client will not focus on his/her physical condition; monitor and process the intervention's effectiveness (or assign "Controlling the Focus on Physical Problems" in *Adult Psychotherapy Homework Planner,* 2nd ed. by Jongsma).

19. Create an ordeal (i.e., a specific task that is necessary in the client's daily life but one that he/she finds unpleasant) for the client to do each time the symptom (physical complaint) occurs; convince the client of the effectiveness of this prescription and monitor for compliance and results.

11. Poll family and friends regarding their concern about physical complaints. (20)

20. Assign to the client the ritual of polling spouse, friends, neighbors, pastors, and so on about how concerned they feel he/she should be, and what they would recommend he/she do each time a physical complaint/concern occurs. Process results.

12. List coping behaviors that will be implemented when physical symptoms appear. (21)

21. Ask the client to try to predict the next attack or physical issue and then plan how he/she will cope with it when it comes.

13. Report on instances of taking active control over environmental events versus passively reacting like a victim. (22)

22. Empower the client to take control of his/her environment rather than continuing in his/her attitude of helplessness, frustration, anger, and "poor me."

14. Engage in normal responsibilities vocationally and socially without complaining or withdrawing into avoidance while using physical problems as an excuse. (23, 24, 25)

23. Reframe the client's worries into a metaphor of "making sure he/she stays healthy." Then issue a prescription and a plan for implementing increased exercise, sex, or joy.

24. Give positive feedback when the client is symptom-free and accepting of his/her body as normal and healthy.

25. Discuss with client the destructive social impact that consistent complaintive verbalizations or negative body focus have on friends and family.

15. Accept referral to a pain clinic to learn pain management techniques. (26)

26. Refer the client to a pain clinic.

EB 16. Cooperate with an evaluation by a physician for psychotropic medication for Body Dysmorphic Disorder. (27, 28)

27. Arrange for an evaluation for a prescription of psychotropic medications (e.g., SSRIs). EB

28. Monitor the client for prescription compliance, side effects, and overall effectiveness of the medication; consult with the prescribing physician at regular intervals. EB

EB 17. Participate in exposure and ritual prevention therapy for Body Dysmorphic Disorder. (29)

29. Enroll the client in a small closed-enrollment group for exposure and ritual prevention therapy for Body Dysmorphic Disorder (see "Cognitive Behavior Group Therapy for Body Dysmorphic Disorder: A Case Series" by Wilhelm, Otto, Lohr, et al. in *Behavior Research and Therapy,* 1999, Vol. 37, pp. 71–75), or conduct the therapy individually. EB

EB 18. Verbalize an understanding of the rationale for treatment. (30)

30. Educate client about the role of biased fears and avoidance in maintaining Body Dysmorphic Disorder; discuss how treatment serves as an arena to desensitize fears, to reality test fears and underlying beliefs, and build

---

EB indicates that the Objective/Intervention is consistent with those found in evidence-based treatments.

confidence in self-acceptance of his/her appearance. ▼

▼19. Identify and replace biased, fearful self-talk and beliefs. (31)

31. Explore the client's schema and self-talk that mediate his/her self-conscious fears and related avoidance behavior; assist him/her in generating thoughts that challenge and correct for the biases (or assign "Negative Thoughts Trigger Negative Feelings" in *Adult Psychotherapy Homework Planner,* 2nd ed. by Jongsma). ▼

▼20. Undergo repeated imaginal exposure to feared external and/or internal cues. (32, 33, 34)

32. Assess external triggers for fears (e.g., persons or situations) and subtle and obvious avoidant strategies (e.g., wearing concealing clothing, only going out at night). ▼

33. Direct and assist the client in construction of a hierarchy of fear triggers; incorporate exposures that gradually increase the degree to which the client hides his/her appearance. ▼

34. Select initial exposures that have a high likelihood of being a successful experience for the client; be a participant model and do cognitive restructuring within and after the exposure. ▼

▼21. Complete homework assignments involving in vivo exposure to feared external and/or internal cues. (35)

35. Assign the client a homework exercise in which he/she repeats the exposure between sessions and records responses (or assign "Gradually Reducing Your Phobic Fear" in *Adult Psychotherapy Homework Planner,* 2nd ed. by Jongsma); review during next session, reinforcing success and providing corrective feedback toward improvement. ▼

22. Implement the use of the "thought-stopping" technique to reduce the frequency of obsessive thoughts. (36, 37)

36. Teach the client to interrupt critical self-conscious thoughts using the "thought-stopping" technique of shouting STOP to himself/herself silently while picturing a red traffic signal and then thinking about a calming scene.

37. Assign the client to implement the "thought-stopping" technique on a daily basis between sessions (or assign "Making Use of the Thought-Stopping Technique" in *Adult Psychotherapy Homework Planner,* 2nd ed. by Jongsma); review.

23. Implement maintenance strategies for managing possible future anxiety symptoms. (38, 39, 40)

38. Identify and rehearse with the client the management of future situations or circumstances in which lapses could occur.

39. Instruct the client to routinely use strategies learned in therapy (e.g., continued exposure to previously feared external or internal cues that arise) to prevent relapse into critical self-conscious fears and avoidance patterns.

40. Schedule periodic "maintenance sessions" to help the client maintain therapeutic gains.

—. ______________________________

—. ______________________________

—. ______________________________

—. ______________________________

—. ______________________________

—. ______________________________

DIAGNOSTIC SUGGESTIONS

Axis I:	300.7	Body Dysmorphic Disorder
	300.11	Conversion Disorder

300.7	Hypochondriasis
300.81	Somatization Disorder
307.80	Pain Disorder Associated With Psychological Factors
307.89	Pain Disorder Associated With Both Psychological Factors and a General Medical Condition
300.81	Undifferentiated Somatoform Disorder
300.4	Dysthymic Disorder
________	________________________________
________	________________________________

SPIRITUAL CONFUSION

BEHAVIORAL DEFINITIONS

1. Verbalization of a desire for a closer relationship to a higher power.
2. Feelings and attitudes about a higher power that are characterized by fear, anger, and distrust.
3. Verbalization of a feeling of emptiness in his/her life, as if something were missing.
4. A negative, bleak outlook on life and regarding others.
5. A felt need for a higher power, but because upbringing contained no religious education or training, does not know where or how to begin.
6. An inability to connect with a higher power, due to anger, hurt, and rejection from religious upbringing.
7. A struggle with understanding and accepting Alcoholics Anonymous (AA) Steps Two and Three (i.e., difficulty in believing in a higher power).

__. ____

____

__. ____

____

__. ____

____

LONG-TERM GOALS

1. Clarify spiritual concepts and instill a freedom to approach a higher power as a resource for support.
2. Increase belief in and development of a relationship with a higher power.
3. Begin a faith in a higher power and incorporate it into support system.
4. Resolve issues that have prevented faith or belief from developing and growing.

__. ____

____

__. ____

____

__. ____

____

SHORT-TERM OBJECTIVES

1. Summarize the highlights of own spiritual quest or journey to this date. (1)
2. Describe beliefs and feelings around the idea of a higher power. (2, 3, 4)
3. Describe early life training in spiritual concepts and identify its impact on current religious beliefs. (5)
4. Verbalize an increased knowledge and understanding of concept of a higher power. (6, 7)

THERAPEUTIC INTERVENTIONS

1. Ask the client to write the story of his/her spiritual quest/journey; process the journey material.
2. Assign the client to list all of his/her beliefs related to a higher power; process the beliefs.
3. Assist the client in processing and clarifying his/her feelings regarding a higher power.
4. Explore the causes for the emotional components (e.g., fear, rejection, peace, acceptance, abandonment) of the client's reaction to a higher power.
5. Review the client's early life experiences surrounding belief in a higher power.
6. Ask the client to talk with a chaplain, pastor, rabbi, or priest regarding the client's spiritual struggles, issues, or questions, and record the feedback.
7. Assign the client to read *God: A Biography* (Miles) or *The History of God* (Armstrong) to build knowledge and a concept of a higher power.

5. Identify specific blocks to believing in a higher power. (8, 9)

8. Assist the client in identifying specific issues or blocks that prevent the development of his/her spirituality.

9. Encourage the client to read books dealing with conversion experiences (e.g., *Surprised by Joy* by Lewis; *Confessions of St. Augustine* by Augustine; *The Seven Storey Mountain* by Merton; *Soul on Fire* by Cleaver).

6. Identify the difference between religion and faith. (10)

10. Educate the client on the difference between religion and spirituality.

7. Replace the concept of a higher power as harsh and judgmental with a belief in a higher power as forgiving and loving. (9, 11)

9. Encourage the client to read books dealing with conversion experiences (e.g., *Surprised by Joy* by Lewis; *Confessions of St. Augustine* by Augustine; *The Seven Storey Mountain* by Merton; *Soul on Fire* by Cleaver).

11. Emphasize that the higher power is characterized by love and gracious forgiveness for anyone with remorse and who seeks forgiveness.

8. Implement daily attempts to be in contact with higher power. (12, 13, 14)

12. Recommend that the client implement daily meditations and/or prayer; process the experience.

13. Assign the client to write a daily note to his/her higher power.

14. Encourage and assist the client in developing and implementing a daily devotional time or other ritual that will foster his/her spiritual growth.

9. Verbalize separation of beliefs and feelings regarding one's earthly father from those regarding a higher power. (15, 16)

15. Assist the client in comparing his/her beliefs and feelings about his/her earthly father with those about a higher power.

16. Urge separating the feelings and beliefs regarding the earthly father from those regarding a higher power to allow for spiritual growth and maturity.

10. Acknowledge the need to separate negative past experiences with religious people from the current spiritual evaluation. (17, 18)

17. Assist the client in evaluating religious tenets separated from painful emotional experiences with religious people in his/her past.

18. Explore the religious distortions and judgmentalism that the client has been subjected to by others.

11. Verbalize acceptance of forgiveness from a higher power. (19, 20)

19. Ask the client to read the books *Serenity* (Helmfelt and Fowler)—all readings related to AA Steps Two and Three; *The Road Less Traveled* (Peck); and *Search for Serenity* (Presnall); process the concept of forgiveness.

20. Explore the client's feelings of shame and guilt that led to him/her feeling unworthy before a higher power and others.

12. Ask a respected person who has apparent spiritual depth to serve as a mentor. (21)

21. Help the client find a mentor to guide his/her spiritual development.

13. Attend groups dedicated to enriching spirituality. (22, 23)

22. Make the client aware of opportunities for spiritual enrichment (e.g., Bible studies, study groups, fellowship groups); process the experiences he/she decides to pursue.

23. Suggest that the client attend a spiritual retreat (e.g., DeColores or Course in Miracles) and report to therapist what the experience was like for him/her and what he/she gained from the experience.

14. Read books that focus on furthering a connection with a higher power. (24)

24. Ask the client to read books to cultivate his/her spirituality (e.g., *Cloistered Walk* by Norris; *Hymns to an Unknown God* by Keen; *The Care of the Soul* by Moore).

__. ____________________

__. ____________________

__. ____________________

__. ____________________

__. ____________________

__. ____________________

DIAGNOSTIC SUGGESTIONS

Axis I:	300.4	Dysthymic Disorder
	311	Depressive Disorder NOS
	300.00	Anxiety Disorder NOS
	296.xx	Major Depressive Disorder
	______	____________________
	______	____________________

SUICIDAL IDEATION

BEHAVIORAL DEFINITIONS

1. Recurrent thoughts of or preoccupation with death.
2. Recurrent or ongoing suicidal ideation without any plans.
3. Ongoing suicidal ideation with a specific plan.
4. Recent suicide attempt.
5. History of suicide attempts that required professional or family/friend intervention on some level (e.g., inpatient, safe house, outpatient, supervision).
6. Positive family history of depression and/or a preoccupation with suicidal thoughts.
7. A bleak, hopeless attitude regarding life coupled with recent life events that support this (e.g., divorce, death of a friend or family member, loss of job).
8. Social withdrawal, lethargy, and apathy coupled with expressions of wanting to die.
9. Sudden change from being depressed to upbeat and at peace, while actions indicate the client is "putting his/her house in order" and there has been no genuine resolution of conflict issues.
10. Engages in self-destructive or dangerous behavior (e.g., chronic drug or alcohol abuse; promiscuity, unprotected sex; reckless driving) that appears to invite death.

__. ____

____

__. ____

____

__. ____

____

LONG-TERM GOALS

1. Alleviate the suicidal impulses/ideation and return to the highest level of previous daily functioning.
2. Stabilize the suicidal crisis.
3. Placement in an appropriate level of care to safely address the suicidal crisis.
4. Reestablish a sense of hope for self and the future.
5. Cease the perilous lifestyle and resolve the emotional conflicts that underlie the suicidal pattern.

—. ______________________________

____

—. ______________________________

____

—. ______________________________

____

SHORT-TERM OBJECTIVES

1. State the strength of the suicidal feelings, the frequency of the thoughts, and the detail of the plans. (1, 2, 3, 4)

THERAPEUTIC INTERVENTIONS

1. Assess the client's suicidal ideation, taking into account the extent of his/her ideation, the presence of a primary and backup plan, past attempts, and family history.
2. Assess and monitor the client's suicidal potential on an ongoing basis.
3. Notify the client's family and significant others of his/her suicidal ideation; ask them to form a 24-hour suicide watch until the crisis subsides.
4. Arrange for the client to take the Minnesota Multiphasic Personality Inventory (MMPI), Beck Depression Inventory (BDI), or Modified Scale for Suicide Ideation (MSSI); evaluate the results for the client's degree of depression and suicide risk.

2. Verbalize a promise to contact the therapist or some other emergency helpline if a serious urge toward self-harm arises. (5, 6, 7, 8)

   5. Elicit a promise from the client that he/she will initiate contact with the therapist or a helpline if the suicidal urge becomes strong and before any self-injurious behavior.
   6. Provide the client with an emergency helpline telephone number that is available 24 hours a day.
   7. Make a contract with the client, identifying what he/she will and won't do when experiencing suicidal thoughts or impulses.
   8. Offer to be available to the client through telephone contact if a life-threatening urge develops.

3. Client and/or significant others increase the safety of the home by removing firearms or other lethal weapons from easy access. (3, 9)

   3. Notify the client's family and significant others of his/her suicidal ideation; ask them to form a 24-hour suicide watch until the crisis subsides.
   9. Encourage significant others to remove firearms or other lethal weapons from the client's easy access.

4. Report suicidal impulses to a designated significant other or helping professional. (3, 5, 10)

   3. Notify the client's family and significant others of his/her suicidal ideation; ask them to form a 24-hour suicide watch until the crisis subsides.
   5. Elicit a promise from the client that he/she will initiate contact with the therapist or a helpline if the suicidal urge becomes strong and before any self-injurious behavior.
   10. Encourage the client to be open and honest regarding suicidal urges, reassuring him/her regularly of caring concern by therapist and significant others.

5. Cooperate with hospitalization if the suicidal urge becomes uncontrollable. (4, 11)

4. Arrange for the client to take the Minnesota Multiphasic Personality Inventory (MMPI), Beck Depression Inventory (BDI), or Modified Scale for Suicide Ideation (MSSI); evaluate the results for the client's degree of depression and suicide risk.

11. Arrange for hospitalization when the client is judged to be uncontrollably harmful to self.

6. Identify life factors that preceded the suicidal ideation. (12, 13, 14)

12. Explore the client's sources of emotional pain and hopelessness.

13. Encourage the client to express feelings related to his/her suicidal ideation in order to clarify them and increase insight as to the causes for them.

14. Assist the client in becoming aware of life factors that were significant precursors to the beginning of his/her suicidal ideation.

7. Increase communication with significant others, resulting in a feeling of understanding, empathy, and being attended to. (15, 16, 17)

15. Probe the client's feelings of despair related to his/her family relationships.

16. Hold family therapy sessions to promote communication of the client's feelings of sadness, hurt, and anger.

17. Meet with significant others to assess their understanding of the causes for the client's distress.

8. Significant others verbalize an understanding of the client's feelings of alienation and hopelessness. (16, 17)

16. Hold family therapy sessions to promote communication of the client's feelings of sadness, hurt, and anger.

17. Meet with significant others to assess their understanding of the causes for the client's distress.

9. Cooperate with a referral to a physician for an evaluation for antidepressant medication. (18)

    18. Assess the client's need for antidepressant medication and arrange for a prescription, if necessary.

10. Take medications as prescribed and report all side effects. (19)

    19. Monitor the client for effectiveness and compliance with prescribed psychotropic medication; confer with prescribing physician on a regular basis.

11. Identify how previous attempts to solve interpersonal problems have failed, leading to feelings of abject loneliness and rejection. (14, 20, 21)

    14. Assist the client in becoming aware of life factors that were significant precursors to the beginning of his/her suicidal ideation.

    20. Encourage the client to share feelings of grief related to broken close relationships.

    21. Review with the client previous problem-solving attempts and discuss new alternatives that are available.

12. Reestablish a consistent eating and sleeping pattern. (22)

    22. Encourage normal eating and sleeping patterns by the client and monitor his/her compliance.

13. Verbally report no longer feeling the impulse to take own life and demonstrate an increased sense of hope for self. (2, 23, 24)

    2. Assess and monitor the client's suicidal potential on an ongoing basis.

    23. Assist the client in developing coping strategies for suicidal ideation (e.g., more physical exercise, less internal focus, increased social involvement, more expression of feelings).

    24. Assist the client in finding positive, hopeful things in his/her life at the present time.

14. Identify the positive aspects, relationships, and achievements in his/her life. (24, 25)

    24. Assist the client in finding positive, hopeful things in his/her life at the present time.

25. Review with the client the success he/she has had and the sources of love and concern that exist in his/her life; ask him/her to write a list of positive aspects of his/her life.

15. Identify and replace negative thinking patterns that mediate feelings of hopelessness and helplessness. (26, 27, 28, 29)

26. Assist the client in developing an awareness of the cognitive messages that reinforce hopelessness and helplessness.

27. Identify and confront catastrophizing tendencies in the client's cognitive processing, allowing for a more realistic perspective of hope in the face of pain.

28. Train the client in revising core schemas using cognitive restructuring techniques.

29. Require the client to keep a daily record of self-defeating thoughts (thoughts of hopelessness, helplessness, worthlessness, catastrophizing, negatively predicting the future, etc.); challenge each thought for accuracy, then replace each dysfunctional thought with one that is positive and self-enhancing.

16. Develop and implement a penitence ritual in which one expresses grief for victims and absolves self of guilt for surviving an incident fatal to others. (30)

30. Develop a penitence ritual for the client with suicidal ideation connected with being a survivor and implement it with him/her.

17. Verbalize a feeling of support that results from spiritual faith. (31, 32)

31. Explore the client's spiritual belief system as to it being a source of acceptance and peace.

32. Arrange for the client's spiritual leader to meet with and support the client.

__. ______________________ __. ______________________

______________________ ______________________

__. ______________________ __. ______________________

______________________ ______________________

__. ______________________ __. ______________________

______________________ ______________________

DIAGNOSTIC SUGGESTIONS

Axis I:	296.xx	Bipolar I Disorder
	300.4	Dysthymic Disorder
	296.2x	Major Depressive Disorder, Single Episode
	296.3x	Major Depressive Disorder, Recurrent
	296.89	Bipolar II Disorder
	______	______________________
	______	______________________
Axis II:	301.83	Borderline Personality Disorder
	______	______________________
	______	______________________

TYPE A BEHAVIOR

BEHAVIORAL DEFINITIONS

1. A pattern of pressuring self and others to accomplish more because there is never enough time.
2. A spirit of intense competition in all activities.
3. Intense compulsion to win at all costs regardless of the activity or cocompetitor.
4. Inclination to dominate all social or business situations, being too direct and overbearing.
5. Propensity to become irritated by the actions of others who do not conform to own sense of propriety or correctness.
6. A state of perpetual impatience with any waiting, delays, or interruptions.
7. Difficulty in sitting and quietly relaxing or reflecting.
8. Psychomotor facial signs of intensity and pressure (e.g., muscle tension, scowling, glaring, tics).
9. Psychomotor voice signs (e.g., irritatingly forceful speech or laughter, rapid and intense speech, frequent use of obscenities).

__. ____
____

__. ____
____

__. ____
____

LONG-TERM GOALS

1. Formulate and implement a new life attitudinal pattern that allows for a more relaxed pattern of living.

2. Reach a balance between work/competitive and social/noncompetitive time in daily life.
3. Achieve an overall decrease in pressured, driven behaviors.
4. Develop social and recreational activities as a routine part of life.
5. Alleviate sense of time urgency, free-floating anxiety, anger, and self-destructive behaviors.

—. ____

____

—. ____

____

—. ____

____

SHORT-TERM OBJECTIVES

1. Describe the pattern of pressured, driven living. (1, 2)
2. Comply with psychological assessment. (3, 4)
3. Identify the beliefs that support driven, overachieving behavior. (5, 6, 7)

THERAPEUTIC INTERVENTIONS

1. Assess examples of pressured lifestyle.
2. Assist the client to see self as others do.
3. Administer measure to assess and track the client's breadth and depth of Type A behavior (e.g., *Jenkins Activity Survey* by Jenkins, Zyzanski, and Rosenman).
4. Review and process results of testing with the client.
5. Probe personal history including family of origin history for role models of and/or pressure for high achievement and compulsive drive.
6. Ask the client to make a list of his/her beliefs about self-worth and the worth of others; process it with the therapist.
7. Assist the client in making key connections between his/her overachieving/driven behavior and the desire to please key parental figures.

4. Verbalize a desire to reprioritize values toward less self-focus, more inner and other orientation. (8, 9)

8. Explore and clarify the client's value system and assist in developing new priorities on the importance of relationships, recreation, spiritual growth, reflection time, giving to others, and so on.

9. Ask the client to read biographies or autobiographies of spiritual people (e.g., St. Augustine, Thomas Merton, Albert Schweitzer, C. S. Lewis); process the key beliefs they lived by.

EBT 5. Verbalize a commitment to emphasize the values of inner and other orientation. (10)

10. Ask the client to commit to attempting attitude and behavior changes to promote a healthier, less Type A lifestyle, learning new approaches to managing self, time, relationships. EBT

EBT 6. Work on one task at a time with less emphasis on pressure to complete it quickly. (11)

11. Encourage and reinforce the client focusing on one activity at a time without a sense of urgency. EBT

EBT 7. Decrease the number of hours worked daily and the frequency of taking work home. (12)

12. Review the client's pattern of hours spent working (at home and office) and recommend selected reductions. EBT

EBT 8. Learn and implement calming skills to manage pressure situations. (13, 14)

13. Teach the client calming techniques (e.g., muscle relaxation, paced breathing, calming imagery) as part of a tailored strategy for responding appropriately to feelings of pressure when they occur. EBT

14. Assign the client to implement calming techniques in his/her daily life when facing trigger situations; process the results, reinforcing success and redirecting for failure. EBT

EBT indicates that the Objective/Intervention is consistent with those found in evidence-based treatments.

9. Increase daily time involved in relaxing activities. (15, 16, 17, 18)

10. Identify and replace distorted automatic thoughts that motivate pressured living. (19)

11. Verbalize a recognition of hostility toward and impatience with others. (20, 21)

12. Verbalize the distinction between respectful assertiveness and insensitive directness or verbal aggression that is controlling. (22, 23)

15. Assign the client to do one noncompetitive activity each day for a week; process this experience.

16. Ask the client to try one area of interest outside of his/her vocation that he/she will do two times weekly for 1 month.

17. Assign the client to watch comedy movies and identify the positive aspects of them.

18. Reinforce all the client changes that reflect a greater sense of life balance.

19. Assist the client in identifying distorted automatic thoughts that lead to feeling pressured to achieve; assist him/her in replacing these distortions with positive, realistic cognitions.

20. Explore the client's pattern of intolerant, impatient interaction with others.

21. Assist the client in identifying his/her critical beliefs about other people and connecting them to hostile verbal and behavior patterns in daily life.

22. Train the client in assertive communication, with emphasis on recognizing and refraining from aggressive ignoring of the rights of others.

23. Monitor, point out, and reframe the client's actions or verbalizations that reflect a self-centered or unempathetic approach to others; practice alternatives using behavioral strategies such as modeling, role-playing, and/or role reversal.

13. Implement problem-solving and/or conflict resolution skills to manage interpersonal problems. (24)

24. Teach the client conflict resolution skills (e.g., empathy, active listening, "I messages," respectful communication, assertiveness without aggression, compromise) and problem-solving skills (e.g., define specifically, brainstorm options, evaluate, implement, reevaluate) using modeling, role-playing, and behavior rehearsal to work through several current conflicts.

14. Implement new calming, communication, and problem-solving skills to manage anger. (25, 26, 27)

25. Assist the client in constructing a client-tailored strategy for managing pressure that combines any of the somatic, cognitive, communication, problem-solving, and/or conflict resolution skills relevant to his/her needs.

26. Select situations in which the client will be increasingly challenged to apply his/her new strategies for managing anger.

27. Use any of several techniques, including relaxation, imagery, behavioral rehearsal, modeling, role-playing, or in vivo exposure/behavioral experiments to help the client consolidate the use of his/her new anger management skills (or assign "Alternatives to Destructive Anger" in *Adult Psychotherapy Homework Planner,* 2nd ed. by Jongsma).

15. Demonstrate decreased impatience with others by talking of appreciating and understanding the good qualities in others. (28, 29, 30, 31)

28. Assign the client to talk to an associate or child, focusing on listening to the other person and learning several good things about that person; process the experience.

29. Assign the client and family to attend an experiential weekend that promotes self-awareness (e.g., high-low ropes course or cooperative tasks); process the experience afterward. EB

30. Assign the client to go with a group on a wilderness camping and canoeing trip, on a work camp project, or with the Red Cross as a disaster worker; process the experience. EB

31. Encourage the client to volunteer for a nonprofit social agency, school, or the like for 1 year, doing direct work with people (i.e., serving food at a soup kitchen or tutoring an inner-city child); process the positive consequences. EB

EB 16. Increase interest in the lives of others as evidenced by listening to others talk of their life experiences, and by engaging in one act of kindness per day. (32, 33, 34)

32. Encourage and monitor the client in doing one random, spontaneous act of kindness on a daily basis and explore the positive results. EB

33. Encourage the client to express warmth, appreciation, affection, and gratitude to others. EB

34. Assign the client to read the book *The Road Less Traveled* (Peck) and to process key ideas with therapist. EB

EB 17. Develop a daily routine that reflects a balance between the quest for achievement and appreciation of aesthetic things. (35, 36)

35. Assign the client to read "List of Aphorisms" in *Treating Type A Behavior and Your Heart* (Friedman and Ulmer) three times daily for 1 or 2 weeks, then to pick several to incorporate into his/her life. EB

36. Ask the client to list activities he/she could engage in for purely aesthetic enjoyment (e.g., visit an art museum, attend a symphony concert, hike in the woods, take painting lessons) and incorporate these into his/her life (or assign "Identify and Schedule Pleasant Activities" in *Adult Psychotherapy Homework Planner,* 2nd ed. by Jongsma). ♥

—. ______________________________

—. ______________________________

—. ______________________________

—. ______________________________

—. ______________________________

—. ______________________________

DIAGNOSTIC SUGGESTIONS

Axis I:	300.3	Obsessive-Compulsive Disorder
	300.02	Generalized Anxiety Disorder
	296.89	Bipolar II Disorder (Hypomanic)
	______	______________________
	______	______________________
Axis II:	301.4	Obsessive-Compulsive Personality Disorder
	______	______________________
	______	______________________

VOCATIONAL STRESS

BEHAVIORAL DEFINITIONS

1. Feelings of anxiety and depression secondary to interpersonal conflict (perceived feelings of inadequacy, fear, and failure) secondary to severe business losses.
2. Fear of failure secondary to success or promotion that increases perceived expectations for greater success.
3. Rebellion against and/or conflicts with authority figures in the employment situation.
4. Feelings of anxiety and depression secondary to being fired or laid off, resulting in unemployment.
5. Anxiety related to perceived or actual job jeopardy.
6. Feelings of depression and anxiety related to complaints of job dissatisfaction or the stress of employment responsibilities.

—. ____

____

—. ____

____

—. ____

____

LONG-TERM GOALS

1. Improve satisfaction and comfort surrounding coworker relationships.
2. Increase sense of confidence and competence in dealing with work responsibilities.
3. Be cooperative with and accepting of supervision of direction in the work setting.

4. Increase sense of self-esteem and elevation of mood in spite of unemployment.
5. Increase job security as a result of more positive evaluation of performance by a supervisor.
6. Pursue employment consistency with a reasonably hopeful and positive attitude.
7. Increase job satisfaction and performance due to implementation of assertiveness and stress management strategies.

—. ____

____

—. ____

____

—. ____

____

SHORT-TERM OBJECTIVES

1. Identify own role in the conflict with coworkers or supervisor. (1, 2)
2. Identify any personal problems that may be causing conflict in the employment setting. (3, 4)
3. Review family of origin history to determine roots for interpersonal conflict that are being reenacted in the work atmosphere. (5)
4. Identify patterns of similar conflict with people outside the work environment. (6)

THERAPEUTIC INTERVENTIONS

1. Clarify the nature of the client's conflicts in the work setting.
2. Help the client identify his/her own role in the conflict, attempting to represent the other party's point of view.
3. Explore possible role of substance abuse in the client's vocational conflicts.
4. Explore the client's transfer of personal problems to the employment situation.
5. Probe the client's family of origin history for causes of current interpersonal conflict patterns.
6. Explore the client's patterns of interpersonal conflict that occur beyond the work setting but are repeated in the work setting.

5. Replace projection or responsibility for conflict, feelings, or behavior with acceptance of responsibility for own behavior, feelings, and role in conflict. (7, 8)

7. Confront the client's projection of responsibility for his/her behavior and feelings onto others.

8. Reinforce the client's acceptance of responsibility for personal feelings and behavior.

6. Identify and implement behavioral changes that could be made in workplace interactions to help resolve conflicts with coworkers or supervisors. (9, 10)

9. Assign the client to write a plan for constructive action (e.g., polite compliance with directedness, initiate a smiling greeting, compliment other's work, avoid critical judgments) that contains various alternatives to coworker or supervisor conflict.

10. Use role-playing, behavioral rehearsal, and role rehearsal to increase the client's probability of positive encounters and to reduce anxiety with others in employment situation or job search.

7. Implement assertiveness skills that allow for effective communication of needs and feelings without aggression or defensiveness. (11)

11. Train the client in assertiveness skills or refer to assertiveness training class.

8. Verbalize more healthy, realistic cognitive messages that promote harmony with others, self-acceptance, and self-confidence. (12, 13)

12. Train the client in the development of more realistic, healthy cognitive messages that relieve anxiety and depression.

13. Require the client to keep a daily record of self-defeating thoughts (e.g., thoughts of hopelessness, worthlessness, rejection, catastrophizing, negatively predicting the future); challenge each thought for accuracy, then replace each dysfunctional thought with one that is positive and self-enhancing.

9. Identify and replace distorted cognitive messages associated with feelings of job stress. (14, 15, 16)

14. Probe and clarify the client's emotions surrounding his/her vocational stress.

15. Assess the client's distorted cognitive messages and schema that

foster his/her vocational stress; replace these messages with positive cognitions.

16. Confront the client's pattern of catastrophizing situations leading to immobilizing anxiety; replace these messages with realistic thoughts.

10. Identify the effect that vocational stress has on feelings toward self and relationships with significant others. (17, 18)

17. Explore the effect of the client's vocational stress on his/her intra- and interpersonal dynamics with friends and family.

18. Facilitate a family therapy session in which feelings of family members can be aired and clarified regarding the client's vocational situation.

11. Develop and verbalize a plan for constructive action to reduce vocational stress. (19)

19. Assist the client in developing a plan to react positively to his/her vocational situation; process the proactive plan and assist in its implementation.

12. Verbalize an understanding of circumstances that led up to being terminated from employment. (20)

20. Explore the causes for client's termination of employment that may have been beyond his/her control.

13. Cease self-disparaging comments that are based on perceived failure at workplace. (21, 22, 23, 24)

21. Probe childhood history for roots of feelings of inadequacy, fear of failure, or fear of success.

22. Reinforce realistic self-appraisal of the client's successes and failures at workplace.

23. Assign the client to separately list his/her positive traits, talents, and successful accomplishments, and then the people who care for, respect, and value him/her. Process these lists as a basis for genuine gratitude and self-worth.

24. Teach the client that the ultimate worth of an individual is not measured in material or vocational success but in service to a higher power and others.

14. Outline plan for job search. (25, 26, 27)

25. Help the client develop a written job plan that contains specific attainable objectives for job search.

26. Assign the client to choose jobs for follow up in the want ads and to ask friends and family about job opportunities.

27. Assign the client to attend a job search class or resumé-writing seminar.

15. Report on job search experiences and feelings surrounding these experiences. (28)

28. Monitor, encourage, and process the client's search for employment.

—. ____________________

—. ____________________

—. ____________________

—. ____________________

—. ____________________

—. ____________________

DIAGNOSTIC SUGGESTIONS

Axis I:	309.0	Adjustment Disorder With Depressed Mood
	300.4	Dysthymic Disorder
	296.xx	Major Depressive Disorder
	V62.2	Occupational Problem
	309.24	Adjustment Disorder With Anxiety
	303.90	Alcohol Dependence
	304.20	Cocaine Dependence
	304.80	Polysubstance Dependence
	______	____________________
	______	____________________
Axis II:	301.0	Paranoid Personality Disorder
	301.81	Narcissistic Personality Disorder
	301.7	Antisocial Personality Disorder
	301.9	Personality Disorder NOS
	______	____________________
	______	____________________

Appendix A

BIBLIOTHERAPY SUGGESTIONS

GENERAL

Many references are made throughout the chapters to a therapeutic homework resource that was developed by the authors as a corollary to this *Complete Adult Psychotherapy Treatment Planner,* Fourth Edition (Jongsma and Peterson). This frequently cited homework resource book is:

Jongsma, A. E. (2006). *Adult Psychotherapy Homework Planner, Second Edition.* New York: Wiley.

ANGER MANAGEMENT

Carter, L. (2003). *The Anger Trap.* San Francisco: Jossey-Bass.
Deffenbacher, J. L., and McKay, M. (2000). *Overcoming Situational and General Anger: Client Manual (Best Practices for Therapy).* Oakland, CA: New Harbinger.
Lerner, H. (1985). *The Dance of Anger: A Woman's Guide to Changing the Patterns of Intimate Relationships.* New York: Harper Perennial.
McKay, M., and Rogers, P. (2000). *The Anger Control Workbook*. Oakland, CA: New Harbinger.
McKay, M., Rogers, P., and McKay, J. (1989). *When Anger Hurts.* Oakland, CA: New Harbinger.
Potter-Etron, R. (2001). *Stop the Anger Now: A Workbook.* Oakland, CA: New Harbinger.
Rosellini, G., and Worden, M. (1986). *Of Course You're Angry.* San Francisco: Harper Hazelden.
Rubin, T. I. (1969). *The Angry Book.* New York: Macmillan.
Smedes, L. (1991). *Forgive and Forget: Healing the Hurts We Don't Deserve.* San Francisco: HarperCollins.
Tavris, C. (1989). *Anger: The Misunderstood Emotion.* New York: Touchstone Books.
Weisinger, H. (1985). *Dr. Weisinger's Anger Work-Out Book.* New York: Quill.

ANTISOCIAL BEHAVIOR

Carnes, P. (1983). *Out of the Shadows: Understanding Sexual Addictions.* Minneapolis, MN: CompCare.
Katherine, A. (1998). *Boundaries: Where You End and I Begin.* New York: MJF Books.
Pittman, F. (1998). *Grow Up!* New York: Golden Books.
Williams, R., and Williams, V. (1993). *Anger Kills.* New York: Time Books.

ANXIETY

Benson, H. (1975). *The Relaxation Response.* New York: William Morrow.
Bernstein, D. A., and Borkovec, T. D. (1973). *Progressive Relaxation Training.* Champaign, IL: Research Press.
Bourne, E. (2005). *The Anxiety and Phobia Workbook.* Oakland, CA: New Harbinger.
Burns, D. (1993). *Ten Days to Self-Esteem!* New York: William Morrow.
Davis, M., Eshelman, E., and McKay, M. (1988). *The Relaxation and Stress Reduction Workbook.* Oakland, CA: New Harbinger.
Hauck, P. (1975). *Overcoming Worry and Fear.* Philadelphia: Westminster Press.
Jeffers, S. (1987). *Feel the Fear and Do It Anyway.* San Diego, CA: Harcourt Brace Jovanovich.
Marks, I. (1980). *Living with Fear: Understanding and Coping with Anxiety.* New York: McGraw-Hill.
McKay, M., Davis, M., and Farming, P. (1998). *Thoughts and Feelings: Taking Control of Your Moods and Your Life.* Oakland, CA: New Harbinger.
Zinbarg, R. E., Craske, M. G., Barlow, D. H., and O'Leary, T. (1993). *Mastery of Your Anxiety and Worry—Client Guide.* San Antonio, TX: The Psychological Corporation.

ATTENTION DEFICIT DISORDER (ADD)—ADULT

Hallowell, E., and Ratey, J. (1994). *Driven to Distraction.* New York: Simon & Schuster.
Kelly, K., and Ramundo, P. (1994). *You Mean I'm Not Lazy, Stupid, or Crazy?! A Self-Help Book for Adults with Attention Deficit Disorder.* Cincinnati, OH: Tyrell and Jerem Press.
Nadeau, K. (1996). *Adventures in Fast Forward.* Levittown, PA: Brunner/Mazel.
Quinn, D., and Stern, J. (1991). *Putting on the Brakes.* New York: Magination Press.
Weis, Lynn. (1994). *The Attention Deficit Disorder in Adults Workbook.* Dallas, TX: Taylor Publishing.
Wender, P. (1987). *The Hyperactive Child, Adolescent, and Adult.* New York: Oxford University Press.

BORDERLINE PERSONALITY

Cudney, M., and Handy, R. (1993). *Self-Defeating Behaviors.* San Francisco: HarperCollins.
Herman, J. (1997). *Trauma and Recovery*. New York: Basic Books.
Katherine, A. (1998). *Boundaries: Where You End and I Begin.* New York: MJF Books.
Kreisman, J., and Straus, H. (1989). *I Hate You—Don't Leave Me.* New York: Avon.
Linehan, M. (1993). *Skills Manual for Treating Borderline Personality Disorder.* New York: Guilford.
Miller, D. (1994). *Women Who Hurt Themselves: A Book of Hope and Understanding*. New York: HarperCollins.
O'Neil, M., and Newbold, C. (1994). *Boundary Power.* Fort Smithy, AR: Sonlight Publishing.
Peurito, R. (1997). *Overcoming Anxiety.* New York: Henry Holt.
Reiland, R. (2004). *Get Me Out of Here: My Recovery from Borderline Personality Disorder*. Center City, MN: Hazeldon Foundation.
Spadlin, S. (2003). *Don't Let Your Emotions Run Your Life: How Dialectical Behavior Therapy Can Put You in Control*. Oakland, CA: New Harbinger.

CHEMICAL DEPENDENCE

Alcoholics Anonymous. (1975). *Living Sober.* New York: A. A. World Service.
Alcoholics Anonymous. (1976). *Alcoholics Anonymous: The Big Book.* New York: A. A. World Service.
Carnes, P. (1989). *A Gentle Path Through the Twelve Steps.* Minneapolis, MN: CompCare.
Gorski, T. (1992). *Staying Sober Workbook.* Independence, MO: Herald House Press.
Gorski, T., and Miller, M. (1986). *Staying Sober: A Guide to Relapse Prevention.* Independence, MO: Herald House Press.
Johnson, V. (1980). *I'll Quit Tomorrow.* New York: Harper & Row.
Kasl-Davis, C. (1992). *Many Roads, One Journey.* New York: HarperCollins.
Nuckals, C. (1989). *Cocaine: From Dependence to Recovery.* Blue Ridge Summit, PA: TAB Books.
Wilson, B. (1967). *As Bill Sees It.* New York: A. A. World Service.

CHEMICAL DEPENDENCE—RELAPSE

Alcoholics Anonymous. (1975). *Living Sober.* New York: A. A. World Service.
Alcoholics Anonymous. (1976). *Alcoholics Anonymous: The Big Book.* New York: A. A. World Service.
Burns, D. (1993). *Ten Days to Self-Esteem!* New York: William Morrow.
Carnes, P. (1989). *A Gentle Path Through the Twelve Steps.* Minneapolis, MN: CompCare.
Doe, J. (1955). *The Golden Book of Resentments.* Minneapolis, MN: CompCare Publishing.

Gorski, T. (1992). *The Staying Sober Workbook.* Independence, MO: Herald House Press.
Gorski, T., and Miller, M. (1986). *Staying Sober: A Guide to Relapse Prevention.* Independence, MO: Herald House Press.
Johnson, V. (1980). *I'll Quit Tomorrow.* New York: Harper & Row.
Kasl-Davis, C. (1992). *Many Roads, One Journey.* New York: HarperCollins.
Larson, E. (1985). *Stage II Recovery: Life Beyond Addiction.* San Francisco: Harper & Row.
Nuckals, C. (1989). *Cocaine: From Dependence to Recovery.* Blue Ridge Summit, PA: TAB Books.
Wilson, B. (1967). *As Bill Sees It.* New York: A. A. World Service.

CHILDHOOD TRAUMAS

Black, C. (1980). *It Will Never Happen to Me.* Denver, CO: MAC Publishing.
Bradshaw, J. (1990). *Homecoming.* New York: Bantam Books.
Bradshaw, J. (1998). *Healing the Shame that Binds You.* Deerfield Beach, FL: Health Communications, Inc.
Copeland, M., and Harris, M. (2000) *Healing the Trauma of Abuse: A Woman's Workbook.* Oakland, CA: New Harbinger.
Gil, E. (1984). *Outgrowing the Pain: A Book for and About Adults Abused as Children.* New York: Dell Publishing.
Kushner, H. (1981). *When Bad Things Happen to Good People.* New York: Schocken Books.
Pittman, F. (1998). *Grow Up!* New York: Golden Books.
Powell, J. (1969). *Why I'm Afraid to Tell You Who I Am.* Allen, TX: Argus Communications.
Smedes, L. (1991). *Forgive and Forget: Healing the Hurts We Don't Deserve.* San Francisco: HarperCollins.
Whitfield, C. (1987). *Healing the Child Within.* Deerfield Beach, FL: Health Communications, Inc.
Whitfield, C. (1990). *A Gift to Myself.* Deerfield Beach, FL: Health Communications, Inc.

CHRONIC PAIN

Benson, H. (1975). *The Relaxation Response.* New York: William Morrow.
Benson, H. (1979). *The Mind/Body Effect.* New York: Simon & Schuster.
Bernstein, D. A., and Borkovec, T. D. (1973). *Progressive Relaxation Training.* Champaign, IL: Research Press.
Burns, D. (1980). *Feeling Good: The New Mood Therapy.* New York: Signet.
Burns, D. (1989). *The Feeling Good Handbook.* New York: Blume.
Burns, D. (1993). *Ten Days to Self-Esteem.* New York: William Morrow.
Catalano, E., and Hardin, K. (1996). *The Chronic Pain Control Workbook: A Step-by-Step Guide for Coping With and Overcoming Pain.* Oakland, CA: New Harbinger.

Caudill, M. (1995). *Managing Pain Before It Manages You.* New York: Guilford.
Duckro, P., Richardson, W., and Marshall, J. (1995). *Taking Control of Your Headaches.* New York: Guilford.
Fields, H. (1987). *Pain.* New York: McGraw-Hill.
Hunter, M. (1996). *Making Peace with Chronic Pain.* Levittown, PA: Brunner/Mazel.
LeShan, L. (1984). *How to Meditate.* New York: Bantam Books.
Morris, D. (1991). *The Culture of Pain.* Berkeley: University of California Press.
Siegel, B. (1989). *Peace, Love, & Healing.* New York: Harper & Row.

COGNITIVE DEFICITS

Ellis, A., and Harper, R. (1974). *A New Guide to Rational Living.* Hollywood, CA: Wilshire Books.

DEPENDENCY

Alberti, R., and Emmons, M. (1990). *Your Perfect Right: Assertiveness and Equality in Your Life and Relationships, Eighth Edition.* San Luis Obispo, CA: Impact.
Beattie, M. (1987). *Codependent No More: How to Stop Controlling Others and Start Caring for Yourself.* San Francisco: HarperCollins.
Evans, P. (1992). *The Verbally Abusive Relationship.* Holbrook, MA: Bob Adams, Inc.
Helmfelt, R., Minirth, F., and Meier, P. (1985). *Love Is a Choice.* Nashville, TN: Nelson.
Katherine, A. (1998). *Boundaries: Where You End and I Begin.* New York: MJF Books.
Norwood, R. (1985). *Women Who Love Too Much.* Los Angeles: Archer.
Pittman, F. (1998). *Grow Up!* New York: Golden Books.
Smith, M. (1985). *When I Say No, I Feel Guilty.* New York: Bantam Books.
Walker, L. (1979). *The Battered Woman.* New York: Harper & Row.
Whitfield, C. (1990). *A Gift to Myself.* Deerfield Beach, FL: Health Communications, Inc.

DEPRESSION

Burns, D. (1989). *The Feeling Good Handbook.* New York: Blume.
Burns, D. (1999). *Feeling Good: The New Mood Therapy*. New York: HarperCollins.
Butler, P. (1991). *Talking to Yourself: Learning the Language of Self-Affirmation.* New York: Stein and Day.
Downs, A. (2003). *The Half Empty Heart.* New York: St. Martin's.
Dyer, W. (1974). *Your Erroneous Zones.* New York: Funk & Wagnalls.
Geisel, T. (1990). *Oh, The Places You'll Go.* New York: Random House.
Gilson, M., and Freemen, A. (2000). *Overcoming Depression: A Cognitive Therapy Approach for Taming the Depression Beast: Client Workbook*. New York: Oxford University Press.

Hallinan, P. K. (1976). *One Day at a Time.* Minneapolis, MN: CompCare.
Hazelden Staff. (1991). *Each Day a New Beginning.* Center City, MN: Hazelden.
Helmstetter, S. (1986). *What to Say When You Talk to Yourself.* New York: Fine Communications.
Knauth, P. (1977). *A Season in Hell.* New York: Pocket Books.
Leith, L. (1998). *Exercising Your Way to Better Mental Health.* Morgantown, WV: Fitness Information Technology.
McKay, M., Davis, M., and Farming, P. (1998). *Thoughts and Feelings: Taking Control of Your Moods and Your Life.* Oakland, CA: New Harbinger.
Miklowitz, D. (2002) *Bipolar Disorder Survival Guide: What You and Your Family Need to Know*. New York: Guilford.
Strauss, C. (2004) *Talking to Depression*. New York: New American Library.
Weissman, M. (2005). *Mastering Depression Through Interpersonal Psychotherapy: Patient Workbook*. New York: Oxford University Press.
Yapko, M. (1999). *Hand Me Down Blues.* New York: Golden Books.
Zonnebelt-Smeenge, S., and DeVries, R. (1998). *Getting to the Other Side of Grief: Overcoming the Loss of a Spouse.* Grand Rapids, MI: Baker Books.

DISSOCIATION

Grateful Members of Emotional Health Anonymous. (1982). *The Twelve Steps for Everyone . . . Who Really Wants Them.* Minneapolis, MN: CompCare.

EATING DISORDER

Fairburn, C. (1995). *Overcoming Binge Eating.* New York: Guilford.
Hirschmann, J., and Munter, C. (1988). *Overcoming Overeating.* New York: Ballentine Books.
Hollis, J. (1985). *Fat Is a Family Affair.* New York: Harper & Row.
Rodin, J. (1993). *Body Traps.* New York: William Morrow.
Sacker, I., and Zimmer, M. (1987). *Dying to Be Thin.* New York: Warner Books.
Siegel, M., Brisman, J., and Weinshel, M. (1997). *Surviving an Eating Disorder.* San Francisco: HarperCollins.

EDUCATIONAL DEFICITS

de Boro, E. (1982). *de Boro's Thinking Course.* New York: Facts of Life Publishing.
Sandstrom, R. (1990). *The Ultimate Memory Book.* Granada, CA: Stepping Stones Books.

FAMILY CONFLICT

Black, C. (1980). *It Will Never Happen to Me.* Denver, CO: MAC Publishing.
Bloomfield, H., and Felder, L. (1983). *Making Peace with Your Parents.* New York: Random House.
Bradshaw, J. (1988). *On the Family.* Deerfield Beach, FL: Health Communications, Inc.

Cline, F., and Fay, J. (1990). *Parenting with Love and Logic.* Colorado Springs, CO: Navpress.
Faber, A., and Mazlish, E. (1987). *Siblings Without Rivalry.* New York: Norton.
Fassler, D., Lash, M., and Ivers, S. (1988). *Changing Families.* Burlington, VT: Waterfront Books.
Ginott, H. (1969). *Between Parent and Teenager.* New York: Scribner.
Ginott, H. (2003). *Between Parent and Child.* New York: Three Rivers Press.
Glenn, S., and Nelsen, J. (1989). *Raising Self-Reliant Children in a Self-Indulgent World.* Rocklin, CA: Prima.
Phelan, T. (1995). *1-2-3 Magic: Training Your Preschoolers and Preteens to Do What You Want.* Glen Ellyn, IL: Child Management, Inc.
Steinberg, L., and Levine, A. (1990). *You and Your Adolescent: A Parents' Guide for Ages 10–20.* New York: Harper Perennial.

FEMALE SEXUAL DYSFUNCTION

Barbach, L. (1982). *For Each Other: Sharing Sexual Intimacy.* New York: Doubleday.
Comfort, A. (1991). *The New Joy of Sex.* New York: Crown.
Heiman, J., and LoPiccolo, J. (1988). *Becoming Orgasmic: A Sexual Growth Program for Women.* New York: Prentice-Hall.
Kaplan, H. S. (1975). *The Illustrated Manual of Sex Therapy.* New York: Quadrangle, The New York Times Book Co.
Kaplan, H. S. (1988). *The Illustrated Manual of Sex Therapy*. Levittown, PA: Brunner/Mazel.
McCarthy, B., and McCarthy, E. (1984). *Sexual Awareness.* New York: Carroll & Graf.
Penner, C., and Penner, C. (1981). *The Gift of Sex.* Waco, TX: Word.
Schnarch, D., and Maddock, J. (2003). *Resurrecting Sex: Solving Sexual Problems and Revolutionizing Your Relationship*. New York: HarperCollins.
Valins, L. (1992). *When a Woman's Body Says No to Sex: Understanding and Overcoming Vaginismus.* New York: Penguin.
Wincze, J., and Barlow, D. H. (1997). *Enhancing Sexuality: A Problem-solving Approach—Client Workbook*. San Antonio, TX: The Psychological Corporation.
Zibergeld, B. (1992). *The New Male Sexuality.* New York: Bantam Books.

FINANCIAL STRESS

Abentrod, S. (1996). *10 Minute Guide to Beating Debt.* New York: Macmillan.
Burkett, L. (1989). *Debt Free Living.* Chicago: Moody Press.
Loungo, T. (1997). *10 Minute Guide to Household Budgeting.* New York: Macmillan.
Ramsey, D. (1997). *Financial Peace.* New York: Penguin.

GRIEF/LOSS UNRESOLVED

Albom, Mitch. (1997). *Tuesdays with Morrie.* New York: Doublesday.
Colgrove, M. (1991). *How to Survive the Loss of a Love.* Los Angeles: Prelude Press.

Kushner, H. (1981). *When Bad Things Happen to Good People.* New York: Schocken Books.
Lewis, C. S. (1961). *A Grief Observed.* New York: The Seabury Press.
Moore, Thomas. (2004). *Dark Nights of the Soul.* New York: Gotham.
Rando, T. (1991). *How to Go on Living When Someone You Love Dies.* New York: Bantam Books.
Schiff, N. (1977). *The Bereaved Parent.* New York: Crown Publications.
Smedes, L. (1982). *How Can It Be All Right When Everything Is All Wrong?* San Francisco: HarperCollins.
Smedes, L. (1991). *Forgive and Forget: Healing the Hurts We Don't Deserve.* San Francisco: HarperCollins.
Tatelbaum, Judy. (1980). *The Courage to Grieve.* New York: Harper & Row.
Westberg, G. (1962). *Good Grief.* Philadelphia: Augsburg Fortress Press.
Wolterstorff, N. (1987). *Lament for a Son.* Grand Rapids, MI: Eerdmans.
Zonnebelt-Smeenge, S., and DeVries, R. (2004). *Living Fully in the Shadow of Death.* Grand Rapids, MI: Baker.
Zonnebelt-Smeenge, S., and DeVries, R. (1998). *Getting to the Other Side of Grief: Overcoming the Loss of a Spouse.* Grand Rapids, MI: Baker Books.

IMPULSE CONTROL DISORDER

Helmstetter, S. (1986). *What to Say When You Talk to Yourself.* New York: Fine Communications.
Kelly, K., and Ramundo, P. (1994). *You Mean I'm Not Lazy, Stupid or Crazy?! A Self-Help Book for Adults with Attention Deficit Disorder.* Cincinnati, OH: Tyrell and Jerem Press.
Wander, P. (1987). *The Hyperactive Child, Adolescent, and Adult.* New York: Oxford University Press.

INTIMATE RELATIONSHIP CONFLICTS

Abrams-Spring, J. (1996). *After the Affair.* New York: HarperCollins.
Bach, G., and Wyden, P. (1976). *The Intimate Enemy: How to Fight Fair in Love and Marriage.* New York: Avon.
Christensen, A., and Jacobson, N. (2000). *Reconcilable Differences.* New York: Guilford.
Colgrove, M., Bloomfield, H., and McWillilams, P. (1991). *How to Survive the Loss of a Love.* Los Angeles: Prelude Press.
Fisher, B. (1981). *Rebuilding: When Your Relationship Ends.* San Luis Obispo, CA: Impact.
Fromm, E. (1956). *The Art of Loving.* New York: Harper & Row.
Gorski, T. (1993). *Getting Love Right: Learning the Choices of Healthy Intimacy.* New York: Simon & Schuster.
Gray, J. (1992). *Men Are From Mars, Women Are From Venus.* New York: HarperCollins.

Gray, J. (1993). *Men and Women and Relationships: Making Peace with the Opposite Sex.* Hillsboro, OR: Beyond Words.
Harley, W. (1994). *His Needs, Her Needs: Building an Affair-Proof Marriage.* Grand Rapids, MI: Revell.
Hendrix, H. (1988). *Getting the Love You Want: A Guide for Couples.* New York: HarperCollins.
Lerner, H. (1989). *The Dance of Intimacy: A Woman's Guide to Courageous Acts of Change in Key Relationships.* New York: Harper Perennial.
Lindbergh, A. (1955). *A Gift from the Sea.* New York: Pantheon.
Markman, H., Stanley S., and Blumberg, S. (1994). *Fighting for Your Marriage.* San Francisco: Jossey-Bass.
Oberlin, L. (2005). *Surviving Separation and Divorce: A Woman's Guide.* Avon, MA: Adams Media.
Schnarch, D. (1997). *Passionate Marriage.* New York: Norton.
Weiner-Davis, M. (1993). *Divorce Busting: A Step-by-step Approach to Making Your Marriage Loving Again.* New York: Simon & Schuster.

LEGAL CONFLICTS

Carnes, P. (1983). *Out of the Shadows: Understanding Sexual Addictions.* Minneapolis, MN: CompCare.
Williams, R., and Williams, V. (1993). *Anger Kills.* New York: Time Books.

LOW SELF-ESTEEM

Branden, N. (1994). *The Six Pillars of Self-Esteem.* New York: Bantam Books.
Burns, D. (1993). *Ten Days to Self-Esteem!* New York: William Morrow.
Helmstetter, S. (1986). *What to Say When You Talk to Yourself.* New York: Fine Communications.
McKay, M., and Fanning, P. (1987). *Self-Esteem.* Oakland, CA: New Harbinger.
Schialdi, G. (2001). *The Self Esteem Workbook.* Oakland, CA: New Harbinger.
Zimbardo, P. (1987). *Shyness: What It Is and What to Do About It.* Reading, MA: Addison-Wesley.

MALE SEXUAL DYSFUNCTION

Comfort, A. (1991). *The New Joy of Sex.* New York: Crown.
Kaplan, H. S. (1988). *The Illustrated Manual of Sex Therapy.* New York: Brunner/Mazel.
McCarthy, B., and McCarthy, E. (1981). *Sexual Awareness.* New York: Carroll & Graf.
Penner, C., and Penner, C. (1981). *The Gift of Sex.* Waco, TX: Word.
Schnarch, D., and Maddock, M. (2003) *Resurrecting Sex: Solving Sexual Problems and Revolutionizing Your Relationship.* New York: HarperCollins.
Wincze, J., and Barlow, D. (1997) *Enhancing Sexuality: A Problem-solving Approach (Client Workbook).* San Antonio, TX: The Psychological Corporation.
Zilbergeld, B. (1992). *The New Male Sexuality.* New York: Bantam Books.

MANIA OR HYPOMANIA

Copeland, M. (2000). *The Depression Workbook: A Guide for Living with Depression and Manic Depression.* Oakland, CA: New Harbinger.
Grateful Members of Emotional Health Anonymous. (1987). *The Twelve Steps for Everyone . . . Who Really Wants Them.* Minneapolis, MN: CompCare.
Miklowitz, D. (2002). *The Bipolar Disorder Survival Guide: What You and Your Family Need to Know.* New York: Guilford.

MEDICAL ISSUES

Friedman, M., and Ulmer, P. (1984). *Treating Type A Behavior and Your Heart.* New York: Knopf.

OBSESSIVE-COMPULSIVE DISORDER (OCD)

Baer, L. (2000). *Getting Control: Overcoming Your Obsessions and Compulsions, Revised Edition.* New York: Plume.
Bourne, E. (2005). *The Anxiety and Phobia Workbook.* Oakland, CA: New Harbinger.
Burns, D. (1993). *Ten Days to Self-Esteem!* New York: William Morrow.
Foa, E. B., and Wilson, R. (2001). *Stop Obsessing! How to Overcome Your Obsessions and Compulsions, Revised Edition.* New York: Bantam Books.
Hyman, B. M., and Pedrick, C. (1999). *The OCD Workbook: Your Guide to Breaking Free from Obsessive-Compulsive Disorder.* Oakland, CA: New Harbinger.
Kozak, M., and Foa, E. B. (1997). *Mastery of Obsessive-Compulsive Disorder: A Cognitive Behavioral Approach.* San Antonio, TX: The Psychological Corporation.
Levenkron, S. (1991). *Obsessive-Compulsive Disorders.* New York: Warner Books.
Penzel, F. (2000). *Obsessive-Compulsive Disorders: A Complete Guide to Getting Well and Staying Well.* New York: Oxford University Press.
Schwartz, J. (1996). *Brain Lock: Free Yourself from Obsessive-Compulsive Behavior.* New York: HarperCollins.
Steketee, G., and White, K. (1990). *When Once is Not Enough: Help for Obsessive Compulsives.* Oakland, CA: New Harbinger.
Steketee, G. (1999). *Overcoming Obsessive Compulsive Disorder—Client Manual.* Oakland, CA: New Harbinger.

PANIC/AGORAPHOBIA

Antony, M., and McCabe, R. (2004). *10 Simple Solutions to Panic: How to Overcome Panic Attacks, Calm Physical Symptoms, and Reclaim Your Life.* Oakland, CA: New Harbinger.
Barlow, D. H., and Craske, M. G. (2000). *Mastery of Your Anxiety and Panic (MAP-3).* San Antonio, TX: Graywind/The Psychological Corporation.

Bourne, E. (2005). *The Anxiety and Phobia Workbook,* Fourth Edition. Oakland, CA: New Harbinger.
Gold, M. (1988). *The Good News About Panic, Anxiety, and Phobias.* New York: Villard/Random House.
Marks, I. (2001). *Living With Fear, Second Edition.* London: McGraw-Hill.
McKay, M., Davis, M., and Farming, P. (1998) *Thoughts and Feelings: Taking Control of Your Moods and Your Life.* Oakland, CA: New Harbinger.
Swede, S., and Jaffe, S. (1987). *The Panic Attack Recovery Book.* New York: New American Library.
Wilson, R. (1996). *Don't Panic: Taking Control of Anxiety Attacks, Second Edition.* New York: Harper & Row.
Wilson, R. (1986). *Don't Panic: Taking Control of Anxiety Attacks.* New York: Harper & Row.

PARANOID IDEATION

Burns, D. (1989). *The Feeling Good Handbook.* New York: Plume.
Cudney, M., and Hard, R. (1991). *Self-Defeating Behaviors.* San Francisco: HarperCollins.
Ross, J. (1994). *Triumph Over Fear.* New York: Bantam Books.

PARENTING

Cline, F., and Fay, J. (1990). *Parenting with Love and Logic.* Colorado Springs, CO: Navpress.
Dobson, J. (2000). *Preparing for Adolescence: How to Survive the Coming Years of Change.* New York: Regal Press.
Edwards, C. (1999). *How to Handle a Hard-to-Handle Kid.* Minneapolis, MN: Free Spirit Publishing.
Faber, A., and Mazlish, E. (1982). *How to Talk So Kids Will Listen and Listen So Kids Will Talk.* New York: Avon.
Forehand, R., and Long, N. (1996) *Parenting the Strong-Willed Child.* Chicago: Contemporary Books.
Forgatch, M. (1994) *Parenting Through Change: A Training Manual.* Eugene, OR: Oregon Social Learning Center.
Ginott, H. (1969). *Between Parent and Teenager.* New York. Macmillan.
Gordon, T. (2000). *Parent Effectiveness Training.* New York: Three Rivers Press.
Greene, R. (1998). *The Explosive Child.* New York: HarperCollins.
Greenspan, S. (1995). *The Challenging Child.* Reading, MA: Perseus Books.
Ilg, F., Ames, L., and Baker, S. (1992). *Child Behavior: The Classic Childcare Manual from the Gesell Institute of Human Development.* New York: Harper Perennial.
Phelan, T. (1995). *1-2-3 Magic: Training Your Preschoolers and Preteens to Do What You Want.* Glen Ellyn, IL: Child Management, Inc.
Renshaw-Joslin, K. (1994). *Positive Parenting from A to Z.* New York: Fawcett Books.

Tracy, F. (1994). *Grounded for Life: Stop Blowing Your Fuse and Start Communicating.* Seattle, WA: Parenting Press.
Turecki, S., and Tonner, L. (1988). *The Difficult Child.* New York: Bantam Books.
Wolf, A. (1992). *Get Out of My Life, But First Could You Drive Me and Cheryl to the Mall?: A Parent's Guide to the New Teenager.* New York: Noonday Press.

PHASE OF LIFE PROBLEMS

Alberti, R., and Emmons, M. (2001). *Your Perfect Right: Assertiveness and Equality in Your Life and Relationships, Eighth Edition.* San Luis Obispo, CA: Impact.
Black, J., and Enns, G. (1998). *Better Boundaries: Owning and Treasuring Your Life.* Oakland, CA: New Harbinger.
Bower, S., and Bower, G. (1991). *Asserting Yourself: A Practical Guide for Positive Change.* Cambridge, MA: Perseus Publishing.
Hollis, J. (2005). *Finding Meaning in the Second Half of Life.* New York: Gotham.
Katherine, A. (1998). *Boundaries: Where You End and I Begin.* New York: MJF Books.
Moore, T. (2004). *Dark Nights of the Soul.* New York: Gotham.
Paterson, R. (2000). *The Assertiveness Workbook: How to Express Your Ideas and Stand Up for Yourself at Work and in Relationships.* Oakland, CA: New Harbinger.
Seuss, Dr. (1986). *You're Only Old Once.* New York: Random House.
Simon, S. (1993). *In Search of Values: 31 Strategies for Finding Out What Really Matters Most to You.* New York: Warner Books.
Simon, S., Howe, L., and Kirschenbaum, H. (1995). *Values Clarification.* New York: Warner Books.
Smith, M. (1975). *When I Say No, I Feel Guilty.* New York: Bantam Books.

PHOBIA

Antony, M. M., Craske, M. C., and Barlow, D. H. (1995). *Mastery of Your Specific Phobia—Client Manual.* San Antonio, TX: The Psychological Corporation.
Bourne, E. (2005). *The Anxiety and Phobia Workbook,* Fourth Edition. Oakland, CA: New Harbinger.
Gold, M. (1988). *The Good News About Panic, Anxiety, and Phobias.* New York: Villard/Random House.
Marks, I. (1980). *Living with Fear: Understanding and Coping with Anxiety.* New York: McGraw-Hill.
McKay, M., Davis, M., and Farming, P. (1998) *Thoughts and Feelings: Taking Control of Your Moods and Your Life.* Oakland, CA: New Harbinger.

POSTTRAUMATIC STRESS DISORDER (PTSD)

Allen, J. (1995). *Coping with Trauma: A Guide to Self-Understanding.* Washington, DC: American Psychiatric Press.

Bradshaw, J. (1988). *Healing the Shame That Binds You.* Deerfield Beach, FL: Health Communications, Inc.

Foa E., Davidson, J., and Frances, A. (1999). The Expert Consensus Guideline Series: Treatment of Posttraumatic Stress Disorder. *Journal of Clinical Psychiatry, 60–66*(16). Also available online at: http://www.psychguides.com/ptsdhe.pdf.

Frankel, V. (1959). *Man's Search for Meaning.* Boston: Beacon Press.

Jeffers, S. (1987). *Feel the Fear and Do It Anyway.* New York: Random House.

Leith, L. (1998). *Exercising Your Way to Better Mental Health.* Morgantown, WV: Fitness Information Technology.

Matsakis, A. (1996). *I Can't Get Over It: A Handbook for Trauma Survivors, Second Edition.* Oakland, CA: New Harbinger.

Rothbaum, B. O., and Foa, E. B. (2004). *Reclaiming Your Life After Rape: Cognitive-Behavioral Therapy for Posttraumatic Stress Disorder—Client Workbook.* New York: Oxford University Press.

Simon, S., and Simon, S. (1990). *Forgiving: How to Make Peace with Your Past and Get On with Your Life.* New York: Warner Books.

Williams, M., and Poijula, S. (2002). *The PTSD Workbook.* Oakland, CA: New Harbinger.

Zehr, H. (2001). *Transcending: Reflections of Crime Victims.* Intercourse, PA: Good Books.

PSYCHOTICISM

Torrey, M., and Fuller, E. (1988). *Surviving Schizophrenia: A Family Manual.* New York: Harper & Row.

SEXUAL ABUSE

Bass, E., and Davis, L. (1988). *The Courage to Heal: A Guide for Women Survivors of Child Sexual Abuse.* San Francisco: HarperCollins.

Bradshaw, J. (1988). *Healing the Shame That Binds You.* Deerfield Beach, FL: Health Communications, Inc.

Burns, D. (1993). *Ten Days to Self-Esteem!* New York: William Morrow.

Davis, L. (1990). *The Courage to Heal Workbook: For Men and Women Survivors of Child Sexual Abuse.* San Francisco: HarperCollins.

Forward, S., and Buck, C. (1978). *Betrayal of Innocence: Incest and Its Devastation.* New York: Penguin.

Fossum, M., and Mason, M. (1986). *Facing Shame: Families in Recovery.* New York: Norton.

Gil, E. (1984). *Outgrowing the Pain: A Book for and About Adults Abused as Children.* New York: Dell Publishing.

Simon, S., and Simon, S. (1990). *Forgiving: How to Make Peace with Your Past and Get On with Your Life.* New York: Warner Books.

Smedes, L. (1991). *Forgive and Forget: Healing the Hurts We Don't Deserve.* San Francisco: HarperCollins.

Copeland, M. E., and Harris, M. (2000). *Healing the Trauma of Abuse: A Women's Workbook.* Oakland, CA: New Harbinger.
Zehr, H. (2001). *Transcending: Reflections of Crime Victims.* Intercourse, PA: Good Books.

SEXUAL IDENTITY CONFUSION

Beam, J. (1986). *In the Life: A Black Gay Anthology.* Boston: Alyson Publications.
Eichberg, R. (1991). *Coming Out: An Act of Love.* New York: Penguin.
Katz, J. (1996). *The Invention of Heterosexuality.* New York: Plume.
Marcus, E. (1993). *Is It a Choice? Answers to 300 of the Most Frequently Asked Questions About Gays and Lesbians.* San Francisco: HarperCollins.
Signorile, M. (1996). *Outing Yourself: How to Come Out as Lesbian or Gay to Your Family, Friends, and Coworkers.* New York: Fireside Books.

SLEEP DISTURBANCE

Dotto, L. (1990). *Losing Sleep: How Your Sleeping Habits Affect Your Life.* New York: William Morrow.
Catalano, E., Morin, C., and Webb, W. (1990). *Getting to Sleep: Simple, Effective Methods for Falling and Staying Asleep, Getting the Rest You Need, and Awakening Refreshed and Renewed.* Oakland, CA: New Harbinger.
Hewish, J. (1985). *Relaxation.* Chicago: NTC Publishing Group.
Leith, L. (1998). *Exercising Your Way to Better Mental Health.* Morgantown, WV: Fitness Information Technology.

SOCIAL DISCOMFORT

Alberti, R., and Emmons, M. (2001). *Your Perfect Right: Assertiveness and Equality in Your Life and Relationships, Eighth Edition.* San Luis Obispo, CA: Impact.
Antony, M., and Swinson, R. (2000). *The Shyness and Social Anxiety Workbook: Proven, Step-by-step Techniques for Overcoming Your Fear.* Oakland, CA: New Harbinger.
Bradshaw, J. (1988). *Healing the Shame That Binds You.* Deerfield Beach, FL: Health Communications, Inc.
Burns, D. (1985). *Intimate Connections: The New Clinically Tested Program for Overcoming Loneliness.* New York: William Morrow.
Burns, D. (1989). *The Feeling Good Handbook.* New York: William Morrow.
Burns, D. (1993). *Ten Days to Self-Esteem!* New York: William Morrow.
Butler, G. (1999). *Overcoming Social Anxiety and Shyness: A Self-help Guide Using Cognitive Behavioral Techniques.* London: Robinson.
Desberg, P. (1996). *No More Butterflies: Overcoming Shyness, Stage Fright, Interview Anxiety, and Fear of Public Speaking.* Oakland, CA: New Harbinger.
Dyer, W. (1978). *Pulling Your Own Strings.* New York: T. Crowell.

Fossum, M., and Mason, M. (1986). *Facing Shame: Families in Recovery.* New York. Norton.
Garner, A. (1997). *Conversationally Speaking: Tested New Ways to Increase Your Personal and Social Effectiveness.* Los Angeles: Lowell House.
Harris, T. (1996). *I'm OK, You're OK.* New York: Avon.
James, M., and Jongeward, D. (1971). *Born to Win.* Reading, MA: Addison-Wesley.
Markway, B., Carmin, C., Pollard, C., and Flynn, T. (1992). *Dying of Embarrassment: Help for Social Anxiety and Phobia.* Oakland, CA: New Harbinger.
Nouwen, H. (1975). *Reaching Out.* New York: Doubleday.
Rapee, R.M. (1998). *Overcoming Shyness and Social Phobia: A Step-by-step Guide.* Northvale, NJ: Jason Aronson.
Schneier, F., and Welkowitz, L. (1996). *The Hidden Face of Shyness: Understanding and Overcoming Social Anxiety.* New York: Avon.
Soifer, S., Zgourides, G. D., Himle, J., and Pickering, N. L. (2001). *Shy Bladder Syndrome: Your Step-by-step Guide to Overcoming Paruresis.* Oakland, CA: New Harbinger.
Stein, M., and Walker, J. (2001). *Triumph Over Shyness: Conquering Shyness and Social Anxiety.* New York: McGraw-Hill.
Steiner, C. (1997). *Achieving Emotional Literacy: A Personal Program to Improve Your Emotional Intelligence.* New York: Avon.
Zimbardo, P. (1987). *Shyness: What It Is and What to Do About It.* Reading, MA: Addison-Wesley.

SOMATIZATION

Benson, H. (1980). *The Mind-Body Effect.* New York: Simon & Schuster.
Claiborn, J., and Pedrick, C. (2002). *The BDD Workbook: Overcome Body Dysmorphic Disorder and End Body Image Obsessions.* Oakland, CA: New Harbinger.
Grateful Members of Emotional Health Anonymous. (1987). *The Twelve Steps for Everyone . . . Who Really Wants Them.* Minneapolis, MN: CompCare.

SPIRITUAL CONFUSION

Armstrong, K. (1993). *A History of God.* New York: Knopf.
Augustine, St. (1949). *The Confessions of St. Augustine.* New York: Random House.
Chopra, D. (2000). *How to Know God.* New York: Three Rivers Press.
Cleaver, E. (1992). *The Soul on Fire.* Grand Rapids, MI: Zondervan.
Dyer, W. (2003). *There's a Spiritual Solution to Every Problem.* New York: Quill.
Foster, R. (1988). *Celebration of Discipline.* San Francisco: HarperCollins.
Helmfelt, R., and Fowler, R. (1990). *Serenity: A Companion for 12 Step Recovery.* Nashville, TN: Nelson.
Lewis, C. S. (1955). *Surprised by Joy.* New York: Harcourt Brace.
Merton, T. (1948). *The Seven Storey Mountain.* New York: Harcourt Brace.
Moore, T. (1992). *The Care of the Soul.* New York: HarperCollins.
Moore, T. (2004). *Dark Nights of the Soul.* New York: Gotham.

Norris, K. (1996). *The Cloister Walk.* New York: Riverhead Books.
Norris, K. (1998). *Amazing Grace.* New York: Riverhead.
Peck, M. S. (1978). *The Road Less Traveled.* New York: Simon & Schuster.
Peck, M. S. (1993). *Further Along the Road Less Traveled.* New York: Simon & Schuster.
Warren, R. (2002). *The Purpose-Driven Life.* Grand Rapids, MI: Zondervan.

SUICIDAL IDEATION

Butler, P. (1991). *Talking to Yourself: Learning the Language of Self-Affirmation.* New York: Stein and Day.
Hutschnecker, A. (1951). *The Will to Live.* New York: Cornerstone Library.
Seligman, M. (1990). *Learned Optimism: The Skill to Conquer Life's Obstacles, Large and Small.* New York: Pocket Books.

TYPE A BEHAVIOR

Charlesworth, E., and Nathan, R. (2004). *Stress Management: A Comprehensive Guide to Wellness.* New York: Ballentine Books.
Friedman, M., and Ulmer, P. (1984). *Treating Type A Behavior and Your Heart.* New York: Knopf.
Glasser, W. (1976). *Positive Addiction.* San Francisco: HarperCollins.
Lehrer, P., and Woolfolk, R. (1993). *Principles and Practice of Stress Management, Second Edition.* New York: Guilford.
Peck, M. S. (1978). *The Road Less Traveled.* New York: Simon & Schuster.
Peck, M. S. (1993). *Further Along the Road Less Traveled.* New York: Simon & Schuster.
Pirsig, R. (1974). *Zen and the Art of Motorcycle Maintenance.* New York: William Morrow.
Robinson, B. (1993). *Overdoing It.* Deerfield Beach, FL: Health Communications, Inc.

VOCATIONAL STRESS

Bolles, R. (1992). *What Color Is Your Parachute?* Berkeley, CA: Ten-Speed Press.
Charland, R. (1993). *Career Shifting: Starting Over in a Changing Economy.* Holbrook, MA: Bob Adams.
Jandt, F. (1985). *Win-Win Negotiating: Turning Conflict into Agreement.* New York: Wiley.
Weiss, R. (1990). *Staying the Course: The Emotional and Social Lives of Men Who Do Well at Work.* New York: Free Press.

Appendix B

PROFESSIONAL REFERENCES FOR EVIDENCE-BASED CHAPTERS

GENERAL

Bruce, T. J., and Sanderson, W. C. (2005). Evidence-based psychosocial practices: Past, present, and future. In C. Stout and R. Hayes (Eds.), *The Handbook of Evidence-Based Practice in Behavioral Healthcare: Applications and New Directions* (pp. 220–243). New York: Wiley.

Chambless, D. L, Baker, M. J., Baucom, D., Beutler, L. E., Calhoun, K. S., Crits-Christoph, P., et al. (1998). Update on empirically validated therapies: II. *The Clinical Psychologist, 51*(1), 3–16.

Chambless, D. L., and Ollendick, T. H. (2001). Empirically supported psychological interventions: Controversies and evidence. *Annual Review of Psychology, 52,* 685–716.

Chambless, D. L., Sanderson, W. C., Shoham, V., Johnson, S. B., Pope, K. S., Crits-Christoph, P., et al. (1996). An update on empirically validated therapies. *The Clinical Psychologist, 49*(2), 5–18.

Nathan, P. E., and Gorman, J. M. (Eds.). (1998). *A Guide to Treatments That Work.* New York: Oxford University Press.

Nathan, P. E., and Gorman, J. M. (Eds.). (2002). *A Guide to Treatments That Work, Volume II.* New York: Oxford University Press.

ANGER MANAGEMENT

Deffenbacher, J., Dahlen, E., Lynch, R., Morris, C., and Gowensmith, W. (2000). An application of Beck's cognitive therapy to general anger reduction. *Cognitive Therapy and Research, 24,* 689–687.

Deffenbacher, J., Oetting, E., Huff, M., Cornell, G., and Dallagher, C. (1996). Evaluation of two cognitive-behavioral approaches to general anger reduction. *Cognitive Therapy and Research, 20,* 551–573.

Deffenbacher, J., Story, D., Brandon, A., Hogg, J., and Hazaleus, S. (1988). Cognitive and cognitive relaxation treatment of anger. *Cognitive Therapy and Research, 12,* 167–184.

DiGiuseppe, R., and Tafrate, R. (2003). Anger treatment for adults: A meta-analytic review. *Clinical Psychology: Science & Practice, 10,* 70–84.

Feindler, E., and Ecton, R. (1986). *Adolescent Anger Control: Cognitive-Behavioral Techniques.* New York: Pergamon.

Meichenbaum, D. (1985). *Stress Inoculation Training.* New York: Pergamon.

Meichenbaum, D. (1993). Stress inoculation training: A twenty-year update. In R. L. Woolfolk and P. M. Lehrer (Eds.), *Principles and Practices of Stress Management* (pp. 373–406). New York: Guilford.

Meichenbaum, D. (2001). *Treatment of Individuals with Anger Control Problems and Aggressive Behaviors: A Clinical Handbook.* Clearwater, FL: Institute Press.

Novaco, R. (1975). *Anger Control: The Development and Evaluation of an Experimental Treatment.* Lexington, MA: Lexington Books.

Novaco, R. (1976). The functions and regulation of the arousal of anger. *American Journal of Psychiatry, 133,* 1124–1128.

Novaco, R. (1977). A stress inoculation approach to anger management in the training of law enforcement officers. *American Journal of Community Psychology, 5,* 327–346.

ANXIETY

Barlow, D. H., Raffa, S. D., and Cohen, E. M. (2002). Psychosocial treatments for panic disorders, phobias, and generalized anxiety disorder. In P. E. Nathan and J. M. Gorman (Eds.), *A Guide to Treatments that Work, Second Edition* (pp. 301–335). New York: Oxford University Press.

Beck, A., and Emory, G. (1990). *Anxiety Disorders and Phobias: A Cognitive Perspective.* New York: Basic.

Brown, T. A., O'Leary, T., and Barlow, D. H. (1994). Generalized anxiety disorder. In D. H. Barlow (Ed.), *Clinical Handbook of Psychological Disorders* (pp. 154–208). New York: Guilford.

Chambless, D., Baker, M., Baucom, D., Beutler, L., Calhoun, K., Crits-Christoph, P., et al. (1998). Update on empirically validated therapies: II. *The Clinical Psychologist, 51*(1), 3–16.

Chambless, D., and Ollendick, T. (2001). Empirically supported psychological interventions: Controversies and evidence. *Annual Review of Psychology, 52,* 685–716.

Craske, M. G., Barlow, D. H., and O'Leary, T. (1993). *Mastery of Your Anxiety and Worry—Therapist Guide.* San Antonio, TX: The Psychological Corporation.

DiNardo, P. A., Brown, T. A., and Barlow, D. H. (1994). *Anxiety Disorders Interview Schedule for DSM-IV: Lifetime Version.* San Antonio, TX: The Psychological Corporation.

Haley, J. (1984). *Ordeal Therapy.* San Francisco: Jossey-Bass.

Meyer, T., Miller, M., Metzger, R., and Borkovec, T. (1990). Development and validation of the Penn State Worry Questionnaire. *Behaviour Research and Therapy, 28,* 487–495.

Rygh, J., and Sanderson, W. C. (2004). *Treating GAD: Evidence-based Strategies, Tools, and Techniques.* New York: Guilford.

BORDERLINE PERSONALITY

Beck, A., Rush, A., Shaw, B., and Emery, G. (1979). *Cognitive Therapy of Depression.* New York: Guilford.

Linehan, M. (1993). *Cognitive Behavioral Treatment for Borderline Personality Disorder.* New York: Guilford.

Linehan, M. (1993). *Skills Training Manual for Treating Borderline Personality Disorder.* New York: Guilford.

Linehan, M., Armstrong, H., Suarez, A., Allmon, D., and Heard, H. (1991). Cognitive-behavioral treatment of chronically parasuicidal borderline patients. *Archives of General Psychiatry, 48,* 1060–1064.

Linehan, M., Cochran, B. N., and Kehrer, C. A. (2001). Dialectical behavior therapy for borderline personality disorder. In D. H. Barlow (Ed.), *Clinical Handbook of Psychological Disorders: A Step-by-Step Treatment Manual, Third Edition* (pp. 332–375). New York: Guilford.

Linehan, M., Heard, H., and Armstrong, H. (1993). Naturalistic follow-up of a behavioral treatment for chronically parasuicidal borderline patients. *Archives of General Psychiatry, 50,* 971–974.

Linehan, M., Schmidt, H., Dimeff, L., Craft, J., Kanter, J., and Comtois, K. (1999). Dialectical behavior therapy for patients with borderline personality disorder and drug-dependence. *American Journal on Addiction, 8*(4), 279–292.

Linehan, M., Tutek, D., Heard, H., and Armstrong, H. (1992). Interpersonal outcome of cognitive behavioral treatment for chronically suicidal borderline patients. *American Journal of Psychiatry, 151*(12), 1771–1775.

Resick, P., and Calhoun, K., (2001). Posttraumatic stress disorder. In D. H. Barlow (Ed.), *Clinical Handbook of Psychological Disorders: A Step-by-Step Treatment Manual, Third Edition* (pp. 60–113). New York: Guilford.

Safer, D., Telch, C., and Agras, W. (2001). Dialectical behavior therapy for bulimia nervosa. *American Journal of Psychiatry, 158*(4), 632–634.

CHEMICAL DEPENDENCE

Abbot, P., Weller, S., Delaney, H., and Moore, B. (1998). Community reinforcement approach in the treatment of opiate addicts. *American Journal of Drug and Alcohol Abuse, 24*(1), 17–30.

Epstein, E., and McGrady, B. (1998). Behavioral couples treatment of alcohol and drug use disorders: Current status and innovations. *Clinical Psychology Review, 18,* 689–711.

Finney, J., and Moos, R. (2002). Psychosocial treatments for alcohol use disorders. In P. E. Nathan and J. M. Gorman (Eds.), *A Guide to Treatments That Work, Volume II* (pp. 157–168). New York: Oxford University Press.

Marlatt, G., and Gordon, J. (1985). *Relapse Prevention: Maintenance Strategies in the Treatment of Addictive Behaviors.* New York: Guilford.

McCrady, B. (2001). Alcohol use disorders. In D. H. Barlow (Ed.), *Clinical Handbook of Psychological Disorders, Third Edition* (pp. 376–433). New York: Guilford.

Miller, W., Andrews, N., Wilbourne, P., and Bennett, M. (1998). A wealth of alternatives: Effective treatments for alcohol problems. In W. R. Miller and N. Heather (Eds.), *Treating Addictive Behaviors, Second Edition* (pp. 203–216). New York: Plenum.

O'Farrell, T., Choquette, K., and Cutter, H. (1998). Couples relapse prevention sessions after Behavioral Marital Therapy for male alcoholics: Outcomes during the three years after starting treatment. *Journal of Studies on Alcohol, 59,* 357–370.

O'Farrell, T., Choquette, K., Cutter H., Brown, E., and McCourt, W. (1993). Behavioral Marital Therapy with and without additional couples relapse prevention sessions for alcoholics and their wives. *Journal of Studies on Alcohol, 54,* 652–666.

Ouimette, P., Finney, J., and Moos, R. (1997). Twelve step and cognitive-behavioral treatment for substance abuse: A comparison of treatment effectiveness. *Journal of Consulting and Clinical Psychology, 65,* 230–240.

Project MATCH Research Group. (1997). Matching alcoholism treatments to client heterogeneity: Project MATCH posttreatment drinking outcomes. *Journal of Studies on Alcohol, 58,* 7–29.

Smith, J., Meyers, R., and Delaney, H. (1998). The community reinforcement approach with homeless alcohol-dependent individuals. *Journal of Consulting and Clinical Psychology, 66,* 541–548.

CHRONIC PAIN

Bradley, L. A., Young, L. D., Anderson, J. O., Turner, R. A., Agudelo, C. A., McDaniel, L. K., et al. (1987). Effects of psychological therapy on pain behavior of rheumatoid arthritis patients: Treatment outcome and six-month follow-up. *Arthritis & Rheumatism, 30,* 1105–1114.

Keefe, F. J., Beaupre, P. M., Gil, K. M., Rumble, M. E., and Aspnes, A. K. (2002). Group therapy for patients with chronic pain. In D. C. Turk and R. J. Gatchel (Eds.), *Psychological Approaches to Pain Management: A Practitioner's Handbook, Second Edition* (pp. 234–255). New York: Guilford.

Keefe, F. J., Caldwell, D. S., Williams, D. A., Gil, K. M., Mitchell, D., Robertson, D., et al. (1990). Pain coping skills training in the management of osteoarthritic knee pain: A comparative study. *Behavior Therapy, 21,* 49–62.

Keefe, F. J., and Gil, K. M. (1986). Behavioral concepts in the analysis of chronic pain syndromes. *Journal of Consulting and Clinical Psychology, 54,* 776–783.

Syrjala, K. L., Donaldson, G. W., Davis, M. W., Kippes, M. E., and Carr, J. E. (1995). Relaxation and imagery and cognitive-behavioral training reduce pain during cancer treatment: A controlled clinical trial. *Pain, 63,* 189–198.

Turk, D. C., Meichenbaum, D., and Genest, M. (1983). *Pain and Behavioral Medicine: A Cognitive-Behavioral Perspective.* New York: Guilford.

Turner, J. A., and Clancy, S. (1988). Comparison of operant-behavioral and cognitive-behavioral group treatment for chronic low back pain. *Journal of Consulting and Clinical Psychology, 58,* 573–579.

DEPRESSION

Beck, A. T., and Steer, R. A. (1988). *Beck Hopelessness Scale.* San Antonio, TX: The Psychological Corporation.
Beck, A. T., Steer, R. A., and Brown, G. K. (1996). *Beck Depression Inventory Manual, Second Edition.* San Antonio, TX: The Psychological Corporation.
Beck, A. T., Rush, A. J., Shaw, B. F., and Emery, G. (1979). *Cognitive Therapy of Depression.* New York: Guilford.
Beck, J. S. (1995). *Cognitive Therapy: Basics and Beyond.* New York: Guilford.
Klerman, G. L., Weissman, M. M., Rounasacille, B. J., and Chevron, E. S. (1984). *Interpersonal Psychotherapy of Depression.* New York: Basic.
Lewinson, P. M. (1974). A behavioural approach to depression. In R. J. Friedman and M. M. Katz (Eds.), *The Psychology of Depression* (pp. 157–186). New York: Wiley.
Lewinsohn, P. M., Antonuccio, D. O., Steinmetz, J. L., and Teri, L. (1984). *The Coping With Depression Course: A Psychoeducational Intervention for Unipolar Depression.* Eugene, OR: Castalia.
Nezu, A. M., Nezu, C. M., and Perri, M. G. (1989). *Problem-Solving Therapy for Depression: Theory, Research, and Clinical Guidelines.* New York: Wiley.
Weissman, M. M., Markowitz, J. C., and Klerman, G. L. (2000). *Comprehensive Guide to Interpersonal Psychotherapy.* New York: Basic.
Zimmerman, M., Coryell, W., Corenthal, C., and Wilson, S. (1986). A self-report scale to diagnose major depressive disorder. *Archives of General Psychiatry, 43,* 1076–1081.

EATING DISORDER

Agras, W., Walsh, B., Fairburn, C., Wilson, G., and Kraemer, H. (2000). A multicenter comparison of cognitive-behavioural therapy and interpersonal psychotherapy for bulimia nervosa. *Archives of General Psychiatry, 57,* 459–466.
Fairburn, C. G., Marcus, M. D., and Wilson, G. T. (1993). Cognitive-behavioral therapy for binge eating and bulimia nervosa. In C. G. Fairburn and G. T. Wilson (Eds.), *Binge Eating: Nature, Assessment, and Treatment* (pp. 361–404). New York: Guilford.
Fairburn, C. G., Jones, R., Peveler, R. C., Carr, S. J., Solomon, R. A., O'Conner, M. E., et al. (1991). Three psychological treatments for bulimia nervosa: A comparative trial. *Archives of General Psychiatry, 48,* 463–469.
Garner, D. M. (1991). *Eating Disorders Inventory–2.* Odessa, FL: Psychological Assessment Resources.
Wilson, G. T., and Pike, K. M. (2001). Eating disorders. In D. H. Barlow (Ed.), *Clinical Handbook of Psychological Disorders: A Step-by-Step Treatment Manual, Third Edition* (pp. 332–375). New York: Guilford.

Wilson, G. T., and Fairburn, C. G. (2001). Treatments for eating disorders. In P. E. Nathan and J. M. Gorman (Eds.), *A Guide to Treatments That Work, Second Edition* (pp. 559–592). New York: Oxford University Press.

Wilson, G. T., Fairburn, C. G., and Agras, W. S. (1997). Cognitive-behavioral therapy for bulimia nervosa. In D. M. Garner and P. Garfinkel (Eds.), *Handbook of Treatment for Eating Disorders* (pp. 67–93). New York: Guilford.

FEMALE SEXUAL DYSFUNCTION

Goldstein, I., Lue, T., Padma-Nathan, H., Rosen, R., Stern, W., and Wicker, P. (1998). Oral sildenafil in the treatment of erectile dysfunction. *New England Journal of Medicine, 338,* 1397–1404.

Heiman, J., and LoPiccolo, J. (1983). Clinical outcome of sex therapy. *Archives of General Psychiatry, 40,* 443–449.

Heiman, J., and Meston, M. (1997). Empirically validated treatment for sexual dysfunction. *Annual Review of Sex Research, 8,* 148–194.

Kaplan, H. (1988). *The Illustrated Manual of Sex Therapy.* Levittown, PA: Brunner/Mazel.

Masters, W., and Johnson, V. (1970). *Human Sexual Inadequacy.* Boston: Little, Brown, and Co.

Wincze, J., and Barlow, D. H. (1997). *Enhancing Sexuality: A Problem-solving Approach—Therapist Guide.* San Antonio, TX: The Psychological Corporation.

Wincze, J., and Carey, M. (1991). *Sexual Dysfunction: A Guide to Assessment and Treatment.* New York: Guilford.

Zimmer D. (1987). Does marital therapy enhance the effectiveness of treatment for sexual dysfunction? *Journal of Sex and Marital Therapy, 13,* 193–209.

INTIMATE RELATIONSHIP CONFLICTS

Baucom, D. H., Shoham, V. M., Kim, T., Daiuto, A. D., and Stickle, T. R. (1998). Empirically supported couple and family interventions for marital distress and adult mental health problems. *Journal of Consulting and Clinical Psychology, 66*(1), 53–88.

Christensen, A., and Heavey, C. (1999). Interventions for couples. *Annual Review of Psychology, 50,* 165–190.

Holtzworth-Munroe, A. S., and Jacobson, N. S. (1991). Behavioral marital therapy. In A. S. Gurman and D. P. Knickerson (Eds.), *Handbook of Family Therapy, Second Edition* (pp. 96–133). Levittown, PA: Brunner/Mazel.

Jacobson, N. S., and Addis, M. E. (1993). Research on couple therapy: What do we know? Where are we going? *Journal of Consulting and Clinical Psychology, 61,* 85–93.

Jacobson, N. S., and Christensen, A. (1996). *Integrative Couple Therapy: Promoting Acceptance and Change.* New York: Norton.

Jacobson, N. S., Christensen, A., Prince, S. E., Cordova, J., and Eldridge, K. (2000). Integrative behavioral couple therapy: An acceptance-based, promising new treatment for couple discord. *Journal of Consulting and Clinical Psychology, 68*(2), 351–355.

Jacobson, N. S., and Gottman, J. (1998). *When Men Batter Women: New Insights into Ending Abusive Relationships.* New York: Simon & Schuster.

Jacobson, N. S., and Margolin, G. (1979). *Marital Therapy: Strategies Based on Social Learning and Behavior Exchange Principles.* Levittown, PA: Brunner/Mazel.

Jacobson, N. S., Schmaling, K. B., and Holtzworth-Munroe, A. (1987). Component analysis of behavioral marital therapy: Two-year follow-up and prediction of relapse. *Journal of Marital and Family Therapy, 13,* 187–195.

Snyder, D. K. (1997). *Marital Satisfaction Inventory—Revised.* Los Angeles: Western Psychological Services.

Spanier, G. B. (1976). Measuring dyadic adjustment: New scales for assessing the quality of marriage and similar dyads. *Journal of Marriage and the Family, 38,* 15–28.

MALE SEXUAL DYSFUNCTION

Goldstein, I., Lue, T., Padma-Nathan, H., Rosen, R., Stern, W., and Wicker, P. (1998). Oral sildenafil in the treatment of erectile dysfunction. *New England Journal of Medicine, 338,* 1397–1404.

Heiman, J., and LoPiccolo, J. (1983). Clinical outcome of sex therapy. *Archives of General Psychiatry, 40,* 443–449.

Heiman, J., and Meston, M. (1997). Empirically validated treatment for sexual dysfunction. *Annual Review of Sex Research, 8,* 148–194.

Kaplan, H. S. (1988). *The Illustrated Manual of Sex Therapy.* Levittown, PA: Brunner/Mazel.

Masters, W., and Johnson, V. (1970). *Human Sexual Inadequacy.* Boston: Little, Brown, and Co.

Wincze, J., and Barlow, D. H. (1997). *Enhancing Sexuality: A Problem-solving Approach—Therapist Guide.* San Antonio, TX: The Psychological Corporation.

Wincze, J. P., and Carey, M. P. (1991). *Sexual Dysfunction: A Guide to Assessment and Treatment.* New York: Guilford.

Zimmer, D. (1987). Does marital therapy enhance the effectiveness of treatment for sexual dysfunction? *Journal of Sex and Marital Therapy, 13,* 193–209.

MANIA OR HYPOMANIA

Falloon, I., Boyd, J., and McGill, C. (1984). *Family Care of Schizophrenia: A Problem-solving Approach to the Treatment of Mental Illness.* New York: Guilford.

Miklowitz, D., George, E., Richards, J., Simoneau, T., and Suddath, R. (2003). A randomized study of family-focused psychoeducation and pharmacotherapy in the outpatient management of bipolar disorder. *Archives of General Psychiatry, 60,* 904–912.

Miklowitz, D., and Goldstein, M. (1997). *Bipolar Disorder: A Family-focused Treatment Approach.* New York: Guilford.

Miklowitz, D., and Hooley, J. (1998). Developing family psychoeducational treatments for patients with bipolar and other severe psychiatric disorders. *Journal of Marital and Family Therapy, 24*(4), 419–435.

Miklowitz, D., Simoneau, T., George, E., Richards, J., Kalbag, A., Sachs-Ericsson, N., and Suddath, R. (2000). Family-focused treatment of bipolar disorder: One-year effects of a psychoeducational program in conjunction with pharmacotherapy. *Biological Psychiatry, 48,* 582–592.

Miklowitz, D. (2001). Bipolar Disorder. In D. H. Barlow (Ed.), *Clinical Handbook of Psychological Disorders: A Step-by-Step Treatment Manual, Third Edition.* New York: Guilford.

Otto, M., and Reilly-Harrington, N. (2002). Cognitive behavioral therapy for the management of bipolar disorder. In S. Hofmann and M. Tompson (Eds), *Treating Chronic and Severe Mental Disorders: A Handbook of Empirically Supported Interventions.* New York: Guilford.

Rea, M., Tompson, M., Miklowitz, D., Goldstein, M., Hwang, S., and Mintz, J. (2003). Family focused treatment vs. individual treatment for bipolar disorder: Results of a randomized clinical trial. *Journal of Consulting and Clinical Psychology, 71,* 482–492.

Simoneau, T., Miklowitz, D., Richards, J., Saleem, R., and George, E. (1999). Bipolar disorder and family communication: Effects of a psychoeducational treatment program. *Journal of Abnormal Psychology, 108,* 588–597.

Wendel, J., Miklowitz, D., Richards, J., and George, E. (2000). Expressed emotion and attributions in the relatives of bipolar patients: An analysis of problem-solving interactions. *Journal of Abnormal Psychology, 109,* 792–796.

OBSESSIVE-COMPULSIVE DISORDER (OCD)

DiNardo, P. A., Brown, T. A., and Barlow, D. H. (1994). *Anxiety Disorders Interview Schedule for DSM-IV: Lifetime Version.* San Antonio, TX: The Psychological Corporation.

Foa, E. B., and Franklin, M. E. (2001). Obsessive-compulsive disorder. In D. H. Barlow (Ed.), *Clinical Handbook of Psychological Disorders: A Step-by-Step Treatment Manual, Third Edition* (pp. 209–263). New York: Guilford.

Franklin, R., March, J., and Foa, E. B. (2002). Obsessive-compulsive disorder. In M. Hersen (Ed.), *Clinical Behavior Therapy: Adults and Children* (pp. 276–303). New York: Wiley.

Goodman, W., Price, L., Rasmussen, S., Mazure, C., Delgado, P., Heninger, G., and Charney, D. (1989). The Yale-Brown Obsessive-Compulsive Scale II. Validity. *Archives of General Psychiatry, 46,* 1012–1016.

Goodman, W., Price, L., Rasmussen, S., Mazure, C., Fleishmann, R., Hill, C., et al. (1989). The Yale-Brown Obsessive-Compulsive Scale I: Development, use, and reliability. *Archives of General Psychiatry, 46,* 1006–1011.

Hiss, H., Foa, E. B., and Kozak, M. J. (1994). A relapse prevention program for treatment of obsessive compulsive disorder. *Journal of Consulting and Clinical Psychology, 62,* 801–808.

McGinn, L., and Sanderson, W. C. (1999). *Treatment of Obsessive-Compulsive Disorder.* Northvale, NJ: Jason Aronson.

Riggs, D. S., and Foa, E. B. (1993). Obsessive-compulsive disorder. In D. H. Barlow (Ed.), *Clinical Handbook of Psychological Disorders, Second Edition* (pp. 189–239). New York: Guilford.

Salkovskis, P. M., and Kirk, J. (1997). Obsessive-compulsive disorder. In D. M. Clark and C. G. Fairburn (Eds.), *Science and Practice of Cognitive Behaviour Therapy* (pp. 179–208). Oxford, UK: Oxford University Press.

Steketee, G. (1993). *Treatment of Obsessive Compulsive Disorder.* New York: Guilford.

Turner, S. M., and Beidel, D. C. (1988). *Treating Obsessive-Compulsive Disorder.* New York: Pergamon.

PANIC/AGORAPHOBIA

Barlow, D. H., Craske, M. G., Cerny, J. A., and Klosko, J. (1986). Behavioral treatment of panic disorder. *Behavior Therapy, 20,* 261–282.

Chambless, D. L, Baker, M. J., Baucom, D., Beutler, L. E., Calhoun, K. S., Crits-Christoph, P., et al. (1998). Update on empirically validated therapies: II. *The Clinical Psychologist, 51*(1), 3–16.

Chambless, D. L., Caputo, G. C., Jasin, S. E., Gracel, E. J., and Williams, C. (1985). The mobility inventory for agoraphobia. *Behaviour Research and Therapy, 23,* 35–44.

Chambless, D. L., and Ollendick, T. H. (2001). Empirically supported psychological interventions: Controversies and evidence. *Annual Review of Psychology, 52,* 685–716.

Clark, D., Salkovskis, P., Hackman, A., Middleton, H., Anastasiades, P., and Gelder, M. (1994). A comparison of cognitive therapy, applied relaxation, and imipramine in the treatment of panic disorder. *British Journal of Psychiatry, 164,* 759–769.

Craske, M. G., Barlow, D. H., and Meadows, E. (2000). *Mastery of Your Anxiety and Panic: Therapist's Guide for Anxiety, Panic, and Agoraphobia (MAP-3).* San Antonio, TX: Graywind/The Psychological Corporation.

Craske, M. G., and Barlow, D. H. (2000). *Mastery of Your Anxiety and Panic (MAP-3): Agoraphobia Supplement.* San Antonio, TX: Graywind/The Psychological Corporation.

DiNardo, P. A., Brown, T. A., and Barlow, D. H. (1994). *Anxiety Disorders Interview Schedule for DSM-IV: Lifetime Version.* San Antonio, TX: The Psychological Corporation.

Nathan, P. E., and Gorman, J. M. (Eds.). (2002). *A Guide to Treatments That Work, Volume II.* New York: Oxford University Press.

Reiss, S., Peterson, R. A., Gursky, D. M., and McNally, R. J. (1986). Anxiety sensitivity, anxiety frequency, and the prediction of fearfulness. *Behaviour Research and Therapy, 24,* 1–8.

PARENTING

Brestan, E., and Eyberg, S. (1998). Effective psychosocial treatments of conduct-disordered children and adolescents: 29 years, 82 studies, and 5,272 kids. *Journal of Clinical Child Psychology, 27,* 180–189.

Forgatch, M., and DeGarmo, D. (1999). Parenting through change: An effective prevention program for single mothers. *Journal of Consulting and Clinical Psychology, 67,* 711–724.

Graziano, A., and Diament, D. (1992). Parent behavioral training: An examination of the paradigm. *Behavior Modification, 16,* 3–38.

Kazdin, A. (1997). Parent management training: Evidence, outcomes, and issues. *Journal of the American Academy of Child and Adolescent Psychiatry, 36,* 1349–1356.

Long, P., Forehand, R., Wierson, M., and Morgan, A. (1994). Does parent training with young noncompliant children have long-term effects? *Behaviour Research and Therapy, 32,* 101–107.

Patterson, G., Dishion, T., and Chamberlain, P. (1993). Outcomes and methodological issues relating to treatment of antisocial children. In T. R. Giles (Ed.), *Handbook of Effective Psychotherapy* (pp. 43–87). New York: Plenum.

Sanders, M., and Dadds, M. (1993). *Behavioral Family Intervention.* Needham Heights, MA: Allyn & Bacon.

Serketich, W., and Dumas, J. (1996). The effectiveness of behavioral parent training to modify antisocial behavior in children: A meta-analysis. *Behavior Therapy, 27,* 171–186.

Webster-Stratton, C. (1994). Advancing videotape parent training: A comparison study. *Journal of Consulting and Clinical Psychology, 62,* 583–593.

PHOBIA

Antony, M. M. (2001). Measures for specific phobia. In M. M. Antony, S. M. Orsillo, and I. Roemer (Eds.), *Practitioner's Guide to Empirically-Based Measures of Anxiety* (pp. 133–158). New York: Kluwer Academic/Plenum.

Bruce, T. J., and Sanderson, W. C. (1998). *Specific Phobias: Clinical Applications of Evidence-Based Psychotherapy.* Northvale, NJ: Jason Aronson.

Craske, M. G., Antony, M. M., and Barlow, D. H. (1997). *Mastery of Your Specific Phobia—Therapist Guide.* San Antonio, TX: The Psychological Corporation.

DiNardo, P. A., Brown, T. A., and Barlow, D. H. (1994). *Anxiety Disorders Interview Schedule for DSM-IV: Lifetime Version.* San Antonio, TX: The Psychological Corporation.

Marks, I. (1978). *Living With Fear.* New York: McGraw Hill.

Ost, L. G., Fellenius, J., Sterner, U. (1991). Applied tension, exposure in vivo, and tension-only in the treatment of blood phobia. *Behaviour Research and Therapy, 29*(6), 561–574.

POSTTRAUMATIC STRESS DISORDER (PTSD)

Bryant, R. A., and Harvey, A. G. (2000). *Acute Stress Disorder: A Handbook of Theory, Assessment, and Treatment.* Washington, DC: American Psychological Association.

Dunmore, E., Clark, D. M., and Ehlers, A. (2001). A prospective investigation of the role of cognitive factors in persistent posttraumatic stress disorder (PTSD) after physical or sexual assault. *Behaviour Research and Therapy, 39,* 1063–1084.

Ehlers, A., and Clark, D. M. (2000). A cognitive model of posttraumatic stress disorder. *Behaviour Research and Therapy, 38,* 319–345.

Falsetti, S. A., and Resnick, H. S. (2001). Posttraumatic stress disorder. In W. J. Lyddon and J. V. Jones, Jr. (Eds.), *Empirically Supported Cognitive Therapies: Current and Future Applications.* (pp. 182–199). New York: Springer.

Foa, E. B., Dancu, C. V., Hembree, E. A., Jaycox, L. H., Meadows, E. A., and Street, G. (1999). A comparison of exposure therapy, stress inoculation training and their combination for reducing posttraumatic stress disorder in female assault victims. *Journal of Consulting and Clinical Psychology, 67,* 194–200.

Foa, E. B., Keane, T. M., and Friedman, M. J. (2004). *Effective Treatments for PTSD: Practice Guidelines from the International Society for Traumatic Stress Studies.* New York: Guilford.

Foa, E. B., and Rothbaum, B. O. (1998). *Treating the Trauma of Rape: Cognitive-Behavioral Therapy for PTSD.* New York: Guilford.

Foy, D. W. (Ed.). (1992). *Treating PTSD: Cognitive Behavioral Strategies.* New York: Guilford.

Marks, I., Lovell, K., Noshirvani, H., Livanou, M., and Thrasher, S. (1998). Treatment of posttraumatic stress disorder by exposure and/or cognitive restructuring: A controlled study. *Archives of General Psychiatry, 55,* 317–325.

McNally, R. J. (2003). *Remembering Trauma.* Cambridge, MA: Harvard University Press.

Meichenbaum, D. A. (1995). *A Clinical Handbook/Practical Therapist Manual for Assessing and Treating Adults with Post-Traumatic Stress Disorder (PTSD).* Ontario, Canada: Institute Press.

Najavits, L. M. (2002). *Seeking Safety: A Treatment Manual for PTSD and Substance Abuse.* New York: Guilford.

Padesky, C., Candido, D., Cohen, A., Gluhoski, V., McGinn, L., Sisti, M., and Westover, S. (2002). Academy of Cognitive Therapy's Trauma Task Force Report. [on-line]. Available: http://academyofct.org./Info/Zoom.asp?InfoID=150 &szparent=127

Resick, P. A., and Calhoun, K. S. (2001). Posttraumatic stress disorder. In D. H. Barlow (Ed.), *Clinical Handbook of Psychological Disorders: A Step-by-Step Treatment Manual, Third Edition* (pp. 60–113). New York: Guilford.

Resick, P. A., and Schnicke, M. K. (1996). *Cognitive Processing Therapy for Rape Victims: A Treatment Manual.* Newbury Park, CA: Sage Publications.

Wilson, J. P., Friedman, M. J., and Lindy, J. D. (Eds.). (2001). *Treating Psychological Trauma and PTSD.* New York: Guilford.

Wilson, J. P., and Keane, T. M. (Eds.). (1997). *Assessing Psychological Trauma and PTSD.* New York: Guilford.

Yule, W. (Ed.). (1999). *Post-Traumatic Stress Disorders: Concepts and Therapy.* New York: Wiley.

SLEEP DISTURBANCE

Bootzin, R. (1972). A stimulus control treatment for insomnia. *American Psychological Association Proceedings,* 395–396.

Bootzin, R., and Nicassio, P. (1978). Behavioral treatments for insomnia. In M. Hersen, R. Eisler, and P. Miller (Eds.), *Progress in Behavior Modification, Volume 6* (pp. 1–45). New York: Academic Press.

Morin, C. (1996). *Insomnia: Psychological Assessment and Management.* New York: Guilford.

Morin, C., Hauri, P., Espie, C., Spielman, A., Buysse, D., and Bootzin, R. (1999). Nonpharmacologic treatment of chronic insomnia: An American Academy of Sleep Medicine review. *Sleep, 22*(8), 1134–1156.

Murtagh, D. R., and Greenwood, K. M. (1995). Identifying effective psychological treatments for insomnia: A meta-analysis. *Journal of Consulting and Clinical Psychology, 63,* 79–89.

Sloan, E., Hauri, P., Bootzin, R., Morin, C., Stevenson, M., and Shapiro, C. (1993). The nuts and bolts of behavioral therapy for insomnia. *Journal of Psychosomatic Research, 37*(Suppl.1), 19–37.

SOCIAL DISCOMFORT

Antony, M. M., and Swinson, R. P. (2000). *Phobic Disorders and Panic in Adults: A Guide to Assessment and Treatment.* Washington, DC: American Psychological Association.

Beidel, D. C., and Turner, S. M. (1998). *Shy Children, Phobic Adults: Nature and Treatment of Social Phobia.* Washington, DC: American Psychological Association.

Bruce, T. J., and Saeed, S. A. (1999). Social anxiety disorder: A common, underrecognized mental disorder. *American Family Physician, 60*(8), 2311–2320.

Chambless, D. L, Baker, M. J., Baucom, D., Beutler, L. E., Calhoun, K. S., Crits-Christoph, P., et al. (1998). Update on empirically validated therapies: II. *The Clinical Psychologist, 51*(1), 3–16.

Chambless, D. L., and Ollendick, T. H. (2001). Empirically supported psychological interventions: Controversies and evidence. *Annual Review of Psychology, 52,* 685–716.

Clark, D. M., and Wells, A. (1995). A cognitive model of social phobia. In R. G. Heimberg, M. R. Liebowitz, et al. (Eds.), *Social Phobia: Diagnosis, Assessment, and Treatment* (pp. 69–93). New York: Guilford.

Cognitive Behavioral Group Therapy for Social Phobia. (Cost = $20.00. Contact: Social Phobia Program, Department of Psychology, Temple University, Weiss

Hall, 1701 N. 13th Street, Philadelphia, PA 19122-6085. Telephone: (215) 204-1575, Fax: (215) 204-2155, e-mail: rheimber@nimbus.ocis.temple.edu)

Crozier, W. R., and Alden, L. E. (2001). *International Handbook of Social Anxiety: Concepts, Research and Interventions Relating to the Self and Shyness.* New York: Wiley.

DiNardo, P. A., Brown, T. A., and Barlow, D. H. (1994). *Anxiety Disorders Interview Schedule for DSM-IV: Lifetime Version.* San Antonio, TX: The Psychological Corporation.

Heimberg, R. G., and Becker, R. E. (2002). *Cognitive-Behavioral Group Therapy for Social Phobia: Basic Mechanisms and Clinical Strategies.* New York: Guilford.

Heimberg, R. G., Liebowitz, M. R., Hope, D. A., and Schneier, F. R. (Eds.). (1995). *Social Phobia: Diagnosis, Assessment, and Treatment.* New York: Guilford.

Hofmann, S. G., and DiBartolo, P. M. (2001). *From Social Anxiety to Social Phobia: Multiple Perspectives.* Needham Heights, MA: Allyn & Bacon.

Hope, D. A., Heimberg, R. G., Juster, H. R., and Turk, C. L. (2000). *Managing Social Anxiety.* Boulder, CO: Graywind Publications.

Mattick, R. P., and Clarke, J. C. (1998). Development and validation of measures of social phobia scrutiny fear and social interaction anxiety. *Behaviour Research and Therapy, 36,* 455–470.

Nathan, P. E., and Gorman, J. M. (Eds.). (2002). *A Guide to Treatments That Work, Volume II.* New York: Oxford University Press.

Paleg, K., and Jongsma, A. E. (2005). *The Group Therapy Treatment Planner, Second Edition.* New York: Wiley.

Rapee, R. M., and Sanderson, W. C. (1998). *Social Phobia: Clinical Application of Evidence-based Psychotherapy.* Northvale, NJ: Jason Aronson.

Schmidt, L. A., and Schulkin, J. (Eds.). (1999). *Extreme Fear, Shyness and Social Phobia: Origins, Biological Mechanisms, and Clinical Outcomes.* New York: Oxford University Press.

Scholing, A., Emmelcamp, P., and Van Oppen, P.(1996). Cognitive behavioral treatment of social phobia. In V. B. Van Hasselt and M. Hersen (Eds.), *Sourcebook of Psychological Treatment Manuals for Adult Disorders* (pp. 123–178). New York: Plenum.

Stein, M. B. (Ed.). (1995). *Social Phobia: Clinical and Research Perspectives.* Washington, DC: American Psychiatric Press.

Turk, C., Heimberg, R. G., and Hope, D. A. (2001). Social anxiety disorder. In D. H. Barlow (Ed.), *Clinical Handbook of Psychological Disorders, Third Edition* (pp. 114–153). New York: Guilford.

Turner, S. M., Beidel, D. C., and Cooley, M. (1997). *Social Effectiveness Therapy: A Program for Overcoming Social Anxiety and Phobia.* Toronto, Canada: Multi-Health Systems.

SOMATIZATION

Hollander, E., Allen, A, Kwon, J., Aronowitz, B., Schmeidler, J., Wong, C., and Simeon, D. (1999). Clomipramine vs. desipramine crossover trial in body dysmorphic disorder: Selective efficacy of a serotonin reuptake inhibitor in imagined ugliness. *Archives of General Psychiatry, 56,* 1033–1099.

Hollander, E., Cohen, L., Simeon, D., Rosen, J., DeCaria, C., and Stein, D. J. (1994). Fluvoxamine treatment of body dysmorphic disorder. *Journal of Clinical Psychopharmacology, 14,* 75–77.

Hollander, E., Liebowitz, M., Winchel, R., Klumker, A., and Klein D. F. (1989). Treatment of body dysmorphic disorder with serotonin reuptake inhibitors. *American Journal of Psychiatry, 146,* 768–770.

McKay, D. (1999). Two-year follow-up of behavioral treatment and maintenance for body dysmorphic disorder. *Behavior Modification, 23,* 620–629.

Newell, R., and Shrubb, S. (1994). Attitude change and behavior therapy in body dysmorphic disorder: Two case reports. *Behavioral and Cognitive Psychotherapy, 22,* 163–169.

Neziroglu, F., and Yaryura, T. (1993). Exposure, response prevention, and cognitive therapy in the treatment of body dysmorphic disorder. *Behavior Therapy, 24,* 431–438.

Perugi, G., Giannotti, D., DiVaio, S., Frare, F., Saettoni, M., and Cassano, G. B. (1996). Fluvoxamine in the treatment of body dysmorphic disorder (dysmorphophobia). *International Journal of Clinical Psychopharmacology, 11,* 247–254.

Phillips, K., Dwight, M., and McElroy, S. (1998). Efficacy and safety of fluvoxamine in body dysmorphic disorder. *Journal of Clinical Psychiatry, 59,* 165–171.

Rosen, J., Reiter, P., and Orosan, P. (1995). Cognitive-behavioral body image therapy for body dysmorphic disorder. *Journal of Consulting and Clinical Psychology, 63,* 263–269.

Schmidt, N., and Harrington, P. (1995). Cognitive-behavioral treatment of body dysmorphic disorder: A case report. *Journal of Behavior Therapy and Experimental Psychiatry, 26,* 161–167.

Veale, D., Gournay, K., Dryden, W., Boocock, A., Shah, F., Willson, R., and Walburn, J. (1996). Body dysmorphic disorder. A cognitive-behavioural model and pilot randomized trial. *Behaviour Research and Therapy, 34,* 717–729.

Wilhelm, S., Otto, M., Lohr, B., and Deckersbach, T. (1999). Cognitive behavior group therapy for body dysmorphic disorder: A case series. *Behaviour Research and Therapy, 37,* 71–75.

TYPE A BEHAVIOR

Deffenbacher, J., McNamara, K., Stark, R., and Sabadell, P. (1990). A combination of cognitive, relaxation, and behavioral coping skills in the reduction of general anger. *Journal of College Student Development, 31,* 351–358.

Deffenbacher, J., and Stark, R. (1992). Relaxation and cognitive relaxation treatments of general anger. *Journal of Counseling Psychology, 39,* 158–167.

Hart, K. (1984). Anxiety management training and anger control for type A individuals. *Journal of Behavior Therapy and Experimental Psychiatry, 15,* 133–139.

Jenkins, C., Zyzanski, S., and Rosenman, R. (1979). *Jenkins Activity Survey.* New York: The Psychological Corporation.

Meichenbaum, D. (1993). Stress inoculation training: A 20-year update. In P. M. Lehrer and R. L. Woolfolk (Eds.), *Principles and Practice of Stress Management,* Second Edition (pp. 373–406). New York: Guilford.

Meichenbaum, D. (1996). Stress inoculation training for coping with stressors. *The Clinical Psychologist, 49*(4), 4–7.

Roskies, E. (1983). Stress management for type A individuals. In D. Meichenbaum and M. Jaremko (Eds.), *Stress Prevention and Reduction* (pp. 39–60). New York: Plenum.

Roskies, E. (1987). *Stress Management for the Healthy Type A: A Skills-training Program.* New York: Guilford.

Suinn, R. (1990). *Anxiety Management Training: A Behavior Therapy.* New York: Plenum.

Appendix C

INDEX OF *DSM-IV-TR* CODES ASSOCIATED WITH PRESENTING PROBLEMS

Alcohol Abuse 305.00
Attention-Deficit Disorder (ADD)—Adult
Chemical Dependence
Chemical Dependence—Relapse
Posttraumatic Stress Disorder (PTSD)

Alcohol Dependence 303.90
Antisocial Behavior
Attention-Deficit Disorder (ADD)—Adult
Chemical Dependence
Chemical Dependence—Relapse
Cognitive Deficits
Dissociation
Family Conflict
Legal Conflicts
Posttraumatic Stress Disorder (PTSD)
Sexual Abuse
Vocational Stress

Alcohol-Induced Persisting Amnestic Disorder 291.1
Chemical Dependence
Chemical Dependence—Relapse
Cognitive Deficits

Alcohol-Induced Persisting Dementia 291.2
Chemical Dependence
Cognitive Deficits

Amnestic Disorder Due to Axis III Disorder 294.0
Cognitive Deficits

Amnestic Disorder Not Otherwise Specified 294.8
Cognitive Deficits

Anorexia Nervosa 307.1
Eating Disorder

Antisocial Personality Disorder 301.7
Anger Management
Antisocial Behavior
Chemical Dependence
Chemical Dependence—Relapse
Childhood Traumas
Family Conflict
Financial Stress
Impulse Control Disorder
Legal Conflicts
Parenting
Vocational Stress

Anxiety Disorder Not Otherwise Specified 300.00
Anxiety
Family Conflict
Intimate Relationship Conflicts
Medical Issues
Obsessive-Compulsive Disorder (OCD)
Sexual Identity Confusion—Adult
Spiritual Confusion

Attention-Deficit/Hyperactivity Disorder, Combined Type 314.01
Parenting

Attention-Deficit/Hyperactivity Disorder Not Otherwise Specified 314.9
Attention-Deficit Disorder (ADD)—Adult

Attention-Deficit/Hyperactivity Disorder, Predominantly Hyperactive-Impulsive Type 314.01
Attention-Deficit Disorder (ADD)—Adult

Attention-Deficit/Hyperactivity Disorder, Predominantly Inattentive Type 314.00
Attention-Deficit Disorder (ADD)—Adult

Cocaine Dependence **304.20**
Antisocial Behavior
Chemical Dependencc
Chemical Dependence—Relapse
Family Conflict
Legal Conflicts
Posttraumatic Stress Disorder (PTSD)
Vocational Stress

Cognitive Disorder Not Otherwise Specified **294.9**
Cognitive Deficits

Conduct Disorder **312.8**
Anger Management
Antisocial Behavior

Conduct Disorder/ Adolescent-Onset Type **312.8**
Parenting

Conversion Disorder **300.11**
Chronic Pain
Somatization

Cyclothymic Disorder **301.13**
Attention-Deficit Disorder (ADD)—Adult
Depression
Mania or Hypomania

Delusional Disorder **297.1**
Paranoid Ideation
Psychoticism

Dementia Due to Axis III Disorder **294.1**
Cognitive Deficits

Dementia Not Otherwise Specified **294.8**
Cognitive Deficits

Dependent Personality Disorder **301.6**
Childhood Traumas
Dependency
Eating Disorder
Family Conflict
Parenting
Sexual Abuse

Depersonalization Disorder **300.6**
Dissociation
Posttraumatic Stress Disorder (PTSD)

Depressive Disorder Not Otherwise Specified **311**
Intimate Relationship Conflicts
Medical Issues
Spiritual Confusion

Disorder of Written Expression **315.2**
Educational Deficits

Disruptive Behavior Disorder Not Otherwise Specified **312.9**
Parenting

Dissociative Amnesia **300.12**
Dissociation

Dissociative Disorder Not Otherwise Specified **300.15**
Dissociation
Posttraumatic Stress Disorder (PTSD)
Sexual Abuse

Dissociative Identity Disorder **300.14**
Childhood Traumas
Dissociation
Posttraumatic Stress Disorder (PTSD)
Sexual Abuse

Major Depressive Disorder **296.xx**
Childhood Traumas
Financial Stress
Low Self-Esteem
Medical Issues
Obsessive-Compulsive Disorder (OCD)
Posttraumatic Stress Disorder (PTSD)
Psychoticism
Sexual Abuse
Sleep Disturbance
Social Discomfort
Spiritual Confusion
Vocational Stress

Major Depressive Disorder, Recurrent **296.3x**
Borderline Personality
Chronic Pain
Depression
Grief/Loss Unresolved
Sexual Identity Confusion—Adult
Suicidal Ideation

Major Depressive Disorder, Single Episode **296.2x**
Depression
Grief/Loss Unresolved
Sexual Identity Confusion—Adult
Suicidal Ideation

Male Dyspareunia Due to Axis III Disorder **608.89**
Male Sexual Dysfunction

Male Erectile Disorder **302.72**
Male Sexual Dysfunction

Male Erectile Disorder Due to Axis III Disorder **607.84**
Male Sexual Dysfunction

Male Hypoactive Sexual Desire Disorder Due to Axis III Disorder **608.89**
Male Sexual Dysfunction

Male Orgasmic Disorder **302.74**
Male Sexual Dysfunction

Mild Mental Retardation **317**
Educational Deficits

Mood Disorder Not Otherwise Specified **296.90**
Attention-Deficit Disorder (ADD)—Adult

Narcissistic Personality Disorder **301.81**
Anger Management
Antisocial Behavior
Intimate Relationship Conflicts
Parenting
Sexual Identity Confusion—Adult
Vocational Stress

Neglect of Child **V61.21**
Parenting

Neglect of Child *(if focus of clinical attention is on the victim)* **995.52**
Childhood Traumas

Nightmare Disorder **307.47**
Sleep Disturbance

Obsessive-Compulsive Disorder **300.3**
Childhood Traumas
Chronic Pain
Obsessive-Compulsive Disorder (OCD)
Type A Behavior

Physical Abuse of Adult *(if focus of clinical attention is on victim)* 995.81
Dependency
Posttraumatic Stress Disorder (PTSD)

Physical Abuse of Child V61.21
Parenting

Physical Abuse of Child *(if focus of clinical attention is on victim)* 995.54
Childhood Traumas
Posttraumatic Stress Disorder (PTSD)

Polysubstance Dependence 304.80
Antisocial Behavior
Chemical Dependence
Chemical Dependence—Relapse
Chronic Pain
Family Conflict
Legal Conflicts
Posttraumatic Stress Disorder (PTSD)
Sexual Abuse
Vocational Stress

Posttraumatic Stress Disorder 309.81
Anger Management
Chemical Dependence
Chemical Dependence—Relapse
Childhood Traumas
Intimate Relationship Conflicts
Posttraumatic Stress Disorder (PTSD)
Sleep Disturbance

Premature Ejaculation 302.75
Male Sexual Dysfunction

Primary Hypersomnia 307.44
Sleep Disturbance

Primary Insomnia 307.42
Sleep Disturbance

Psychological Symptoms Affecting (Axis III Disorder) 316
Medical Issues

Pyromania 312.33
Impulse Control Disorder

Reading Disorder 315.00
Educational Deficits

Schizoaffective Disorder 295.70
Depression
Mania or Hypomania
Psychoticism

Schizoid Personality Disorder 301.20
Intimate Relationship Conflicts

Schizophrenia 295.xx
Psychoticism

Schizophrenia, Paranoid Type 295.30
Paranoid Ideation
Psychoticism

Schizophreniform Disorder 295.40
Psychoticism

Schizotypal Personality Disorder 310.22
Paranoid Ideation
Social Discomfort

Sedative, Hypnotic, or Anxiolytic Dependence 304.10
Chemical Dependence
Chronic Pain